FRIENDS OF LIBERTY

FRIENDS OF LIBERTY

Thomas Jefferson, Tadeusz Kościuszko, and Agrippa Hull

A Tale of Three Patriots, Two Revolutions,
and a Tragic Betrayal of Freedom
in the New Nation

GARY B. NASH

and

GRAHAM RUSSELL GAO HODGES

BASIC
BOOKS

A Member of the Perseus Books Group
New York

Library of Congress Cataloging-in-Publication Data
Nash, Gary B.
   Friends of liberty : Thomas Jefferson, Tadeusz Kosciuszko, and
Agrippa Hull / Gary Nash and Graham Russell Gao Hodges.
      p.   cm.
   Includes bibliographical references and index.
   ISBN-13: 978-0-465-04814-4 (hardcover : alk. paper)
   ISBN-10: 0-465-04814-5
   1. United States—History—Revolution, 1775-1783—Biography.
2. United States—History—Revolution, 1775-1783—Social aspects.
3. United States—History—1783-1815.
4. Jefferson, Thomas, 1743-1826.   5. Kosciuszko, Tadeusz,
1746-1817.   6. Hull, Agrippa, 1759-1848.   7. Slavery—
United States—History—18th century.   8. Liberty—United States.
9. Poland—History—Revolution of 1794.   I. Hodges, Graham
Russell, 1946-   II. Title.
   E206.N36 2007
   973.3—dc22

Books published by Basic Books are available at special discounts for
bulk purchases in the United States by corporations, institutions, and
other organizations. For more information, please contact the Special
Markets Department at the Perseus Books Group, 2300 Chestnut
Street, Suite 200, Philadelphia, PA 19103, or call (800) 255–1514,
or e-mail special.markets@perseusbooks.com.

Designed by Brent Wilcox

10 9 8 7 6 5 4 3 2 1

*For Cindy Shelton and Gao Yunxiang,
for their patience and love during constant
ruminations over the lives of the Three Patriots.*

Can America be happy under a government of her own? As happy as she please; she hath a blank sheet to write upon.

THOMAS PAINE, 1776

CONTENTS

INTRODUCTION

This book is about three men who came of age as the storm clouds of the American Revolution gathered. All three served the Revolution in different ways. Two of them gained fame on both sides of the Atlantic; the other became a picaresque and highly respected figure in a remote New England village. The trio lived for many years after the war, their longevity surpassing that of most of their cohort in the age of revolutions.

Born in 1743, Thomas Jefferson was the eldest. He grew up in Virginia in the most favorable circumstances. In his eighty-fourth year he died with spectacular symbolism on July 4, 1826, exactly a half century after the signing of the famous document he drafted. Tadeusz Kościuszko entered the world in a small village in eastern Poland three years after the birth of the Virginian who became his cherished friend. He lived to age seventy-one, his life shortened by grievous battle wounds from hand-to-hand combat with the Russians that nearly caused his death when he was forty-eight. Born in Northampton, Massachusetts, in 1759 in the middle of the Seven Years War, Agrippa Hull lived to the ripe age of eighty-nine, dying as the Mexican-American War broke out in 1848. He outlived his friend Kościuszko by thirty-one years and Jefferson by twenty-three.

It is an odd trifecta: a lowly circumstanced black New Englander, a Polish noble turned military engineer and revolutionary, and a visionary, Southern, slaveowning squire who became a living symbol of liberty. Their lives were braided together by the issues of freedom, race, and identity, which were thrown into question on both sides of the Atlantic. Such influences were not always direct. Thomas Jefferson and Agrippa Hull saw each other only once or twice and may never have spoken to each other. But they were connected by ideas and visions of America's future.

Kościuszko was the pivotal figure in the triangular relationship. Crossing the Atlantic to join the American colonists' "glorious cause," he came to know the fatherless Agrippa Hull, a free black youth from western Massachusetts who joined Washington's Continental Army in 1777. Over the four years that Hull served as Kościuszko's orderly, a special bond developed between the Polish officer and the black enlisted man. Together they endured more than fifteen hundred days under some of the severest conditions of the long war, and the experience would define them both in the years that followed.

Kościuszko and Jefferson had only scant contact during the Revolution but developed an intense friendship after meeting in Paris in 1784. They resumed their relationship thirteen years later, after Kościuszko returned to the United States, having led a revolution to reclaim Poland's independence from foreign enemies. From this friendship that blossomed in Paris, Philadelphia, and Monticello came an extraordinary pact that had the potential to alter the course of American history. In this pact, sworn by Kościuszko and Jefferson, the Virginian agreed eventually to help educate and emancipate scores of enslaved people and strike a mighty blow against the system of slavery. Paradoxically, the celebrated herald of freedom in American history would ultimately block his Polish friend's effort to end slavery.[1]

Each of these three revolutionary patriots believed ardently in securing the unalienable rights of all humankind but played his role in a different way. Their lives are part of the story of our nation's origin and, at the same time, part of larger-scale transatlantic struggles for universal rights. For each of them, freedom was the great hope of humanity and oppression the great enemy. But freedom had disparate meanings for Hull, Jefferson, and Kościuszko. Each grappled differently with methods for battling oppression in America, where by 1800 one million humans were enslaved, and also in Europe, where most people languished in serfdom and miserable poverty.

Agrippa Hull's story is part of long-forgotten African American history. Hull was one of many African Americans—some Patriots, though many more fought alongside the British—whose wartime experiences sparked quests for landownership, citizenship, and respect in the new nation and beyond its borders. Their voices long ignored or muted, African Americans like Hull are now beginning to enter the national consciousness.

Tadeusz Kościuszko's valor is remembered and celebrated especially among Polish Americans, who commemorate him as their homeland's George Washington. His death-defying bravery, first demonstrated during seven years of American revolutionary service, reached legendary proportions during the Polish insurrection of 1794, which he led against the Russian army. Ever since, it has been known as the Kościuszko Insurrection, studied by every Polish schoolchild to this day. Less well-known is the story of how Kościuszko's ideas about the abolition of serfdom in his homeland were fueled by the abolitionist ideas he absorbed in Paris and America. Kościuszko was one of many enlightened Europeans who pledged their blood and honor as volunteers in the American Revolution. But he was one of the few overseas friends of America, rivaled only by Lafayette, who exhorted the Patriots after the Revolution to fulfill the promise of their doctrine of unalienable birthrights by ending slavery.[2]

Thomas Jefferson's supreme role in American history has never been in doubt. Jefferson has become the touchstone and watchword of American democracy. Even more than George Washington, Benjamin Franklin, or John Adams, he is the national and international embodiment of such tenets of modern liberal democracy as universal suffrage, freedom of religion, public education, the erasure of all vestiges of feudalism, and careers open to talent. "If Jefferson is wrong," wrote an early biographer, "America is wrong. If America is right, Jefferson is right."[3]

Notwithstanding his acknowledged greatness, Jefferson's reputation has been tarnished in recent years. Jeffersonian scholars have explored his weak defense of civil liberties, deplored his tortured ruminations about inherent black inferiority while refusing to credit accomplished blacks, and shaken their heads at his long-standing liaison with his enslaved domestic Sally Hemings while he publicly condemned interracial mixing. Above all, his buoyant proclamation of freedom and justice for all was badly undercut by his refusal to draw on his immense moral and political capital to help bring slavery to an end. His antislavery compact of honor with Kościuszko was the climax of his moral dilemma.

Given the very different backgrounds of the three men, it is hardly surprising that the historical record of their activities and influence on one another is highly uneven. Jefferson's writings are mountainous—a blizzard of correspondence, voluminous state papers, and one of the most widely read books of the era, in which he opened his mind and bared his soul with unusual clarity. On the other hand, Kościuszko's paper trail is sporadic and faint. He was neither a notable writer nor a deeply read political theorist. Worse, he was careless about his correspondence and lost many, if not most, of his letters as he moved from country to country. We are left with less than a hundred mostly short, matter-of-fact letters; a few public documents, some indeed notable; a number of his sketches and watercolors; and a few sheets of music. As for Agrippa Hull, only a single letter and a few public documents remain. But many of his spoken words have come down to us through affidavits he signed and through the reportage of those who observed and admired him. Much of Hull's mind has to be inferred by what he did, his actions serving as clues to his deeply held beliefs and commitments.

Recovering the life and mind of Agrippa Hull has been unusually challenging, but at the same time it has been one of our delights over the last several years, for hidden in the lives of largely unvisited figures in our history are important and instructive American examples of lives well lived. Meanwhile, sifting through and reevaluating the prolific studies of Kościuszko and Jefferson have allowed us to uncover overlooked connections and disinter the explosive story of Jefferson's retreat from a promise he made to his Polish friend.

Reconstructing and interweaving the lives of three such different characters involve the complicated question of influences. Agrippa Hull had no direct effect on Jefferson. Yet "Grippy," as he came to be known, influenced Kościuszko in ways that led to several of the Pole's most important decisions, including one that brought his relationship with Jefferson to a pitch. If Jefferson had chanced to tour New England, he might have seen in Hull what Kościuszko admired: a virtuous and hardworking farmer, sober and honest, a man combining small mixed farming with a jack-of-all-trades search for economic security—in short, a man anything but innately inferior.

Kościuszko's effect on Hull was palpable, and vice versa. In the annealing crucible of war, the black New Englander came to admire the Pole greatly and built his life around his experiences in the field with the good-hearted and self-effacing military engineer. With Hull constantly at his side, Kościuszko grew to admire the courage of black American soldiers as he saw them perform in the heat of battle during the Revolution. As this bond with his orderly grew, Kościuszko grew increasingly dismayed that white Americans were fighting for universal principles that they denied to half a million blacks. Returning to Europe with another African American, who served Kościuszko for over twelve years of military conflict and imprisonment, the Pole acted on his antislavery convictions by fighting to secure peasant freedom in Eastern Europe.

Kościuszko's extended wartime experiences with Hull also figured in the Pole's special relationship with Jefferson. The remarkable bequest that Kościuszko drew up after he and Jefferson developed a close friendship in Philadelphia at the end of the eighteenth century betokened the regard for the future of African Americans that Kościuszko gained through his years of close contact with Hull.

There were great differences among these three inheritors of Enlightenment thought—from skin color to place of birth, to education and status, and, most of all, to the career opportunities that befell them. Even their personalities were unalike. Kościuszko and Hull were selfless and playful, while Jefferson was a polymath too busy trying to satisfy his omnivorous curiosity for frolic or banter. Hull's antic humor and storytelling became legendary in western Massachusetts. Kościuszko was a soldier's soldier, his breezy disregard for personal safety in the heat of battle inspiring those who served with him. Jefferson hated rough-and-tumble politics (though he was a crafty political operative) and retreated to Monticello to find refuge in his books and gardens. While Jefferson steeped himself in political theory, philosophy, science, architecture, and literature, Kościuszko held to uncomplicated ideas about government, economy, and society. In bucolic Stockbridge, Hull grew to become the American equivalent of a West African griot—a homespun storyteller full of folk wisdom and vivid tales drawn from his own revolutionary experiences.

Yet these three sons of the American Revolution shared much in their temperaments and commitments. In their dedication to the principles of the Revolution they were of one mind, all sailing on "the boisterous sea of liberty," as Jefferson called it. None was reckless or given to public display, though Jefferson's lavish hautebourgeois, Paris-imported furnishings at Monticello contrasted sharply with the simple, even spare, lives of Kościuszko and Hull. All three were deeply attached to family and friends. Kościuszko never married, however, and Jefferson spent most of his adult life as a widower. Of the three, Hull alone went through his adult life in a state of marriage.

In bringing together the lives of Agrippa Hull, Tadeusz Kościuszko, and Thomas Jefferson, we are mindful that written history and public memory have treated them very differently. Though Grippy became a colorful and celebrated figure after the Revolution, his reputation was strictly local, confined to the Housatonic River valley of western Massachusetts. Beyond the Berkshire hill country, few Americans have ever heard of him.[4] Not even a roadside marker commemorates him in Stockbridge, Massachusetts, where he lived the last sixty-four years of his life. "Lived inequalities," advises the philosopher-historian Michel-Rolph Trouillot, "yield unequal historical power."[5]

Jefferson, of course, stands at the other end of the spectrum of recognition and fame. There is hardly a state without a Jefferson county named for him, a city without a Jefferson school or Jefferson street commemorating him, or a nation without postage stamps bearing his image. The public memory of him has been secure for the 182 years since he was buried at Monticello. The eulogies after his death had barely been published before sculptors got busy fashioning his likeness so that he looks down on passersby in scores of cities in the United States and abroad. His face on Mount Rushmore and his memorial in the tidal basin of the nation's capital are only two of the most visible monuments to his towering role in American history. Biographers got busy too, detailing and dissecting his life, and they are still earnestly at it, offering up new books on Jefferson to an appreciative, history-minded, still-hungry populace. Jefferson once said, "I cannot live without books," and it might be said that Americans cannot live without new books about Jefferson. We can't seem to leave Jefferson alone because he is one of the touchstones of American history.[6]

Kościuszko's fame—at least in the United States—has gone through several stages. At first, the outpouring of grief at his death kept his memory alive. English poets such as Samuel T. Coleridge and John Keats lauded him in verse—"O what a loud and fearful shriek was there, as though a thousand souls one death-groan pour'd!" It was not long before biographers sought to seal his fame. John Quincy Adams contributed his own error-strewn biographical account in 1835. West Point cadets had done their mite to memorialize him a few years before by contributing twenty-five cents a month from their meager wages to build a monument honoring him—the first to rise on the Hudson River heights.

But Kościuszko could never compete with homebred revolutionaries such as Jefferson, Adams, Washington, Franklin, and Hamilton, or even with "friends of liberty" from abroad such as General Friedrich Von Steuben, Jean Baptiste Rochambeau, and Lafayette. Nonetheless, some Americans wanted to assure his place by fastening his name on the landscape. Such was the case in Indiana when John B. Chapman, a veteran himself of the War of 1812, heard from old revolutionary warriors of "the noble traits of character of Kościuszko." As an elected Indiana legislator, he named one of the new counties being surveyed in the 1830s after the Polish hero. In 1833 the grandson of a revolutionary officer who had known Kościuszko during the war named Mississippi's Attala County seat Kościuszko. In time, a national park, Australia's highest mountain, a town in Texas, an island in Alaska, a bridge connecting Long Island and Brooklyn, New York, and streets in Detroit, Los Angeles, Milwaukee, Chicago, and many other cities came to bear Kościuszko's name.[7]

Not until the twentieth century, however, did statues of Kościuszko begin to spring up in marble and bronze in the United

States. This was usually the work of the Polish American heritage societies that started to organize after Poles joined the late nineteenth- and early twentieth-century tidal wave of immigrants from Eastern Europe. The statues first appeared in Milwaukee, Cleveland, and Chicago in 1904–05; another arose in Washington, D.C.'s Lafayette Square across the street from the White House in 1910; others were erected over the next several decades in Yonkers, West Point, Boston, Philadelphia, Saratoga National Historic Park, and St. Petersburg, Florida. Today chapters of the Polish American Congress in forty-one states gather annually to lay wreaths before Kościuszko monuments—with recent Polish immigrants much in evidence. The creation of the Kosciuszko Foundation in New York City in 1925 to promote educational and cultural exchange between Poland and the United States brought further attention to Kościuszko's place in American history, though he was still far from a household figure. To this day in some parts of the country Kościuszko is thought to be an Indian name.

The bicentennial of the American Revolution in 1976 brought new attention to Kościuszko as well as Jefferson. Four years before, through congressional authorization, the National Park Service (NPS) had acquired the house in Philadelphia where Kościuszko and Jefferson had become friends. The support of Polish American organizations permitted NPS to memorialize Kościuszko's contributions to the American Revolution and his lifelong struggle for freedom. Today, the house at Third and Pine streets is furnished in the same style as when the Pole was its occupant.

The revival of Poland after its liberation from Soviet control two decades ago has given new life to the Kościuszko story of patriotism and sacrifice on two continents. In the entryway to the old Jewish synagogue in Kraҟow, tourists today can find a plaque mounted in 1990 inscribed: "Here, in the old synagogue, in the days of the insurrections of 1794, Tadeusz Kościuszko called the Jews to arms in the fight for the liberation of the country. The Jews proved to the world, that whenever humanity can gain, they would not spare their lives." In other places Kościuszko is still regaining his place in public memory. In 2004, Polish Americans turned out to dedicate a Kościuszko monument in front of the Kościuszko County Courthouse in Indiana, while the U.S. government contributed to the building of a Kościuszko monument in Minsk, Belarus, in 2005.

While Jefferson's historic role was long ago fixed in the public mind on both sides of the Atlantic and Kościuszko's name has always resonated more in Poland than the United States, Agrippa Hull is only just beginning to take his place in American history. In Massachusetts and New York many secondary school students study curricular materials on the Stockbridge patriot, but his place is yet to become secure in the national consciousness.

1

Starting a Revolution

LOCAL LORE HANDED down for more than two centuries relates that he always claimed he was the son of an African prince. Revolutionary war records show that just after his eighteenth birthday the black youth enlisted in the revolutionary army and fought alongside two celebrated generals, one from Massachusetts, the other from Poland. His life after the war was of no special significance to most people, certainly not of the kind that would have earned him a place in the history books. Yet in the town of Stockbridge, where he lived for sixty-six years after the American Revolution, he came to embody the strength of small-town America: modesty, community-mindedness, wit, loyalty, and frugality. More than a century and a half after his death in 1848, he is hardly remembered beyond the Berkshire hill towns. At the Stockbridge Public Library his portrait gazes down next to those of white bankers, inventors, poets, and politicians for whom the quiet village along the Housatonic River is celebrated.[1]

Agrippa Hull was born on March 7, 1759, in the Connecticut River town of Northampton, part of Hampshire County. His parents, Amos and Bathsheba Hull, were among a handful of black residents; even rarer, they had gained their freedom. By the year of

Agrippa's birth, the French and Indian War had sucked up nearly half of the town's eligible men and almost bankrupted the colony of Massachusetts, stressing Hull's family, like all others, with heavy taxes.[2]

If Agrippa's claim that he was born to an African prince was true, then his father must have been captured in the early eighteenth century during one of the tribal wars that racked West Africa for two centuries after the Atlantic slave trade began in the late fifteenth century. No records have survived to confirm Agrippa's claim to princely heritage, and not a scrap of evidence remains to trace his parents' arrival in America. Who, after all, cared to set down the family tree of Africans snared in the net of the vicious slave system that brought some eleven million Africans across the Atlantic from the 1490s to the 1870s? Certainly not slave ship captains or the African sellers of slaves on the West African coast or the purchasers of slaves once they reached the Americas. In all but a handful of cases, the family history of slaves was preserved only through stories passed down orally from generation to generation. Yet Agrippa Hull's assertion of royal birth—"He always claimed that he was the son of an African prince," recorded the grandson of the first high-ranking officer who knew Agrippa Hull intimately—has a certain ring of truth about it.[3] From the records of his military service, he displayed an unusual bearing, a spiritedness, a love of ceremony, and a notable folk wisdom. We can never know for sure, but Hull acted like a displaced prince and lived out his life like someone born to be something other than a member of a demeaned caste.

It is unknown how Hull's parents came to a corner of the Americas where enslaved Africans constituted only a tiny portion of the population during the eighteenth century. In Massachusetts as a whole, black Bay Staters made up less than 2 percent of the population, most laboring on the seaport docks facing the Atlantic or on coastal vessels. In western Massachusetts, along the Connecticut and Housatonic rivers, not even one of every hundred settlers was black.[4]

Though living amid a sea of whites limited companionship and restricted the search for marriage partners to a small community of African Americans, the Hulls were snugly imbedded in village life. Agrippa's parents were members of the Congregational church, admitted along with seven other blacks during Jonathan Edwards's ministry. It was natural, therefore, that they took the infant Agrippa, like his two brothers and two sisters, to be baptized in the Congregational church. Within church walls, harder social barriers melted. "We are made of the same human race," wrote the Reverend Edwards some years before. As for master and slave, "their Maker made 'em alike with the same nature." Listening to Edwards's sermons, Amos and Bathsheba Hull must have learned of one of his favorite themes—how the New Testament Agrippa II, the powerful son of Herod Agrippa I, persecuted Christians but then, after his encounters with the apostle Paul, strove to find the truth of the gospel. Here was an appropriate name for their third son.[5]

Born free, Hull had advantages over most black New Englanders born into slavery. Yet he had a far from sunny upbringing. Two of his siblings died early—a sister, probably in infancy, and a brother at age three. His father died under unknown circumstances in 1761 as the French and Indian War was winding down, and this curbed his mother's ability to support her family. Within a few years she lost title to a small plot of Northampton land. In 1766, forced to take to the road like so many other women widowed during the war, Bathsheba sent her seven-year-old son to live under the care of her friends Joab and Rose Binney, a well-positioned black family living in Stockbridge, forty miles west of Northampton.[6]

Living on their fifty-acre farm on Evergreen Hill, just across the Housatonic River from Stockbridge village, Joab and Rose Binney provided what Agrippa Hull's mother could not: security, rudimentary education, and a stable family environment. Growing up in Stockbridge, young Agrippa experienced the rough equality of the frontier and something better than the low expectations available to

The Stockbridge Indian tribe sold their "Ancient Burial Ground" to Oliver Partridge, the town's doctor, in 1809. Agrippa Hull knew many of the Indians buried here and became Partridge's friend. Stockbridgians erected the monument in 1877 with the inscription reading, "The Ancient Burial Place of the Stockbridge Indians, 1734. The Friends of our Fathers." Today, during pilgrimages from their Wisconsin reservation, Stockbridge Indians visit this sacred spot. Monument to Housatonic Indians, Stockbridge, Massachusetts, Stockbridge Library Association.

coastal blacks. To begin with, the town was very new, founded in 1734, just thirty-two years before Agrippa arrived as a seven-year-old. Nearly everyone there, regardless of status, was a pioneer. Stockbridge was also situated in a hauntingly beautiful valley surrounded by low mountains, watered plentifully by the sinuous Housatonic River, and blessed with fertile soil suitable for cropping hay and grain. But more unusual, Stockbridge was mostly an Indian town, where only a few dozen white families and four free black families lived among several hundred Mahican, Wappinger, and Mohawk Indians, remnants of larger tribes that had been devastated by disease and war. The last of the "praying Indian towns" established in the old Puritan colony, Stockbridge stood athwart the main Indian warpath that ran from Canada southward into western Massachusetts. This was no accident; the Massachusetts General Court had established Stockbridge as a mission town in 1736 in order to enfold the Mahicans and Mohawks and inoculate them against the influence of Catholic French Canadians and their Indian allies.[7]

Indian-dominated Stockbridge must have given Hull an unusual outlook on life as he approached adolescence. The color line deeply inscribed in most colonial communities was less pronounced there. Young boys—black, white, and Indian—played together so frequently and so free of stigma that one of Jonathan Edwards's sons at first spoke Mohawk and Mahican more fluently than English. Free black men sometimes married Mahican women, as in the case of Hannibal, who took Mahican Hannah Mhuttawampe as his wife.[8] Also notable, the town was governed by a board of selectmen—three Indian and two white—an unprecedented form of village governance in New England. Mahican families controlled the village center with its mission school and church as the principal structures.

But Stockbridge was changing rapidly as Agrippa entered his teens. By the 1770s Massachusetts no longer needed the town as a buffer against the French on the western frontier because France, the loser in the Seven Years War, had relinquished Canada to the British Crown. This led to an onrush of land-hungry Massachusetts farmers and speculators, who plied the Stockbridge Indians with alcohol and acquired their land by unscrupulous manipulations and trickery. Between the time of Agrippa's arrival as a seven-year-old and his enlistment in the army eleven years later, the Mahicans had lost their seats in town government, seen their ownership of Stockbridge land shrink from 75 percent to a mere 6 percent, and fallen into impoverished despair.[9] The young Agrippa matured as tragedy enveloped the Stockbridge Indians. Their conversion to Christianity and their attempts to follow their minister's advice to remake themselves as devout Massachusetts farmers counted for little when land speculators arrived to swindle and exploit them.

While circumstances tore apart the Stockbridge Indians, Agrippa's family re-formed. In 1771, five years after Hull's mother sent him to

Stockbridge to live under the watchful eye of Joab and Rose Binney, Bathsheba returned to town with a new husband, Philemon Lee. For several years, she, her second husband, and Agrippa's sister had been part of the colony's "strolling poor," looking for work in western Massachusetts river towns. But now Bathsheba and Philemon Lee rejoined the twelve-year-old Agrippa. Taking up a few acres of land, they settled in with a handful of other free black farmers.[10] It was a familiar story—of families enduring death and separation, while striving to repair rents in the family fabric.

Three years later, in 1774, events far to the east of the Massachusetts frontier began to shake the earth and forever change the course of Agrippa Hull's life. Massachusetts had been the thin end of the wedge between England and its American colonies for a decade after England passed the Stamp Act in 1765, forcing the colonists to contribute to the maintenance of ten thousand British regulars left in the colonies after the end of the French and Indian War. Stamp Act riots had exploded up and down the Atlantic seaboard, compelling England to withdraw the detested tax on newspapers, college diplomas, playing cards, and other forms of paper. But more duties came with the Townshend Act in 1767, which renewed the violence-filled jockeying between the restless colonies and discipline-minded England. Most of the action occurred along the seaboard, where local politicians, lawyers, newspaper editors, merchants, and artisan leaders formed the vanguard of an incipient revolutionary movement. Even the Boston Massacre of 1770 and the Boston Tea Party in 1773 registered only mildly among some thirteen hundred villagers in faraway, backwater Stockbridge, where local nabobs held sway and few newspapers circulated the inflammatory reports that fanned the embers of discontent elsewhere.[11]

But 1774 was different. After the British Parliament passed the Coercive Acts of 1774, the spirit of militant resistance reached all the way to the Berkshire mountains. England had thrown down the gauntlet by issuing the "Intolerable Acts." They choked off colony-wide commerce by closing the port of Boston until the city paid for the tea dumped in Boston Harbor; they barred local courts from trying British soldiers and officials for acts committed while suppressing civil disturbances; they beefed up the powers of the royal governor of Massachusetts, General Thomas Gage. In an attempt to defang the recalcitrant elected provincial legislature, the British limited town meetings intended to elect local officers to one time per year.

Fifteen years old, Agrippa Hull, along with every other resident of tiny Stockbridge, surely marveled at the sight of sixty country leaders gathering in the sleepy Indian mission town in a county convention on July 6, 1774, to express their outrage at the Intolerable Acts and sign a Solemn League and Covenant that promised to boycott all English imports. Three days later, the town buzzed with the news that downriver, ten miles away in Great Barrington, stave- and ax-wielding farmers and craftsmen closed the Berkshire County Court, which would never function again under English rule. This was rebellion, plain and simple, rising out of the Berkshire hill towns.[12]

Attempting to squelch such grassroots militancy, Governor General Thomas Gage, commanding a formidable force of British redcoats who held Boston, quick-marched to Concord and Lexington on April 19, 1775, to seize the weapons, shot, and powder thought to be cached in arsenals there. This begat the firefight, first at Concord Bridge and then at Lexington, that echoed around the world.

Agrippa watched the town's militia quickly mobilize to hurry eastward to stand with other Massachusetts villagers. Among the first to leave were thirty-four Mahican warriors, who volunteered for militia service as soon as the shocking news arrived, revealing that British regulars fired on the minutemen at Concord and Lexington. Nor could Hull have missed the commissioning of Stockbridge's Jehoiakim Metoxin (Mtohksin), a strongly built twenty-four-year-old Mahican, as a second lieutenant in the Indian militia company, led by the town's Captain William Goodrich. All of Stockbridge turned out to watch the Berkshire County militia trudge east to join General

George Washington's raw and ragged Continental Army at Cambridge. Arriving at the end of April, they waded into the thick of the bloody Battle of Breed's (Bunker's) Hill. Seven months later, at a Berkshire County convention in Stockbridge, town Patriots vowed not to recognize the British-tainted provincial legislature as the legitimate government of their colony.[13]

Agrippa Hull did not follow Stockbridge's young Mahican and white townsmen who enlisted in the army during this early stage of the war. He was, after all, just sixteen, and his mother must have depended in part on her son's labor. It was also not clear that he would be welcome in the army, for in November 1775 Washington issued an order at the instigation of senior Southern officers that banned the enlistment of any blacks, whether slave or free. Though Southern lawmakers remained adamant in their opposition to enrolling black soldiers, Washington rescinded this order six weeks later, fearful that he would be unable to maintain a large fighting force. Quickly the Massachusetts legislature passed a militia act that excluded free blacks, slaves, and Indians from militia service and reaffirmed this ban the next year.

Revolutionary ideology as well as military necessity soon removed racial strictures. For several years in the North, slaves had been petitioning legislatures to bring an end to slavery, and some white revolutionary leaders had been quick to point out the blatant inconsistency between the unalienable rights proclaimed in the Declaration of Independence and the perpetuation of slavery. This figured in the decision of the Massachusetts legislature in May 1777, when facing a request for fifteen regiments for Washington's Continental Army, to pass a new law exempting only Quakers from military service. Agrippa could now enlist as a volunteer, but he was under no obligation to do so. A year later, in April 1778, Massachusetts removed all ambiguity by specifically sanctioning the enlistment of blacks.[14]

With the door to military service reopened, many New England blacks rushed to join local militias or Continental Army units.

Those who were free were attracted by enlistment bounties, while those who were enslaved often bargained with masters to serve as substitutes in the army. Agrippa Hull's motives were probably mixed. Family tensions may have played a role. Stockbridge's first historian wrote in 1854 that Agrippa "had little affection for his step-father."[15] But equally important, it seems, was genuine patriotism and martial ardor. It may have occurred to Agrippa, as it did to many other black Bay Staters, that a blow for freedom against tyrannical English authorities and legislators might also be a blow for freedom from slavery, which manacled almost one-fifth of the colonial population. And like many other young men, he was probably eager to prove himself.

Hull did not have to seek out the war; rather the war came to him. Whatever insulation Stockbridge residents may have felt earlier from the war raging to the east, it ended in early 1777. Well before the spring thaw of 1777, the British struck to bring the war to a quick end by splitting the colonies in half. The British planned to drive south from Canada, with a well-equipped army rich with artillery, to Lake Champlain, onward to Lake George, and finally down the Hudson River all the way to New York, where another part of the British army had occupied New York City. If this strategy succeeded, the British would sever New England from the middle and Southern states and fatally cripple the American bid for independence.

Word of preparations for this massive assault down the vital corridor only thirty miles or so west of the Housatonic River brought new enlistments from towns such as Stockbridge, Lenox, and Great Barrington. Agrippa Hull was among the new recruits. The muster rolls tell us that on May 1, 1777, he signed up with tavern-keeper Isaac Marsh's First Stockbridge Company for "a term of three years or during the war," whichever was longer. The muster master for Berkshire County wrote out a terse description: "Stature, 5 ft., 7 in.; complexion, black; hair, wool." Seven weeks after his eighteenth birthday, Private Agrippa Hull was now in the army.

He was not the only black man in his company. A German officer brought to America to fight as a mercenary with the British reported shortly after Agrippa's enlistment that numerous blacks were
shouldering arms. He saw no regiment west of Boston without "a
lot of Negroes and there are well-built, strong, husky fellows among
them." From Stockbridge alone, eleven free black men answered the
call to arms. This was part of a pattern; when able, black northerners joined the Patriot units as enthusiastically as whites.[16]

Shortly after enlisting, Hull was assigned as an orderly to
Colonel John Paterson. Forthright and Yale-educated, Paterson had
moved in 1774 from Connecticut to Lenox, six miles north of
Stockbridge. There he gained respect as the son of a militia officer
who had fought in the Seven Years War. His reputation grew as an
able town officer and delegate to Massachusetts conventions assembled in defiance of royal authority. Ramrod straight, athletic, and
more than six feet tall, Paterson was the obvious choice as the
elected colonel of a regiment formed mostly from Berkshire County
companies. Originally appointed to induce the Stockbridge Indians
to form a company as part of his regiment in 1775, Paterson proved
a brilliant success.[17]

By the time Agrippa joined him in May 1777, Paterson was already a hardened leader with two years of war behind him. Since
June 1775, his regiment had been attached to Washington's Continental Army. He and his troops had been in the thick of the fighting
at the siege of Boston. Later, they had been deployed to fight near
Montreal at the Battle of the Cedars, and had retreated to Crown
Point and Ticonderoga in the summer of 1776. His unit, like so
many others, suffered dreadfully when a terrifying outbreak of
smallpox in June killed far more soldiers than did British guns. Paterson's decimated regiment—only 220 of the 600 who first mustered—moved south with Washington's battered, retreating army in
November 1776. Paterson and his men soon participated in the battles at Trenton and Princeton in December 1776 and January 1777.

In late April, Paterson was promoted by the Continental Congress to the rank of brigadier general. Under new orders, he hastened northward with his regiment to defend Ticonderoga. It was there that Hull joined him on May 1, assigned as his orderly.[18]

Very likely, Agrippa carried no arms. The militia law under which Hull enlisted gave a bounty of twenty pounds—today that would be about $2,000—to each man who could furnish his own gun, bayonet, hatchet, jack knife, blanket, knapsack, canteen, and ammunition. For a poor youth like Hull equipping himself in this manner would have been difficult, and no evidence of his six years in the army shows that he was an arms-bearing soldier. So he had to content himself, it seems, with the fifteen-and-a-half-pound bounty given to enlistees unable to fit themselves out.[19]

Soon known as "Grippy" by his fellow soldiers, Hull joined a tattered, disease-riddled, and desperately underprovisioned army. Conditions within the regiment were bleak. General Paterson's letter to the Massachusetts government, one day after Agrippa Hull's enlistment, tells us of the conditions: "The soldiers are chiefly destitute of blankets, some are without shoes or stockings. . . . The want of which renders it extremely difficult, indeed almost impracticable, to keep up the necessary duty, such as scouting, guarding, fatigue, etc. which in this rainy, cold climate . . . is very detrimental to the health of the army unless supplied with these very necessary articles." Sickness stalked the camp at Ticonderoga, Paterson explained, and the exhaustion of sugar and rum denied even these small amenities to the sick.[20]

Paterson and his men would soon face the world's most formidable military machine, a significant part of it under General John Burgoyne, who at the moment was preparing to bear down on Fort Ticonderoga, a key American fortification on Lake Champlain. No one would have predicted that the undisciplined and ill-equipped American forces could blunt Burgoyne's offensive and bring his crack seven-thousand-man army to its knees at the battles of

Saratoga in September and October 1777. But that is precisely what happened in one of the turning points of the war. As Paterson's orderly, Hull waited on his table, tended to his clothes and horse, and probably served as a courier. Many years later, when applying for a military pension, Hull remembered that he was there when Burgoyne surrendered on October 17, 1777. As the American band played "Yankee Doodle Dandy," Burgoyne's five thousand British, German, and Canadian troops, now prisoners of war, readied themselves for a long march that would take them to be sequestered first in the Boston area and then, a year later, southward through the mid-Atlantic states to Virginia, where they would wait out the war.

During the four months before the epic battle at Saratoga, Hull encountered a man who would figure importantly for the rest of his life. Serving table at Fort Ticonderoga, where General Paterson was supping with four subordinate officers on May 8, 1777, Hull met the sixth dinner guest—an officer from Poland who had come to fight with the Americans in their struggle for independence.[21] Before long, he would be reassigned to serve as the Pole's orderly.

If, upon this first meeting, Agrippa Hull may have mistaken Tadeusz Kościuszko for just another ambitious foreign officer, he would soon learn that the Polish immigrant officer was, like himself, the product of a difficult and complicated upbringing. And in time Hull would learn that the Pole held views about race and human equality that were more enlightened than those espoused by most of his American compatriots. Hull would also learn that Kościuszko came from a nation that was troubled, defiant, and, like his own, struggling for democracy while chafing under repression from powerful external foes. Born February 12, 1746, Andrzej Tadeusz Bonaventura Kościuszko was the youngest of Ludwik Tadeusz and Tekla Ratomska Kościuszko's four children. Tadeusz was born in a wooden, thatched-roof house in a small town in eastern Poland. For generations his family had been minor gentry landholders who rarely involved themselves in political affairs and were content to remain within orthodox Roman Catholic traditions. His father, a widely respected district notary with important connections, had revived the family's precarious fortunes through active involvement in the district council. This led to a colonelcy appointment in the Lithuanian Field Regiment, a largely ceremonial rank given to district leaders but nonetheless an emblem of distinction.[22]

As a young man, Kościuszko came in frequent contact with Polish serfs, who lived under laws that so restricted their mobility and freedom that they were nearly as encumbered as American slaves. As members of the lesser rural gentry, the Kościuszkos were small landowners and held perhaps a village or two under their power. Like all other members of the Polish Lithuanian gentry, they depended on extracting their income from the serfs' earnings in the fields. Every nobleman was a law unto himself, so abstract ideas of freedom held little force in gentry-peasant relations. At the time of Kościuszko's birth, Polish society faced a crisis over the historic oppression of serfs and new calls for reform.[23]

Gradually serfdom had enveloped the lives of Polish and Lithuanian peasants, as the two nations joined in a commonwealth in 1569. Beginning in 1496, peasants were forbidden to leave their villages without the masters' permission. After 1520, peasants who lived in these tiny enclaves owed labor service to their masters. By steps, the amount of work done for the nobleman increased from a day or two to a norm of four days a week by the early eighteenth century. Such incremental loss of freedom could afflict a family over several generations or as fast as a calendar year, depending on the place. Peasants could not appeal to the king for justice in disputes with their lords after 1518.

As capitalist methods crept into the gentry-serf relationship, the advantage largely accrued to the master. As the nobility concentrated in the cities, gentry families who lived a distance from a village property could convert it into rental units, a practice that guaranteed profits for the owners and allowed only a meager profit to the peasants. Hampering the peasants' ability to save cash was the gentry's monopolistic control of commodities like salt, herrings, and especially alcohol.

By Kościuszko's day, the peasant lacked every kind of freedom. He owed the bulk of his time to the nobleman; he could be bought, sold, and loaned out; and he could not hold a trade without permission. The master had the power of life or death over a peasant with no more penalty than a small fine—a noble was fined only fifteen livres for killing a peasant, for example—while any resistance by serfs incurred harsh penalties. The peasant's conditions of life might be softened on a larger estate, but on a small one, such as the Kościuszkos', life was bleak. The farther east in Kościuszko's home territory, where the best cash crop, wheat, was primarily grown for the gentry, the worse the conditions.

Thus Kościuszko matured in an atmosphere of crisis over the condition of the peasantry. Resistance was deeply imbedded in peasant culture, and historically peasant resistance lay chiefly in flight, even if only to a nearby town or farm. By the 1740s and 1750s, however, armed peasant revolts, often spurred by disaffected and poorer gentry, became a major problem in Lithuania, especially on the properties of the important Radziwill family. Peasant violence, never far beneath the surface, required suppression by regular troops and private militias. Folk memories of legendary Cossacks, armed horsemen of peasant stock, mixed with a potent nationalism and memories of freer times, fueled peasant resistance.

As Polish peasants suffered from economic distress, Kościuszko's family experienced a severe shock when Tadeusz's father died in 1758, leaving behind a widow and four children, including the twelve-year-old Tadeusz. Schooled at home for his first nine years, he took pride in his father's memory and drew strength from his mother, who instilled respect in her children for the history and culture of the Polish nation. Kościuszko later remembered that an elderly uncle assisted her in teaching him draftsmanship, mathematics, and French and "ignited his zeal for sacrifice by telling him stories of great heroes." Later, at an advanced high school operated by the Piarist Fathers at Lubieszow, near Pinsk, Kościuszko received a sound liberal arts education to strengthen the values inculcated by his family. He devoured Plutarch's *Lives* and was particularly impressed by the saga of Timoleon, the Corinthian who had freed his people from tyrannical oppression in Sicily and fought for the freedom of Syracuse. Kościuszko recalled in later years that Timoleon was his role model because he "burned with hatred toward all tyranny," overthrew tyrants, set up republics, and never demanded power for himself. By Kościuszko's late teens, the seed of a free-thinking Polish nationalist was germinating rapidly.[24]

Though his early lessons in Polish history bolstered his self-esteem, Kościuszko was keenly aware of his family's shaky economic status. While the Kościuszkos were members of the Polish nobility (*szlachta*), theoretically equal to any other noble family, formidable barriers to Tadeusz's ambitions stood in his way. The rights and privileges of the nobility had accumulated over the centuries, providing all of them with religious toleration, equality before the law, freedom of speech, control over the peasantry and townspeople, and a veto power over the king. The most politically free of any nobility before the French Revolution, they were fiercely proud of their perceived equality. But this pretended equality cloaked harsh economic realities facing most of Poland's nobility.

Economically, the noblemen's world was highly structured. Accounting for about 7 percent of Poland's population, the nobility controlled over 70 percent of the land. However, ownership was spread so unevenly that the richest and poorest noble families were separated by a yawning chasm. At the bottom languished the landless *szlachta*, who could rarely hold office or participate in business; often reduced to begging, tramping, and domestic work, they were despised by the upper nobility. Above the thousands of "sparrow gentry" were small landowners who had to cultivate their farms by themselves with only a legal nicety making them different from the peasantry. Higher still were the petty nobles, who owned a single village—or a share of it—as well as its serfs. It was among this group that the Kościuszko family lived. We do not know the Kościuszko family's exact income, but reliance on the earnings of a single village left gentry owners like them highly vulnerable to poor harvests. More insulated from economic downturns were about 750 landowners, who controlled multiple villages. At the top were about sixteen noble families who controlled over 60 percent of the serf population and whose annual wealth rivaled that of the most prosperous English aristocrats.[25]

Though the Kościuszkos were precariously situated in this highly stratified *szlachta* world, his mother's persistence and the support of the important Czartoryski family, one of Poland's wealthiest and most influential, gained Kościuszko admission at age nineteen to a new Royal Military Academy in Warsaw. Created by the king to lift up the middling and lesser nobility, the school enjoyed the financial support of King Stanislaw August Poniatowski and the wealthy Czartoryski family. The school's mission was to instill free thought and a secular morality, to develop individual character, and to teach by exploration and example rather than rote learning.

Shaping its curriculum was a wandering Oxford-trained Englishman, John Lind, who, after reaching Warsaw, attracted the attention of the king. Engaged to superintend the military academy, Lind shaped a curriculum that emphasized classical and modern literature, history, geography, law, mathematics, and military engineering. Lind boldly attacked the debilitating system of peasant serfdom, subversively arguing that the peasantry should eventually graduate into citizenship. In one of their texts, Kościuszko read, "You who now find your Homeland in the most lamentable state conceivable should populate it with citizens' ardent for its glory, for increasing its internal vigor and its international prestige, for improving its government, which is the worst possible of its kind. . . .

May you, the new generation, change the old form of your country." Kościuszko and his classmates were enthralled by this call, which combined patriotism with new liberal ideas of greater democracy and personal freedom.[26]

Kościuszko excelled at the cadet academy in geometry and drawing, and, from 1765 to 1769, he learned French and English. His excellence in his studies brought him to the attention of King Stanislaw and Prince Adam Casimir Czartoryski, the cadet school's commandant; contact with these eminent men and their powers of patronage captured the young man's loyalty. Further expanding his intellectual world was Kościuszko's residence in Warsaw, the center of Poland's intellectual life and the residence of many foreigners, especially the French, who added to the cosmopolitanism of the growing city.[27]

Lessons at the school instilled in the young Kościuszko an understanding of the paradoxes of Polish history. For centuries, Poland had been the battleground for ambitious European nations. Struggle against invading Germans, Mongols, and Turks and destructive wars with Sweden, Russia, and the Ottoman Empire became a critical theme of Polish literature, poetry, and art. Renditions of Polish history in paintings and words bred patriotism, the ideal of self-sacrifice, and sympathy for the independent aspirations of other peoples such as the insurgent Americans. At the same time, as keen students such as Kościuszko knew, Poland's way of governing itself had produced an unstable mix of progressive and retrogressive elements. Also painfully evident to Kościuszko was that Poland was unable to defend itself.

Kościuszko and his classmates could see the legacy of their history in contemporary Polish society and government. As in other Eastern European countries, Poland's largest noble landowners monopolized government and society at large. Meeting in some fifty local assemblies, the noblemen authorized and collected taxes, maintained their own small armies, and created a loose confederation of little republics. The gentry in each republic sent deputies to a national parliament, or

Sejm. The burghers of the towns, in contrast to those of Western Europe, counted for little and were excluded from representation in the Sejm as early as 1501. The peasants counted for nothing. They were the subjects not of the king but of their lords, and these lords, as a lawbook of 1742 stated, had "the right of life and death over [their] subjects attached to the soil, not otherwise than as slaves were considered to be among the Romans."[28]

Gaining power over the years, the Polish Sejm steadily limited royal power and increased the influence of the nobles at a time when Western European nations were moving toward absolutism. The weak king sat on his throne not by divine right or direct descent from an earlier king but because he was elected by the Sejm. This unusual power-sharing between the king and the Sejm included some progressive elements. One was respect for individual faith, legally enacted in 1573 through the first document in European history to ensure religious tolerance. Another was (for the gentry) the guarantee of personal liberty and freedom from imprisonment without a court trial. Poles also enjoyed a form of habeas corpus lacking even in the English parliamentary system. Further advances secured over the centuries for the agrarian landlords included injunctions against laws declared without the consent of the Sejm. Only the Sejm could legislate or raise taxes, and it had uncontested power over all important national decisions. Polish citizens had the right to withdraw their allegiance to the king if he broke any law passed by the Sejm or breached the specific conditions of his election.[29]

Compounding the problem of one-class political rule, where kingly power had been emasculated and the town burghers and peasants excluded altogether, was the peculiar liberum veto. Through this ancient provision, the vote of a single deputy in the Sejm could block any legislation under consideration and even force the dissolution of the Sejm. This often made effective government nearly impossible. Some Poles hailed this unique power wielded by single deputies as a radical form of republicanism, practiced in a golden age when a deputy invoking the liberum veto became a tribune of the people and a guardian of Polish liberty. But in reality the liberum veto led to a tragic decay of government itself. As Kościuszko knew, forty-eight of the fifty-five meetings of the Sejm between 1652 and 1764 were dissolved through the use of the liberum veto by minority interests or even a single deputy, in effect burying the notion of majority rule. At the reform-minded Piarist school in Warsaw where Kościuszko had studied, the lessons celebrating the liberum veto, now seen as a source of Poland's misfortunes, were changed.[30]

Kościuszko also learned in his studies how the use of the liberum veto paved the way for international competition for control of the sizable but weak country in the eighteenth century. Unscrupulous politicians in the Sejm, working with foreign intriguers, used the veto to stalemate political reforms intended to strengthen military defenses, which in Kościuszko's youth were represented by a paltry twenty-four thousand cavalrymen. With the noblemen bowing to no one, the door was open for the plundering of Poland. Foreign interests—first the Swedes and then the Russians—installed pliable kings. During Kościuszko's youth, Stanislaw August Poniatowski was able to reign as monarch because he was sponsored by Catherine of Russia, who had earlier taken Poniatowski as a lover.

Within a year at the Royal Military Academy, Kościuszko earned an officer's commission and an appointment as an instructor in the Cadet Corps. In 1768 he advanced to the rank of captain and earned a stipend from the king to complete his studies in France. After several years of study, Kościuszko, still supported by the Czartoryskis, continued his military engineering education in the small French seacoast of Brest, where he studied the science of fortifications. His career ascending, the maturing Kościuszko traveled to Paris, the center of eighteenth-century Enlightenment thought and the place where his intellectual horizons would now expand.

Arriving in Paris in 1769, Kościuszko studied at the famous Académie Royale de Peinture et de Sculpture, mingling with artists and intellectuals. Converting from his earlier Catholic orthodoxy, Kościuszko became a committed Deist, believing that God's involvement with the world was limited to its creation and that the divinity had equipped humankind with the potential for autonomous development. Kościuszko became convinced that government's purpose was to provide for the happiness of all people, not just its nobility. "During the five years of my life spent in foreign countries," he later wrote, "I have endeavored to master those arts which pertain to a solid government, aiming at the happiness of all, also economics and military art; I earnestly tried to learn this, inasmuch as [I] had a natural passion for these things."[31]

When studying in Paris, Kościuszko was attracted to the writings of François Quesnay and Jean-Jacques Rousseau, whose analyses of European societies provided the young idealist with blueprints for a better Poland. Quesnay's physiocratic theory, emphasizing the primacy of agricultural production in underpinning a nation's wealth, pictured the profit-starved, freedom-deprived peasants as a terrible drag on the economy. A titan of Enlightenment thought, Rousseau diagnosed Poland's problems with a devastating clarity that attracted much attention. Famous for his *The Social Contract*, published seven years before Kościuszko's arrival in France, Rousseau contended that Poland could never survive with its feeble king, all-powerful agrarian landlords, weak army, appalling class divisions, inhuman treatment of serfs, and exclusion of the town burghers from a significant political role. Poland must devise new "national institutions" that would bring Poles together with respect for each other and a willingness to serve the state in its hour of need. Never could a "spiritual solidarity or common basis of loyalty" emerge in Poland amid one-class rule and the denial of basic freedoms to three-quarters of the population writhing in abject servility.[32]

Key to the arguments about freedom and individual liberty in the writings of Rousseau and other Enlightenment thinkers was an attack on slavery. Kościuszko's views on equality and race took form during his four years in Paris. His later words and actions owed much to Rousseau and to the radical antislavery polemicist Abbé Guillaume Thomas Raynal. For Rousseau, writing in *The Social Contract*, human beings were born free and equal. Since slavery was based on brute force, it had no moral validity, leaving slave traders and slave masters bereft of any principle upon which to justify their enslavement of fellow humans. Rousseau's arguments quickly became part of the radical antislavery jeremiads that were at the core of the French Enlightenment thought by the time Kościuszko reached Paris.[33]

Intensifying the critiques of slavery that burned in Kościuszko's mind were the radically antislavery and anticolonial ideas of Abbé Raynal, whose inflammatory treatise *Philosophical and Political History of the Settlements and Trade of Europeans in the East and West Indies* burst onto the Paris scene in 1770 with the force of an exploding meteor. Without "natural liberty, . . . the right granted by nature to every man to dispose of himself at pleasure," wrote Raynal, "no man can be either a husband, a father, a relation, or a friend; he hath neither country, a fellow citizen, nor a God." That the French government sent Raynal into exile and that the French clergy condemned the book were enough to make it the talk of salons and cafés throughout the city. Representing the radical fringe of Enlightenment thought, Raynal's history shattered the notion of the New World as a "land of natural innocence and new hope for mankind." Rather, Raynal argued, in Europe's overseas colonies rapaciousness and violence were leading toward a historic retrogression in human progress. No greater proof of this could be found than the ruthless slaughter and enslavement of the Native peoples of America and the millions of Africans brought across the Atlantic in chains. Because of the great crimes against humanity perpetrated against slaves of the Americas, Raynal called for the rise of a "Black Spartacus" to "avenge the rights of nature."

For Kościuszko, Raynal's words connected the plight of American slaves with ancient Polish problems. As the writings of these philosophers opened Kościuszko's eyes to the plight of American slaves, he must have found much analogous in the suffering of the Polish peasantry. The peasant, like the slave, could not dispose of his own resources and could not move without permission. The estate owner could buy, sell, bequeath, or inherit a peasant, much as could be done with an American slave. Kościuszko's absorption of penetrating critiques of slavery in French Enlightenment thought, conditioned by his experiences and comprehension of Polish history, made him uniquely capable of grasping connections between serfdom and slavery.[34]

Another influence upon Kościuszko's thinking was the swirling conflict developing in North America. Throughout the 1760s he could read the frequent Polish and French press reports on the imperial wrangle between England and its American colonies. The Stamp Act crisis of 1765 attracted much attention, and Poles saluted the protest activities of the Sons of Liberty, seeing the impending war as a worthy struggle for independence.[35]

The American protests were all the more poignant to Kościuszko because the Poles were going through a similar crisis. As the American Patriots groped their way toward independence, a national protest against Russian influence in Poland in 1768 had led to an insurrection against the king. Emerging as leaders were the Pulaski family, led by father Józef and his son, Casimir, who led more than a dozen confederate battles. Though the Poles frequently lost, Casimir Pulaski aroused respect and admiration for rallying his troops. "I expect no other benefit than death for the honor of God and the homeland, which, surrounded by hazards," wrote Pulaski, "it becomes me to await in impeccable virtue."[36] Kościuszko remained loyal to the Polish king, who was his patron, but he had to be deeply moved by such words of selflessness.

Kościuszko's loyalty to the king proved wise when, after several years of fighting, the insurgency collapsed. Under indictment for attempted regicide and shouldering the guilt of the movement when most supporters denied involvement in it, Pulaski fled to America to support the Patriot insurrection against England. Although the insurgency failed, its breadth and persistence demonstrated the weakness of the entire political system and stimulated government reformers to make an all-out effort to expel foreigners.

Kościuszko and his fellow Poles writhed in humiliation as stronger European powers carved up their nation. Fearful that Russia, ruled by Catherine the Great, would annex the entire Polish state, Frederick II of Prussia, supported by the French and the English, persuaded the czarina to share the bounty. The first partition of Poland in 1772 reduced the country by a third, with Russia taking 93,000 square kilometers in the east, Austria another 81,900 in the south, and Prussia 36,300 square kilometers in the strategically and economically important northwest of Poland. France and England allowed the partition because they believed it was the only way to keep Russia from completely dominating Poland. Demonstrating Poland's helplessness, this first partition further convinced the anguished young Kościuszko of the need for action.[37]

Kościuszko's personal life mirrored his nation's plight. After his glorious time studying in France, he returned home in 1774. There he found his family estate near bankruptcy, much of it squandered by his older brother.[38] Kościuszko's bleak future seemed to be that of half of Poland's nearly landless noblemen, who, owning no serfs, plodded into the fields to do the farm labor themselves, often hanging their sword on a tree while plowing and harvesting. As a partitioned Poland fell into a deep slough, only a sense of class superiority based on birth, equestrian skills, and physical bravery remained for such impecunious gentry.

To support himself, Kościuszko took an appointment as tutor for the daughters of the important provincial governor Sosnowski, scion of a wealthy noble family. Kościuszko soon fell in love with the eighteen-year-old Ludwika Sosnowski. Her father refused Kościuszko's request for her hand, sternly lecturing him that "ringdoves are not for sparrows, and the daughters of magnates are not for the sons of the szlachta." Tadeusz and Ludwika planned to elope, but her father discovered the plot. Attacked, wounded, and driven from the estate, the heartbroken twenty-nine-year-old Kościuszko borrowed funds and abandoned Poland in search of a career. For the rest of his life, he carried a lock of Ludwika's hair nestled near his heart.

Kościuszko's self-exile did not lead him immediately to North America. In search of a new life, he traveled first to Dresden, where he unsuccessfully requested an appointment in the King of Saxony's army. By mid-1776 Kościuszko had returned to Paris still adrift. Knowing that the Americans badly needed military engineers to win their struggle against the mighty British war machine, he decided to cross the Atlantic to join the American cause, though he had nothing to assure him of an appointment in Washington's Continental Army. Disconsolate with his personal life, highly educated but without a settled career, he must have regarded the conflict in America as a chance to define his life while applying the Enlightenment ideals imbibed in Paris and Warsaw.

Kościuszko left Europe as a dedicated son of the Enlightenment, afire with civic idealism and unswervingly dedicated to national self-government, personal liberty, tolerance of divergent religious and cultural traditions, and a general humanitarianism spanning all classes and varieties of people. He was by no means a systematic thinker, still reacting emotionally to Poland's agonies and still puzzling out the possibilities of reform afforded by Enlightenment thinking. What he knew most definitely was that his military experience, fortified by a republicanism as ardent as could be found among the most radical American Whigs, effectively equipped him to join the rebellious Americans. Completely uncertain about the future, Kościuszko cast himself as an international friend of liberty, eager to learn what awaited a displaced Pole in the midst of a revolution thousands of miles west of his native land. He now joined a stream of "friends of liberty" journeying across the Atlantic to throw in their lot with what the Americans were now calling "the glorious cause."

His route to America is partially lost to history, but Kościuszko probably sailed from Bordeaux in the summer of 1776. From there he apparently proceeded to Saint Domingue, France's slave-based coffee and sugar island, and then made the trip of several weeks to mainland North America, a route favored by European émigrés wishing to join the American forces and avoid unpleasant questions from an intercepting British navy. By late August 1776 Kościuszko was in Philadelphia, where he immediately requested a commission from the Continental Congress in the American army. But the thirty-year-old Pole had to cool his heels because Congress was beset with foreign adventurers, often presenting themselves in resplendent uniforms as military geniuses, demanding lavish pay and regiments of their own.

Sustaining himself with his own funds, Kościuszko gained the attention of the Pennsylvania Council of Safety, which was frantically trying to fortify the Delaware River approach to Philadelphia. By designing and overseeing the construction of a river island fortress at Billingsport, twelve miles below the city, Kościuszko captured Congress's notice. By mid-October 1776 he received a colonel's commission—just three days after the British army defeated Washington's forces in the Battle of Long Island and chased them across New Jersey in a humiliating rout. Kościuszko spent the winter of 1776–77 constructing additional fortifications at Red Bank, seven miles south of Philadelphia on the New Jersey side of the Delaware River.

Washington's surprise Christmas victory over Hessian troops at Trenton at the end of 1776 and his follow-up victory at Princeton the next month held the British off from an assault on Philadelphia. About this time, Kościuszko made a crucial political connection. The American forces badly needed the engineering skills he possessed, and this led to a warm friendship with the former British officer General Horatio Gates, who assumed command of Philadelphia in

February 1777. By that March, when Washington convinced Gates to assume the position of adjutant general—second only to Washington in the Continental Army—the thirty-one-year-old Kościuszko had gained Gates's confidence and proven himself a valuable officer in the American forces.[39]

Shortly after Kościuszko's arrival in Philadelphia in August 1776, he may have encountered Thomas Jefferson, who served in the Continental Congress before returning to Monticello on September 2. If so, Kościuszko would have been duly impressed with the young planter who had recently authored the Declaration of Independence. As had Kościuszko, Jefferson had climbed from obscurity as part of the minor gentry, but now he was a celebrated leader in the American drive for independence.

In 1743, three years before Kościuszko's birth, the first son of Peter and Jane Jefferson entered the world in a plain frame building not unlike that of the Pole's natal home. Situated in the rolling upcountry lands of Virginia's piedmont region, with vistas of the Blue Ridge, the Jefferson plantation of one thousand acres was a far cry from the tidewater plantations spread across many thousand acres. Yet it had the potential to make young Tom a man of substance among Virginia's planter elite.

Managing a slave-based tobacco and wheat plantation, however, was not the young Jefferson's ambition; law and politics preoccupied him, and he buried himself in books. His education at William and Mary in the early 1760s, when Kościuszko was studying military engineering thousands of miles to the east, swept Jefferson up into eighteenth-century Enlightenment thought, including the central idea that freedom was meant for all humans. But slavery shadowed him at college, for he took with him Jupiter, the slave just Jefferson's age whom Peter Jefferson had assigned to him as a body servant at age fourteen.

In Jefferson's early adulthood, slavery and freedom, joined at the hip, were never far from his mind. His legal studies, for which his principal tutor was George Wythe, an early opponent of slavery, led to a first career as a country lawyer and local officeholder. At the same time, his love for the land and a fascination with planting took hold of him. But with land came slaves. The eldest of eight children, Jefferson, at age twenty-one, inherited fifty-two slaves from his father in 1764.

As with Kościuszko in France, he had imbibed the Enlightenment's uncompromising attacks on chattel bondage, and like some Virginia planters, he felt disquiet over the collision of antislavery ideals and the reality of slave-based plantation society. Arthur Lee's "Address on Slavery," published in 1767 in the *Virginia Gazette*, the most widely circulated newspaper in the southern colonies, may have had a special effect on Jefferson, for Lee was no airy salon philosopher distant from slave societies but the son of an eminent land-rich and slaveowning Virginia family. "Freedom is unquestionably the birth-right of all mankind, of Africans as well as Europeans," wrote Lee, "slavery is in violation of justice and religion," and destroys the morals of masters as well as slaves. Such was the outcry from the rattled Virginia's slave aristocracy that the owner of the *Virginia Gazette* refused to publish a sequel essay. Yet slaves who heard of the controversy must have taken satisfaction that the son of one of the colony's most important families had challenged the system of bondage.[40]

Two years later, in 1769, the rangy twenty-six-year-old Jefferson, just admitted to the Virginia bar and newly elected to Virginia's House of Burgesses, tried himself to strike blows against slavery. First, a fair-skinned indentured servant named Thomas Howell, two years older than Jefferson, had appeared at the young lawyer's door in hopes that Jefferson could rescue him from a lifelong sentence stemming from Virginia legislators' hatred of the offspring of mixed-race love. Fleeing from his master's plantation, Howell explained how he had been consigned to thirty-one years of labor because of the racial intermingling of his white mother and grandmother. Both had been trapped by laws passed in 1705 and 1723 that sanctioned the sentencing of the offspring of a white woman and a black or mulatto man to thirty-one years of labor. The law held further that any child born of such a white woman, even if the father was white, should be held in servitude for thirty-one years if the mother conceived the child while still an indentured servant.

Jefferson took the case to Virginia's highest court in 1770. The neophyte jurist argued that while the law was clear about enslaving the children of mixed-race love, there was no clear legislation specifying that the grandchildren should be held in bondage. Jefferson maintained that Howell, as a grandchild of the illicit union, should be freed. "Under the law of nature," he argued, "all men are born free, every one comes into the world with a right to his own person, which includes the liberty of moving and using it at his own will. This is what is called personal liberty, and is given him by the author of nature." Here was the seed of the all-powerful idea that Jefferson would advance in the Declaration of Independence. In this instance, Jefferson's appeal found little support in Virginia's legal system. The court ordered Howell to return to his master, fearing any leniency that might lighten slavery's strictures, should Jefferson's case succeed.[41]

At the same time, Jefferson attempted to chivy a slightly larger crack in the wall of slavery. In 1769, as a freshman legislator, he drafted a bill that would give slaveowners permission to free a slave without legislative approval, as required by Virginia's old rules. But Jefferson knew that a junior burgess stood little chance of succeeding with such a measure. Maneuvering for advantage, he turned to his cousin Richard Bland, twice his age and an unrivaled scholar of English constitutional law, to introduce the bill. This was an apt choice, for four years before, Bland had shocked fellow Virginians by proclaiming that "under an English government all men are born free." A member of the House of Burgesses for many years, Bland agreed to carry the bill.

Now it was Jefferson's turn to be shocked. He later recalled that "though one of the oldest, ablest, and most respected members" of the House, Bland "was denounced as an enemy of his country and treated with the grossest indecorum."[42] The legal wall protecting slavery stood firm, and the young legislator learned the price of challenging the Virginia slaveocracy. It was a lesson he never forgot.

While navigating the tricky waters of Virginia's legislative and judicial system, Jefferson simultaneously encountered examples of slave attempts to dismantle perpetual bondage. All Virginians rested uneasy with their long history of slave resistance and slave rebellion, and Jefferson saw that unease resurface in 1769. Just as he began building a plantation seat at Monticello, with his slaves doing most of the construction work, slaves in two counties to the east demonstrated that their bondage was a highly unstable proposition. Forty to fifty slaves at Bowler Cocke's plantation in Hanover County seized the overseer and whipped him as they had been whipped, "from neck to waistband." Taking refuge in a barn while white neighbors assembled to squelch the rebellion, the slaves fought desperately. Three died, and five others were wounded in the battle. Others, after capture, were sentenced to death. For years afterward people in Hanover County spoke of the uprising as "Bloody Christmas."[43]

To Jefferson, the uprising demonstrated once more the hazards of slavery and the need to plan for a better future. From his father, who did not regard excessive punishment of slaves as fruitful, Jefferson had learned to hate the use of the whip and to regard the separation of slave families through sales as an affront to the basic humanness of the enslaved. Nonetheless, he had to run a large plantation, where effective management was built on discipline, regularity, and—hardest of all—instilling in slaves a belief that their lives could not be improved by resisting the slave system. Such a belief, when purveyed by a son of the Enlightenment, was on its face contradictory, but living with contradictions of this sort was the price of maintaining one's inherited property while pondering some remedy to Virginia's Achilles heel.

One Virginia planter, an acquaintance of Jefferson, took a bold step that tugged at Jefferson's conscience. Robert Pleasants, a Quaker planter who owned eighty slaves, dumbfounded his gentry friends in 1772 by announcing that his father and brother had chosen to emancipate all of their slaves and that he would follow their lead. Virginia courts blocked this move for many years, but Pleasants soon established the first abolition society in the southern colonies. All of Virginia knew of this, and the observant Jefferson would have been among the most interested. To make sure, Pleasants in 1772 sent Jefferson—and also Patrick Henry, George Washington, and James Madison—a copy of *Some Historical Account of Guinea*, a passionate attack on slavery and the slave trade by the Philadelphia Quaker activist Anthony Benezet.[44] Embarking upon a career of pricking the conscience of his Virginia gentry neighbors, Pleasants was but the first of Jefferson's fellow planters who strived to absolve themselves of the sins of slavery by emancipating their bondpeople.

One of life's important milestones pushed Jefferson in a different direction from that taken by Pleasants. Almost thirty, his marriage to the widow Martha Wayles Skelton in 1772 brought additional slaves to Monticello. When her father died a year later, she inherited about eleven thousand acres and another 135 slaves. The Virginian who was becoming an apostle of Enlightenment thought, in which ideas were meant to lead to progressive action to improve the human condition, had suddenly become the second largest slaveowner in Albemarle County. It was a contradiction with which he would wrestle for the rest of his life.

For now, Jefferson could accept a certain amount of contradiction amid a blossoming family life and a growing political reputation. While building his gracious mansion at Monticello and starting a family—Jefferson's wife bore two daughters between

1773 and 1776—Jefferson burst into public view as a leading spokesman of the revolutionary movement. Joining a group of hot-headed legislators, he participated in drafting a resolution calling for committees of correspondence in each colony and another protesting the Coercive Acts of 1774. Then he placed his *Summary View of the Rights of British America*, a close-grained recital of colonial grievances, before Virginia's House of Burgesses, which had been meeting extralegally since Lord Dunmore, Virginia's royal governor, had dismissed it in mid-1774. After the *Summary View* was published in Williamsburg and Philadelphia in late 1774, Jefferson's name was on the lips of everyone along the Atlantic seaboard.

Elected the next year by the House of Burgesses as one of Virginia's delegates to the Continental Congress meeting in Philadelphia, Jefferson embarked on a lifelong inner struggle of priorities—between a public leader of political reforms and the private patriarch of what he always referred to as his "family" at Monticello. Charged with drafting the Declaration of Independence in May 1776, he worked concurrently on the other document for which he earned great respect, even though it was not adopted—a constitution for a Virginia unshackled from British rule. As he devised these world-shaking documents, Jefferson found himself confronting the great American paradox: that the creation of prosperity and freedom for white colonists had been built on the backs of African slave labor. It was a paradox that would bedevil Jefferson all his days.

While crafting the Declaration of Independence and a constitution for Virginia during his stints of service in the Continental Congress—from June 21 to late August 1775 and again from May 14 to September 2, 1776—Jefferson was exposed to the most intense antislavery activity on the continent. In Philadelphia a small Quaker contingent had just established the first abolition society in the Western world. Their steely members, strangers to compromise, were taking their first steps to lobby legislators to consider the contradiction between colonial protests against British tyranny and the exercise of a far worse tyranny against one-fifth of the colonial population. The young doctor Benjamin Rush and the recent immigrant Thomas Paine had produced hard-hitting pamphlets widely distributed in the city. Rush denounced slavery as one of those "national crimes" that would "require national punishments," while Paine had asked "with what consistency" could American slaveholders "complain so loudly of attempts to enslave them, while they hold so many hundred thousand in slavery."[45] By the time Jefferson reached the city, Philadelphians had been bombarded by a score of pamphlets and newspaper essays condemning slavery, including a few by Virginians. Rush had claimed, perhaps too enthusiastically, that three-quarters of Philadelphians "cry out against it [slavery]." But there was no discounting the surge of abolitionist sentiment.

If Jefferson's developing friendship with Rush did not bear forcibly upon the Virginian's thoughts on slavery, a missive from the North could not help but do so. Samuel Hopkins, minister of a Congregationalist church in Newport, Rhode Island, addressed his "A Dialogue Concerning the Slavery of the Africans" specifically to "the Honorable Members of the Continental Congress." What might Jefferson have thought upon reading Hopkins's charge that half a million enslaved Africans "are shocked with the glaring inconsistence" of "the sons of liberty oppressing and tyrannizing over many thousands of poor blacks who have as good a claim to liberty as themselves"? One might also speculate about his thoughts when reading Hopkins's reminder that "our oppressors have planned to gain the blacks, and induced them to take up arms against us, by promising them liberty, on this condition"—a clear reference to the electrifying proclamation of Lord Dunmore, Virginia's royal governor, who in November 1775 had triggered the flight of hundreds of Virginia slaves to the British colors by promising them freedom if they reached the British lines.[46]

Matching the worrisome flight of slaves in Virginia to the British colors were clear signs of the crumbling of slavery in eastern Pennsylvania. Jefferson received daily reminders of this from the increasing volume of runaway slave advertisements in the Philadelphia newspapers. Even more instructive were the actions of the Society of Friends. Moving from rhetoric to action, the Philadelphia Quaker Yearly Meeting, constituting the Friends' leadership cadre, had taken a startling step in 1775. Twenty years before, they had banned Quakers from trafficking in slaves, but now they instituted a ban on slave ownership. By the time Jefferson was writing the Declaration of Independence, he could look down from his rented rooms on bustling Market Street to see the former slaves of Quakers walking the city as free men and women. Just as Jefferson was leaving Philadelphia to return to Monticello in September 1776, the Yearly Meeting's Quaker leaders agreed to reject members who were slaveowners who would not respond to moral cudgeling while they urged local monthly meetings to step up their efforts to obtain manumissions.[47] The Master of Monticello had personally witnessed the disintegration of slavery in its most important urban setting on the continent.

It was amid this barrage of pamphleteering and abolitionist activity that Jefferson produced drafts of the Declaration of Independence and a constitution for the state of Virginia in a six-week burst of productivity. Jefferson grappled brilliantly with fundamental questions of the unalienable rights of humankind and the right of freeborn English citizens to rebel against tyrannical power exercised against them. The phrases for which the Declaration and the preamble of the Virginia constitution are justly famous still come down to us two centuries later as rolling thunder.

Less well-known, however, are the words Jefferson penned in the Declaration of Independence as he wrestled with the question of slavery. These are the words that signal his deep ambivalence about the coerced labor system that formed the cornerstone of Virginia's economy and, even closer to home for Jefferson, provided the muscle and skill poured into the building of North America's finest mansions. "The Christian king of Great Britain," charged Jefferson in his first draft of the Declaration of Independence, "has waged cruel war against human nature itself, violating its most sacred rights of life and liberty in the persons of a distant people, who never offended him, captivating and carrying them into slavery in another hemisphere, or to incur miserable death in their transportation thither." American colonists were blameless in this account of how African slavery came to the British colonies; Jefferson wrote as if the English kings had forced slaves upon them. Committing "crimes against the liberties" of the Africans, English monarchs had "obtruded" them upon the colonists.

In these powerful words, Jefferson acknowledged that slavery was an offense to humankind and a violation of rights that all humans possessed. Among the growing number of American antislavery advocates these were welcome words affirming universal natural rights. But Jefferson's statement that it was the king who conducted the slave trade and forced the Africans on the colonists was preposterous. Jefferson himself owned more than one hundred slaves at the time, was making no attempt to free them in order to restore their unalienable rights, and understood perfectly well that his planter friends had clamored for slaves for generations. Laboring to impassion his readers, Jefferson used bloated language to suggest that the colonists were unwilling partners in the slave trade and not complicit in instituting chattel bondage.[48]

Not surprisingly, this language did not survive the scrutiny of the full Congress, which replaced it with a brief phrase that the king had "excited domestic insurrections amongst us"—a pointed reference to Dunmore's Proclamation. Delegates from South Carolina and Georgia, avid to continue importing slaves, insisted on striking the language while other delegates were conscious of representing thousands of colonists who gladly profited from slavery. Learning of

Jefferson's vehement language directed at the king, John Lind, the man who had headed the cadet school where Kościuszko had studied and now a writer for the English ministry, taunted the Americans. "It is their boast," he wrote in a widely distributed pamphlet, "that they have taken up arms in support of these their own self-evident truths—that all men are created equal, that all men are endowed with unalienable rights of life, liberty, and the pursuit of happiness." If so, why were they complaining to the world "of the offer of freedom held out [by the British] to these wretched beings [slaves], of the offer of reinstating them in that equality which in this paper [the Declaration of Independence] is declared to be the gift of God to all?" Lind then turned credit for freedom upside down. After all, it was the British who had "offered freedom to the slaves of these assertors of liberty." Were the Americans the true tyrants and the British the true liberators? It was the British who were extending to the slave "a motive . . . that the load which crushed his limbs shall be lightened, that the whip which harrowed his back shall be broken, that he shall be raised to the rank of a freeman and a citizen."[49]

In an extraordinary feat of draftsmanship, Jefferson simultaneously penned a plan of government for Virginia as he polished the Declaration of Independence, producing three drafts in thirteen days and handing the scrawled Virginian document to his old mentor, George Wythe, for transmission to Williamsburg. His charges against the English king for foisting slavery on the colonies also appeared in the preamble to the Virginia constitution, but that was not the heart of the matter. Rather, what would the constitution of the state with by far the largest number of slaves do about slavery? In 1774, in his *Summary View of the Rights of British America*, Jefferson had signaled the Virginia he hoped would emerge from the Revolution. "The abolition of domestic slavery," he had written, "is the great object of desire in those colonies where it was unhappily introduced in their infant state." Twenty months later, he proposed a

concrete way of bringing about the end of slavery: that "no person
hereafter coming into this country [Virginia] shall be held in slavery
under any pretext whatever." If adopted, this would have stopped
the Virginia slave trade dead in its tracks. To be sure, it would not
have abolished slavery outright, but since virtually all Virginians believed that slavery could not perpetuate itself without fresh infu-
sions of African bodies, banning the slave trade was equivalent to
signing a death sentence for slavery itself.[50]

Jefferson's draft of the Virginia constitution was entirely consistent with George Mason's Declaration of Rights written to introduce it. The first article stated "that all men are born equally free
and independent and have certain inherent natural rights, of which
they cannot, by any compact, deprive or divest their posterity;
among which are the enjoyment of life and liberty." Jefferson agreed
with this. But the outcry was immediate. Most of the slaveowning
Virginia legislators shrank from this inherently dangerous clause because, in the words of conservative delegate Robert Carter
Nicholas, it would "have the effect of abolishing" slavery or might
be "the forerunner of . . . civil convulsion."[51]

To the rescue rode Edmund Pendleton, a shrewd lawyer and expert wordsmith, who devised loophole language that made white
Virginians seem like sentinels of natural inborn rights while short-
circuiting slaves from those rights. The accepted rewording stated:
"All men are by nature equally free and independent" but acquired
these rights only "when they enter into a state of society."[52] In subscribing to this clause slaveowners could maintain that slaves were
not in a state of society but stood outside it and therefore had no
rights whatsoever. Though many Virginians were already on record
saying that Africans were part of humanity and therefore as possessed of natural rights as Europeans, Asians, or anyone else, such
sophistry would do for the moment. However, Jefferson's draft of
the constitution had arrived after other gentleman legislators (with
George Mason as the principal architect) had come up with a plan

of government. Jefferson's draft was left for future amendments; for now, his hopes to end slavery were dashed.

After he returned to Virginia in September 1776 and took his place in the new state legislature, Jefferson embraced another chance to clasp figurative hands with the friends of universal freedom. Appointed to the Council of Revisors, which also included the openly abolitionist George Wythe, Jefferson embarked on revising the state's law code. In this regard, he is remembered in history for a burst of reformist zeal: he seized the opportunity to provide a counterweight to Virginia's conservative constitution, which, unlike those of other states, maintained the narrowly held power of the slaveocracy. He hoped to accomplish a thoroughgoing reform of Virginia society that would end "its feudal holdovers, unnatural privileges, its slavery, and massive ignorance."

In this attempt to lay a foundation for a truly republican society, he succeeded in abolishing entail and primogeniture, limiting capital punishment to treason and willful murder, ending the Anglican Church's spiritual rule in Virginia, and laying down a blueprint for public education. But on the slavery question he did not get his way. The Council of Revisors, in whose writings Jefferson's thoughts if not his personal writing style can be discerned, drafted an abolition plan specifying that all slaves born after passage of the law would gain freedom at reaching adulthood (usually defined as age twenty-one) but would be colonized at some unspecified place outside Virginia. "It was thought better that this should be kept back," Jefferson later wrote, "and attempted only by way of amendment, whenever the bill should be brought up." Jefferson had stepped forward with the first concrete plan to end slavery but then yielded with the observation that "the public mind would not yet bear the proposition."[53]

Early in his career, his dreams of Virginia taking the lead in creating a nation based upon universal freedom, and thus cleansing it of slavery, ran into steadfast opposition. Jefferson nonetheless

realized that advocating the eradication of bondage in the Old Dominion was not quite political suicide, for he was elected to the legislature after proposing just such a thing. But planter-legislators
ready to support him on a concrete plan for gradual abolition were
discouragingly few, and Jefferson saw greater political strength in
adopting a conciliatory posture. The rebellious Americans were,
after all, at war with a cruel and mighty master, though it was this
same British master who was enticing slaves to flee their American
owners. So the matter of abolition would have to be delayed,
though questions of freedom and slavery, inextricably linked, would
remain at the heart of the revolutionary battle. As for freeing any of
his own slaves, action on that too had to await another day.

2

Fighting for Freedom

WHEN AGRIPPA HULL witnessed the supper that brought Tadeusz Kościuszko and John Paterson together at Fort Ticonderoga on May 16, 1777, he was standing on the edge of some of the most dramatic events of the American Revolution. What he experienced as General Paterson's orderly furnished him with memories that would last a lifetime. For many years after the war the people of Stockbridge, young and old, would gather around him to listen to what he had seen, heard, participated in, and in some cases influenced. Like a West African storyteller—a griot—he "never tired of telling them stories of the Revolution."[1]

Like everyone else involved, Hull understood the desperation of the American army as Paterson arrived to assume command of Fort Ticonderoga and as Colonel Kościuszko joined him to plan new fortifications for defending the strategic redoubt. Hundreds of men, African Americans among them, frantically set to work on the fortifications. But little could be done to repair the sorry condition of the 2,500 soldiers.

When General John Burgoyne, with some 7,100 regulars and about 2,500 Indian and Tory auxiliaries, swooped down to lay siege at Ticonderoga on July 5, the Americans retreated speedily. Many

Kościuszko looks down on us with the air of a European nobleman. The painting became part of the National Portrait Gallery at Independence National Historic Park in Philadelphia after the Polish National Alliance gave it to the National Park Service in 1897. Portrait of Tadeusz Kościuszko by Julian Rys after Josef Grassi's portrait (1792), Independence National Historic Park Collection, given by the Polish National Alliance.

years later, General James Wilkinson recalled how they were "badly armed, and both men and officers half naked, sickly, and destitute of comforts. Our troops . . . lost spirit" and retreated "with great disorder and its usual accompaniment, frequent desertion." Another eyewitness saw the fatigue and indiscipline of the New England fighting men so pronounced that they had been "converted . . . in a great degree into a rabble," having "lost all confidence in themselves and their leaders." "I met some of the militia on retreat," Kościuszko testified, "and having expressed my surprise at their not staying to fight for their country, they answered, they were willing to stay, but their officers would not."[2]

Fleeing in disorder, General Paterson's regiment regrouped at Fort Edward, twenty-three miles south of Ticonderoga. Meanwhile, Kościuszko threw into the breech all his military engineering skill to hamper Burgoyne's southward advance. From early July to late September, Kościuszko prepared an American defense at Bemis Heights and turned the twenty-three-mile winding route Burgoyne would have to negotiate into a living hell. Surveying the land route surrounded by heavily wooded hills and infested with swampy lowland areas that reminded him of the Polish marshlands, Kościuszko transformed the terrain into an endless series of booby traps. Paterson's brigade was among those who destroyed bridges along the overland route and felled huge trees to dam streams that turned the road into a horrendous morass. As Kościuszko and Paterson worked closely together, Hull, the general's orderly, was in almost daily contact with the Polish engineer.[3]

When Burgoyne's army reached Fort Edward on July 29, after twenty days of slogging through the torturous route, his men were exhausted and demoralized. They also found that the American army, now under General Philip Schuyler, had vanished. Burgoyne spent the next six weeks preparing to assault the American army farther south at Saratoga. But this provided time for the bedraggled, small, and pox-ravaged American army, much diminished by desertions, to regroup. Agrippa, by the side of General Paterson, witnessed Stockbridge men setting out for home, unwilling to extend their short terms of service.[4]

The American picture brightened with the arrival of Connecticut infantry and detachments from Washington's main army positioned to the south. Especially important were sharpshooting riflemen and light infantry recruited from Pennsylvania, Maryland, and Virginia and from Carolina frontiersmen. The trained eye of Kościuszko then provided a key advantage. Selecting a wooded hill not far from the Hudson River, he directed the construction of redoubts and entrenchments that would funnel the attacking British onto a killing field. Here on Bemis Heights the British forces of 5,800 men engaged 6,300 Americans on September 19, 1777. Attending the man he had come to admire, Grippy was there to see the Continental brigades absorb the attacks of General Baron von Riedesel's light infantrymen and grenadiers from Brunswick, Germany, on the Americans' right wing.

For the next month, the battle swayed back and forth. But then, reported a British officer, "the farmers left their ploughs, the smith his anvil, cobbler and tailor followed . . . [and] the militia came marching in from all the provinces of New England." On October 17, 1777, amid the red and gold of the fall trees, Burgoyne surrendered his mixed English and German, provision-short army of about 3,500. Kościuszko's engineering talent enabled inexperienced American troops to defeat some of Europe's finest professional soldiers, and his use of shovel, saw, and ax was vital in thwarting Burgoyne's plan to split the infant nation. Knocking out one-fifth of the British army, the victory paved the way for the crucial French entry into the war on the American side, stiffened the sinew of the American army, and galvanized public support for continuing the war. Many years later, Hull testified that he was there "at the taking of General Burgoyne."[5]

Kościuszko's vital role at Saratoga was long remembered. On the bicentennial of the victory, Congress authorized a plaque to be placed near Kościuszko's tomb in Krakøw's Wawel Cathedral with the inscription: "A grateful America remembers Thaddeus Kościuszko, fighter for your and our freedom." To this day, West Point plebes study the importance of Kościuszko's military engineering in achieving this epic victory. General Horatio Gates, the crusty former British officer, was the first to commend him. Congratulated by Philadelphia's Benjamin Rush for the Saratoga victory, Gates wrote, "Stop, Doctor, stop, let us be honest. . . . In the present case, the great tacticians of the campaign were hills and forests, which a young Polish engineer was skillful enough to select for my encampment."[6] This was the kind of story that Agrippa Hull would tell for the rest of his life as Stockbridgians gathered around to hear his revolutionary tales.

With Hull serving him faithfully, General Paterson marched south to join Washington's army of about 12,000 at Valley Forge. Here Grippy spent the winter of 1777–78, and here he became better acquainted with the Polish engineer. General Paterson "formed an especially close and intimate friendship [with Kościuszko]," recounted Paterson's great-grandson, "often, from the necessity of war, sleeping in the same bed."[7]

As a brigadier general's orderly, Hull no doubt fared better than most of the enlisted men at Valley Forge. But he could see the misery all around him—an exhausted, discouraged, and ill-provisioned army fighting merely to survive the winter. Joseph Plumb Martin, whose account has become a classic of the ordinary man's revolutionary experience, wrote of how

> the army was now not only starved but naked. The greatest part were not only shirtless and barefoot but destitute of all other clothing, especially blankets. I procured a small piece of raw cowhide and made myself a pair of moccasins, which kept my feet (while they lasted) from the frozen ground, although as I well remember the hard edges so galled my ankles while on a march that it was with much difficulty and pain that I could wear them afterwards; but the only alternative I had was to endure this inconvenience or to go barefoot, as hundreds of my companions had to, till they might be tracked by their blood upon the rough frozen ground.[8]

Some two thousand men died, and several thousand deserted; by February the army had dwindled down to six thousand, about half its original size.

Hull met two other men at Valley Forge who surely moved him deeply and whom, in turn, he seems to have impressed. First was the Marquis de Lafayette, the young French nobleman who had left his seventeen-year-old wife to join the American struggle for freedom. Arriving in June 1777, not quite twenty years of age but eager to fight for the "glorious cause," he had been commissioned by the Continental Congress as a major general without command. Joining George Washington, he fought bravely at Brandywine later that year, where he

limped off the field with a leg wound that filled his boot with blood.
When General Paterson and Hull arrived at Valley Forge, Lafayette
was already developing distinct views of American slavery and American blacks. During the course of the war, as his hatred of American
slavery grew, Lafayette cemented an emotional bond with Washington
that soon turned into a surrogate father-son relationship.[9]

Certainly making his mark on Hull was John Laurens, the handsome, urbane twenty-three-year-old South Carolinian who became
one of Washington's aides-de-camp. Sent abroad for his education by
his wealthy father, a South Carolina slaveowning planter of great prestige and the state's representative to the Continental Congress, the
young Laurens also burned with indignation over chattel slavery. Writing to a friend in April 1776, Laurens asked, "How can we whose jealousy has been alarmed more at the name of oppression sometimes
than at the reality, reconcile our spirited assertions of the Rights of
Mankind [with] the galling abject slavery of our Negroes?"[10]

While Washington and others bombarded Congress to provide
the basic requirements of a fighting army, the Continental Line
struggled to survive the winter. By spring they had been shaped into
a respectable force. Then their numbers grew as newly recruited
units came in after the first winter thaws. By this time, Congress's
Board of War had reassigned Kościuszko to General Israel Putnam,
who was charged with fortifying the Hudson Highlands, the highest
Hudson River terrain between Albany and New York City. Leaving
Paterson and Hull for the time being, Kościuszko began planning
fortifications at West Point in March 1778.[11]

When the campaign of 1778 began in early summer, General Paterson and his orderly went on the march again. In late June they
fell out of the Valley Forge encampment, with the Continental Army
now 12,000 strong, to pursue the British army and its supply train
of fifteen hundred wagons, which had evacuated Philadelphia to
head northward to New York. After worrying the rearguard of the
British army, the Americans met them in force on June 28, 1778, at

Monmouth Courthouse, New Jersey. With John Laurens's unit nearby, Paterson's Third Massachusetts Brigade fought with great bravery on a day so sweltering that as many men were felled by heat exhaustion as by bullets. The battle was a stalemate. Grippy added this famous battle—the last major engagement in the Northern states—to his store of revolutionary experiences.[12]

From Monmouth, Paterson's brigade spent time in Danbury and Hartford, Connecticut, and then by December 1778 moved to West Point, where Paterson was given command of the post that Kościuszko had been busily fortifying since February. Through the summer of 1779, Paterson renewed his friendship with Kościuszko, who had turned the "key to America," as it was called, into impressive fortifications that blocked British attempts to move their army units in Canada southward to join their compatriots in New York City. It was here at "the Point" that the young black Stockbridgian who had served as Paterson's orderly for two years found himself reassigned to the Polish engineer he had come to admire.[13]

Surviving war records yield no details on why Paterson arranged Hull's reassignment to Kościuszko, but it could hardly have been done without the Polish engineer's interest in Hull. A century later, Paterson's great-grandson repeated what he heard of how Hull "was intelligent and unusually bright" and how "his aptness and wit and his readiness in repartee, as well as the intelligent manner in which he performed all his duties, made him a great favorite with all the officers of the army stationed at 'the Point.'" After Kościuszko "took a fancy" to him, he recounted, "and, after a time, became much attached to him," Paterson "gave him to [Kościuszko] as a servant." This happened in May 1779, for all accounts agree that Hull served Paterson for two years before being transferred to Kościuszko, whom he would now serve for fifty months.[14]

In the early days of Hull's service with Kościuszko, the growing warmth of their relationship was revealed in one of the most colorful incidents of Hull's life, to be retold many times. Indeed, it seems to have been a defining moment that bonded the two men. In the telling of Hull's friend and Stockbridge's first historian, having "made Grippy his confidential and head servant" and entrusted him with his wardrobe, Kościuszko left West Point to reconnoiter across the Hudson River for several days. With the cat away, the mice began to play. Hull called together "all the black servants in the camp" for a festive dinner. Befitting the son of an African prince, he donned Kościuszko's Polish uniform, resplendent with a "crown-shaped cap and a showy cluster of nodding ostrich plumes." Lacking officer's boots, Hull blacked up his legs to shine like polished boots. With the officers' wine flowing freely, great hilarity broke out among the black men.

Unable to cross the Hudson River, Kościuszko returned unexpectedly. Leaving his horse near his quarters, he approached Grippy's noisy party and peered from behind a screen placed by the black soldiers to shield the frolic "from the view of passers-by." Much amused, Kościuszko watched as the black party toasted Grippy's health, addressing him as General Kościuszko. Whether he knew it or not, Kościuszko was witnessing a festivity long practiced by black New Englanders. Often organized by Africans of princely background, these so-called election day celebrations chose black leaders—faux governors and kings—to commemorate African customs and provide a king-for-a-day relief from the drudgery of slavery or ill-paid free black life. Elaborate dress was de rigueur for these festivities, and the elected governor or king, usually the servant of an important white figure, was expected to provide food and liquor for proper celebrating.[15]

The biographer of Kościuszko's boon friend John Paterson related how "General Kosciusko suddenly sprang in among them, causing such commotion that had a Satan himself appeared in their midst it could not have resulted in a greater stampede." Mortified, Grippy "fell prostrate at the general's feet, crying, 'Whip me, kill me, Massa; do anything with me, Mr. General.'" Rising to the occasion, Tadeusz, with "great formality" befitting the setting, clasped Grippy's hand and said, "Rise, Prince, it is beneath the dignity of an African prince to prostrate himself at the feet of any one." Placing the ostrich-plumed hat back on Grippy's head, Tadeusz marched his orderly to General Paterson's quarters, where, playing it to the hilt, the Polish officer continued the role reversal game by erecting a throne before Paterson's quarters and commanding Grippy to ascend to it. "After going through many mock ceremonies of presentation to royalty that afforded the throng a world of sport, they closed by smoking with him the calumet of peace." For the rest of his long life, Grippy delighted in telling the story, and his listeners delighted in hearing it.

It is evident from the way he rescued Hull from a mortifying moment that the Polish general was at ease with the free black men with whom he mingled. Kościuszko's admiration for black Americans grew as the war wore on, and so did his revulsion at chattel slavery. In twenty-eight months of constructing fortifications at West Point, he found the brawn and skill of black craftsmen and laborers indispensable in felling trees, erecting fortifications of earth and stone, and building bridges and roadways.[16]

Kościuszko must have been confirmed in his positive feelings about African Americans after hearing about the bravery of black American soldiers in the Battle of Newport on August 29, 1778. Americans hoped that a French naval force combined with an American army of ten thousand would dislodge the British in occupied Newport, Rhode Island. But the unexpected withdrawal of the French fleet, a severe three-day storm, and the wholesale desertion of American militiamen left the Patriot troops in a difficult position. The British had become the attackers instead of the attacked.

A newly raised regiment of black Rhode Islanders saved the day. Composed of slaves promised their freedom after whites could not be found to fill the depleted ranks of the First Rhode Island Regiment, this new regiment fought with uncommon bravery to repel three furious assaults by Hessian regulars. Though a Franco-American fiasco, leaving an important shipping lane under British control, it was a triumph for the black men only months out of slavery and hastily trained. Withstanding the charges of the smartly dressed Hessian regulars in blue and yellow, one of the most effective professional units under British command, the black troops attracted the admiration of Lafayette, who led troops in the Rhode Island engagement. When word of the blacks' valor reached West Point a few days later, Kościuszko surely felt confirmed in his view that black Americans, thought by many whites to be poor soldier material, were as daring and leather-necked as the toughest plowman-turned-militiaman.[17]

Through the winters of 1778–79 and 1779–80, the latter the most severe in the memory of those at West Point, Paterson and Kościuszko were in constant contact as the work of fortifying the Hudson River fortress went forward. Whereas the French engineers assigned to the project argued for seventeenth-century Vauban-style fortifications, which emphasized parallel high towers, the Polish engineer built a unique series of sixteen fortified positions in three defensive rings that utilized sheer walls and rocky obstacles to adapt each stronghold to its nearby terrain.[18] By late 1779, the nearly impregnable Hudson Heights fortress had neutralized the British campaign in the Northern states. Bottled up in New York City, Sir Henry Clinton, responding to the decisions of the British military planners, moved his British forces south. With some 8,700 troops aboard, a British flotilla left New York City in December 1779 to pursue the fight in the Southern states that George III's strategists hoped would end the war.

Restless at West Point and eager to ride to the sound of guns, Kościuszko negotiated his way southward to join the climactic stage of the war. Having already announced that "I suppose to be myself at this time more than half a Yankee," he received Washington's appointment to serve as the principal engineer of the Southern army under Horatio Gates's command. With him went Agrippa Hull with the consent of Colonel Ebenezer Sprout, from whose Massachusetts unit Hull still drew his pay.

In seeking Washington's approval of this arrangement, the ever-careful Kościuszko noted that Hull was the only orderly willing "to go with me so far off." This was a remarkable comment. It suggested that men assigned to officers had some right to refuse service if it promised to carry them far from home. Also, it spoke to the limited horizons of ordinary New Englanders, who were unwilling to journey far from the region that constituted their entire cognitive universe. Further, it testified to the bond that had grown between Kościuszko and Hull. The lowborn black New Englander, now turning twenty-one, was willing to accompany the Polish engineer of noble birth, thirteen years his senior, on an arduous trek of many hundred miles—and one of unpredictable duration.[19]

For the three ensuing years, related below, Hull served Kościuszko during the Southern campaign, regarded by historians as the most vicious, life-draining, and spirit-crushing chapter of the American Revolution. It was during this time, it seems, that Hull honed the force of character that carried him through life and stocked his mind with experiences that served him well for many years. In a time when armies fought without furloughs or Christmas home leaves, the two men lived most of their waking hours in close contact. Week in and week out, for more than 1,500 days, their lives were entwined. In army protocol, social distance was an essential part of how officers maintained discipline among enlisted men. Because social familiarity was believed to undermine military discipline and erode the blind obedience soldiers owed their officers, eating, drinking, game playing, and even conversational bantering were proscribed in the field or in camp. The fate of a junior officer who failed to honor the distinction between himself and the rank and file was usually court-martial. However, the relationship between a senior officer and his orderly was blurred, partially because they were in such intimate daily contact and partly because high-ranking officers could be more flexible,

secure in their military authority and social status. In the case of
Kościuszko and Hull, a special bond grew. Paradoxically, the education that the Polish gentry-born, serf-owning officer received in Warsaw and Paris equipped him with more democratic instincts than
many of the American officers with whom he served.

Heading south from West Point in early August 1780, just two
days after Benedict Arnold was appointed to command West Point,
Kościuszko, his assistant engineer named Joseph Dalzian, and Hull
stopped to pay respects to General Washington at Orangetown (also
called Tappan). Here, almost certainly, Hull met Washington's body
servant William Lee, who was never far from the general's side. From
there, Kościuszko, Dalzian, and Hull made their way to Philadelphia.

Passing through the Quaker capital, the three men witnessed the
damage the British had inflicted on the city during their nine-month
occupation several years before, and they probably heard how
Pennsylvania slaves had gained their freedom by fleeing to the
British. Hull also had a chance to hear of how the Pennsylvania legislature had enacted the nation's first gradual abolition, which had
taken effect just eight months before. As of January 1, 1780, the
child born of any slave after that date was guaranteed freedom at
age twenty-eight. Though slaveowners would have the labor of
newborn black children for much of their working lives, this was
the first time any government in the Americas had moved this far.
Perhaps Kościuszko read the abolition act's preamble, which eloquently expressed what would become his bedrock belief in the uni-
tary nature of humankind. "It is not for us to enquire why, in the
creation of mankind," read the preamble, "the inhabitants of the
several parts of the world were distinguished by a difference in fea-
ture or complexion. It is sufficient to know that all are the work of
an Almighty Hand . . . who placed them in their various situations
[and] hath extended equally his care and protection to all."[20]

Continuing south, Kościuszko, Dalzian, and Hull detoured to
visit Traveler's Rest, Horatio Gates's piedmont Virginia plantation,

to pay their respects to the general's wife and gravely ill son. This took them through Richmond, which they reached in mid-September. Oblique references in letters between Jefferson and Gates, who three months before had been called out of retirement to command Washington's Southern Continental Army, suggest that Kościuszko and Hull briefly met Virginia's wartime governor. For Agrippa Hull, it must have been eye-opening to see a battery of slaves from Monticello attending the celebrated Patriot leader.

Moving farther south through North Carolina, Kościuszko and Hull finally rendezvoused with General Gates's army in October 1780. They surely were struck by the pitiful condition of Gates's battered troops. The British had begun their Southern campaign with a flourish. Seizing Savannah, Georgia, on New Year's Day, 1779, they swept northward through Georgia and captured an American army of 3,300 men with all their supplies and matériel at Charleston, South Carolina, in their biggest victory of the war. Upon arriving in North Carolina to take command in late July, Gates found a demoralized remnant of the Continental Line and the raw, unreliable militia units from Virginia and the Carolinas. "A vast number of men" had deserted "to the enemy," wrote one officer, as the only way to avoid starvation in an area where the farmers, many of them Loyalists, would provide little if anything to the troops.[21]

Kościuszko soon learned of Gates's rash decision to push his half-starved, poorly armed army south into South Carolina through a Loyalist-infested region to attack the British garrison at Camden, South Carolina, in August 1780. In this ill-advised foray, the debilitated, half-naked militiamen, bolstered by only a thousand soldiers from the Continental Army, fled from a British assault and suffered the most ignominious American defeat of the war.[22] By the time Kościuszko reached his old friend Gates in October at Hillsborough, North Carolina, where Gates had retreated with his shattered army, the former British professional soldier was a disgraced man.

Upon their arrival, Kościuszko and Agrippa Hull could see the desperate conditions in the South. The army bivouacked at Hillsborough was so barren of supplies that Kościuszko had to share his cloak as a blanket with his bunk mates, Brigadier General Isaac Huger and Dr. William Read, the army's chief physician. But at least these officers' boots were intact. While Kościuszko and other officers rode horses, Hull walked. His shoes worn through from the six-hundred-mile trek southward, the blanketless Grippy got through the winter, the worst in memory, only after a pair of shoes "for Colonel Cusiasko's Servant" arrived.

Begging North Carolina's governor to support the remnants of the army, Nathanael Greene, who had replaced Gates, described what Kościuszko and Hull could see with their own eyes. "Of our troops at this time," he agonized, "more than one half . . . are unfit for any kind of duty; hundreds being without shirts, stockings, or any other clothing." Six days later, writing to Washington, Greene described his troops "as ragged and naked as the Virginia blacks" he had seen when passing through the state that was home to Jefferson, Madison, and Washington. Greene shortly dismissed most of the Virginia Second Regiment in the severe winter for lack of blankets, shoes, breeches, and food, the latter in such short supply that the men received only half a pound of flour each day and occasionally half a pound of beef "so miserably poor that scarce any mortal could make use of it."[23]

Compounding the agonies suffered by dint of the broken commissary system, where procuring basic essentials became a daily travail, was the loyalism of about half the Carolinians and Georgians. In no part of the country other than New York were so many Americans ready to join the British whenever they approached. On top of these defections from the Patriot cause, Greene's troops were further whittled down by the defection of thousands of slaves fleeing their Patriot owners to claim the freedom promised them if they reached the British army. "Their property [in slaves] we need not seek," gloated John André, the famous British spy. "It flies to us and famine follows."[24]

To witness this massive slave defection must have astounded Kościuszko and Hull. No paper trail remains for historians to consult, so imagining how they felt about what they saw and heard can only be surmise. But *nobody* in the American South in the latter stages of the revolutionary war was unaware of the vicious civil war and the black flight to the British that enveloped the region. Throughout the war, white Southerners—Patriot and Loyalist, seaboard and interior, Upper South and Lower South—were absorbed with the problem of how to control some four hundred thousand restive slaves who saw the American Revolution as a breaking dawn they had hoped for almost since their arrival on American shores. It was common knowledge that slaves belonging to Patriot masters were deserting in droves whenever the proximity of the British army gave them a fighting chance to escape, while slaveowners, knowing that the British would not free the slaves of Americans loyal to the Crown, were thus more likely to join the fray under British colors.

The crisis had begun in 1775, when Lord Dunmore, Virginia's royal governor, had issued a proclamation offering freedom to enslaved and indentured people willing to join His Majesty's Army to help repress the Patriot forces. Announced in November 1775, the proclamation unleashed the first black surge for freedom, terrifying white Patriot Southerners in the process. The problem for white slaveowners subsided when the British army moved north in early 1776. However, the British return to the South in 1779 reignited the black insurgency. "All the Negroes, men, women, and children," remembered Banastre Tarleton, the brutal and much vilified British cavalry officer, "upon the approach of any detachment of the King's troops, thought themselves absolved from all respect to their American masters and entirely released from servitude. Influenced by this idea, they quitted the plantations and followed the army."[25]

Kościuszko and Hull arrived in the middle of this second wave of slave rebellion, and it could not help but shape their attitudes toward slavery. Perhaps it inspired them to think about how America might be transformed in the crucible of war.

Kościuszko also knew—it was on everyone's lips—that in the previous year Congress had urged Georgia and South Carolina to raise three thousand slaves. This desperate action was designed to repulse the British Loyalists, especially thousands of blacks seeking freedom through service to the king, aided by swarms of Southern Loyalists. Eager to play a leading role in this recruitment was the dashing John Laurens, whom Hull had encountered at Valley Forge. Hoping that an America unshackled from British tyranny might break the chains of some half million slaves, Laurens had proposed a compensated emancipation for slaves whose masters would allow them to volunteer to join all-black regiments. This would be fitting for "those who are unjustly deprived of the rights of mankind." But Washington refused to support the plan, believing that black men under arms would become the advance guard of an uncontrollable liberation movement. Freed slaves, he reasoned, would become "more irksome to those who remain in it."[26]

As Patriots mulled over the use of black troops, an important change occurred near the top of the American army. Congress relieved Kościuszko's friend General Horatio Gates of his command of the Southern army and replaced him with the thirty-nine-year-old Rhode Islander General Nathanael Greene. For the duration of the war Greene relied on Kościuszko as his primary military engineer; in turn, Kościuszko depended on Hull to serve him faithfully in ways that military officers expected of orderlies in the eighteenth century.[27]

Like Gates before him, Greene found himself commanding a provision-starved tatterdemalion Continental Army with a paper strength of only 2,457 men, a mere third of whom were decently equipped and clothed. Local militiamen, he soon understood, answered a call to arms as if it were a matter of choice. And only by requisitioning food from local farmers almost at gunpoint could he provision his troops. In this unenviable situation, Greene had to respond to the British military strategy in the fall of 1780, which was to hold only Charleston and Savannah on the coast and commit most of their forces to strike north through North Carolina to Virginia. Leading the British army was General Charles Cornwallis, who had drubbed General Gates's army at Camden.[28]

Through the winter of 1780–81, Greene and Cornwallis played hare and hound, feigning attacks, terrorizing the countryside, and skirmishing in guerilla-style, hit-and run probes. Roving through hundreds of miles, Kościuszko and Hull became part of one of the ugliest chapters of the war for independence. As the advance officer for Greene's heroic attempts to harry the much superior British force as they moved northward for a strike that they hoped would end the long war, Kościuszko used his practiced eye to survey unfamiliar terrain. Reconnoitering and mapping the Catawba, Pee Dee, and Yadkin rivers, he supervised the construction of small flat-bottomed boats that could be moved from one river line to the next by wagon and oversaw the removal of obstructions that would impede navigation.[29]

The viciousness of the bushwhacking, partisan warfare that Kościuszko and Hull witnessed in 1781–82 almost beggars description. Patriot and Tory militia stripped the country of food and forage to keep their enemies at bay and starve them into submission. "The whole country," Greene wrote the Continental Congress in December 1780, "is in danger of being laid waste by the Whigs and Tories who pursue each other with as much relentless fury as beasts of prey." Fifteen months later, riding one hundred miles eastward toward the seacoast through Georgia's backcountry, General William Moultrie described a countryside previously flush with "live-stock and wild fowl of every kind ... now destitute of all. ... Not the vestiges of horses, cattle, hogs, or deer was to be found. The squirrels and birds of every kind were totally destroyed," and his dragoons assured him that "no living creature was to be seen, except now and then a few camp scavengers [vultures], picking the bones of some unfortunate fellows, who had been shot or cut down, and left in the woods above ground." General Greene, in the same year, wrote Washington that "I feel for the country, for I believe Saxony [in the] last war was not plundered and ravaged with more severity than this."[30]

In this maelstrom of war, Kościuszko had many opportunities to witness the Southern plantations reeking of misery, even as the fabric of slavery was shredding, and to think about how black bondage might come to an end. What thoughts raced through Agrippa Hull's mind remains an open question, but we can draw some inferences from what is known about his lengthy service in the Lower South.

Barely six weeks after Kościuszko and Hull met up with General Greene, they experienced the ebb and flow of the Southern campaign. Kościuszko had selected an encampment on the Pee Dee River, some sixty miles north of Camden, for Greene's small army, and he had worked with local militia to build a stockade nearby.[31] It was there that two of the crack units of the British and Continental armies met on the North and South Carolina border at Cowpens in an action long remembered as one of the war's most vicious. When General Cornwallis learned that Colonel Dan Morgan's dragoons and light infantrymen were operating in the deep foothills of the interior 120 miles west of Greene's main force, he determined to use his superior forces to eliminate this pesky American unit that had performed brilliantly at Saratoga. To annihilate Morgan's unit of 600 veteran Continentals and 450 militiamen from Virginia, Maryland, and Delaware, Cornwallis sent Banastre Tarleton's greatly feared green-jacketed cavalry to run Morgan down and cut his men to pieces. Morgan chose to make a stand at Cowpens, a tree-dotted upcountry pasturing ground. It was an unconventional battleground on which to take a stand against the flower of Cornwallis's army: Morgan had an impassable river at his back, while the open meadows provided a terrain most favorable to Tarleton, the cocky twenty-six-year-old leader of lightning cavalry charges.[32]

Kościuszko and Hull saw vivid examples of the courage of black troops in this bloody battle between English troops headed by Colonel Banastre Tarleton and Americans soldiers commanded by Colonel Dan Morgan. The bugle boy, still nameless to this day, is on the left. William Ranney, *Battle of Cowpens*, from the Collection of the State of South Carolina.

At the height of the battle, initiated at dawn on January 17, 1781, a black youth saved the life of an important American officer. With 200 British kilted Scottish Highlanders in the center of the action, bagpipes skirling, William Washington, George Washington's powerfully built second cousin, repelled a bayonet charge on the right flank and then attacked Tarleton's elite unit with a mounted saber charge. Slashing at the officer next to Tarleton, Washington broke his saber off at the handguard. As a British officer poised to run Washington through with his sword, a fourteen-year-old black bugle boy dropped the officer with a pistol shot to his shoulder. At this, Tarleton fled, and the battle was over. This incident further impressed Kościuszko that African American soldiers, even as young as fourteen years old, could fight courageously and that their willingness to pledge their lives for the American cause might help the cause of abolishing slavery.

Of Tarleton's 1,150 men, 100 were slain, 229 wounded, and 600 captured, including 70 former slaves who had fled to the British to gain their freedom. Surveying the booty left on the battlefield, the Americans were now in possession of a hundred prize dragoon horses, eight hundred muskets, thirty-five supply wagons, many bugles and bagpipes, and two "grasshoppers" (small British cannon). In the course of the action 12 Americans had been killed and 60 wounded. The stunning American victory saved half of Greene's army, decimated one of Cornwallis's hardened and most prized units, and boosted the much-punctured Patriot morale. Not since Bunker Hill had Patriot marksmen performed so gallantly. It encouraged more Southern Patriot militia to turn out and inspired the Northern states to send more matériel to see the war through.[33]

While black courage on the Patriot side was on display, Kościuszko and Hull repeatedly saw Southern slaves risking their lives for the British cause in exchange for freedom. One vivid example occurred in May and June 1781, at the siege of the fort in Ninety-Six, South Carolina, the British stronghold in the state's hilly interior. American attempts to direct fire at the fort from zigzag trenches they dug at night were thwarted when British colonel John Cruger, the New York Loyalist and former mayor of New York City, sent out South Carolina Loyalist militiamen and escaped slaves to fill in the trenches. Kościuszko then contrived a tunneling effort to blow up the British fortifications while the siege prevented the British from replenishing their desperately lacking supplies of food and water. Colonel Cruger countered, as a British officer described it, by sending out "naked African-Americans who brought a scanty supply [of water] from within pistol shot of the American pickets, their bodies not being distinguishable in the night from fallen trees, with which the place abounded." Learning of British reinforcements marching to Ninety-Six, General Greene broke off the siege and withdrew. From that point forward, the Americans had to get used to former slaves fighting with the British and even officering black troops, many of whom served in cavalry units as experienced horse-men. One former slave, a man named March, was dubbed "the Negro General" after he lost his life in April 1782 in a skirmish on the Ashley River with part of Lee's Legion from Virginia.[34]

Slaves served the British not only as soldiers but also as spies, scouts, messengers, and drummers. Drawing on African expertise, many Southern slaves in Hessian and British regiments sent field di-rections through drumming. In July 1781, as Cornwallis's army in Virginia moved toward the James River, Lieutenant Colonel Banas-tre Tarleton dispatched an escaped slave who had joined the British army to slip into General Lafayette's American encampment, where he pretended he had deserted the British. This allowed him to give the Americans false information about the positioning of British units. In the consequent engagement at James Island, misled by the Tory black, Americans suffered four times as many casualties as the British. Thereafter, General Greene's military correspondence was sprinkled with remarks about how the slaves who had fled to the British knew intimately the creeks, coves, bays, and marshes, much to the advantage of the British troops combating the Americans.[35]

Their warm friendship notwithstanding, Tadeusz would occa-sionally detach Grippy for temporary service on the killing fields. For example, at Eutaw Springs, South Carolina, Kościuszko volun-teered to lead troops onto the field and sent Hull to assist the army doctors. This task was to mark Agrippa Hull's memory indelibly. Called by General Greene "by far the most bloody and obstinate [battle] I ever saw," the fight at Eutaw Springs on September 8 hor-rified Hull. In the battle that began early in the morning, General Greene used his reprovisioned and augmented force of 2,200 to at-tack 1,800 British regulars at the junction of South Carolina's Eutaw Creek and the Santee River. In the last major engagement in the Lower South, the flow of battle swayed back and forth, with bayonet and cavalry charges supplemented by six-pounder cannons. The Americans suffered fearful casualties but managed to stalemate the British forces, which suffered the highest percentage losses of any revolutionary war battle—nearly 40 percent.[36]

When the British and American units disengaged, the work of battlefield surgeons began. Among the casualties was Colonel William Washington, who was bayoneted in the chest and captured after his horse was shot from under him. But far worse off were the maimed. Hull was assigned to pinion some of the 375 badly wounded Americans, as field surgeons amputated their mangled limbs. His horror can be imagined from the field reports. Leading a large contingent of African Americans with entrenching tools, Kościuszko engineered a withdrawal of the mangled army over the Santee River and through swamp lands to reach the hills above the river. But many of the wounded, lying amid a landscape of corpses, were so severely injured that they had to be left near the Santee. "The condition of the wounded," wrote Colonel Otho H. Williams, "was deplorable. We found them without necessaries, some of them scarcely attended, and others wholly neglected. Many had their wounds animated with fly blows [eggs of flies usually found in the open flesh of animals] and all together they exhibited one of the most humiliating and distressing scenes I ever beheld. Their moans indicating pain, want and despair impressed the spirits of every humane spectator with that pathetic sorrow which inclines to inactivity and despondence." Sorely lacking medicine—it was long before the advent of anesthesia—Williams could do little to "alleviate their misery." Hull remembered this blood-drenched battle and his assignment in it for the rest of his life.[37]

Even though the British held their ground, they failed to vanquish the Americans and lost heart for more action. Withdrawing to Charleston, the key Southern seaport they had held since May 1780, they awaited the outcome of another battle looming in Virginia. It was here that Thomas Jefferson, architect of the Declaration of Independence, would encounter how passionately slaves yearned for freedom.

A man with no stomach for the battlefield, Jefferson, after drafting the Declaration of Independence, had spent several years back in Virginia at his Monticello plantation, with part of each year in Williamsburg, the Virginia capital. Here the legislature entrusted him, along with four other eminences, to prescribe key reforms to the state's laws. This difficult process took several years to accomplish. Among the reforms were laws to prohibit further importations of African slaves; to abolish the ancient practice of entail, which froze land and slave property within a family; to institute public education; to scale back capital punishment; to use western lands to open up opportunity for the poor and landless; and to end the privileged place that the Anglican Church enjoyed as Virginia's established religion.

Given Jefferson's proclivities for philosophical and legal ruminations, he was not the right man to lead Virginia during a crisis precipitated by a British invasion in 1780. Nonetheless, on June 1, 1779, the legislature elected Jefferson to succeed Patrick Henry as the state's governor. The timing could hardly have been worse for a man better armed with pen than sword, for just before Jefferson became governor, a British fleet sailed into the tidewater area, disembarked 1,800 troops, and plundered tidewater Virginia.

Black insurgency resumed, as slaves fled to the British in shoals. A quick British withdrawal stopped this. But red-coated forces returned in October 1780 for a second incursion that inspired further slave escapes. The main invasion came on December 30, 1780, led by Brigadier General Benedict Arnold, who just a few months before had betrayed the Americans at West Point. Storming up the James River, facing little Virginia resistance, on January 4, 1781, Arnold laid siege to Richmond, where Jefferson had moved his state government only a few months earlier. Jefferson and the legislature scurried for their lives. After destroying war matériel and buildings, the British fell back down the James River. Four months later they attacked again, this time retaking Richmond and forcing Jefferson and the legislature to turn tail for Charlottesville. Jefferson's flight was aided by a Monticello blacksmith who deceived the British by shoeing his master's horse backwards. Other Jefferson slaves saved the family silver by hanging it on iron hooks inside a well. But some of his slaves plotted to save themselves from lifelong servitude by fleeing to the onrushing British army.[38]

While Virginians ran from the British army, their slaves fled to the British, seizing the best chance for freedom they had ever encountered. James Madison's father wrote him that "families within the sphere of his [Arnold's] action have suffered greatly. Some have lost 40 [slaves], others 30, and one a considerable part of their slaves." When Cornwallis's troops reached Jefferson's several plantations in early June, another twenty-three of his slaves fled to join the British and throw off their shackles. Robert Honyman, Jefferson's doctor, reported that slaves "flocked to the enemy from all quarters, from even remote parts . . . Some lost 30, 40, 50, 60, or even 70 Negroes . . . [and] some plantation entirely cleared and not a single Negro remained." Many others totted up their losses, including Thomas Nelson, Jefferson's successor as governor, who lost all but eighty to a hundred of his seven hundred slaves.[39]

British raids up the Potomac River in April 1781 again stirred the hopes of slaves longing for freedom. Robert Carter, one of the largest slaveowners of the area, lost thirty slaves to the British. At Mount Vernon, Washington lost seventeen. Even today, counting up the losses is difficult. The best estimate may be that of Johann Ewald, the Hessian officer who believed that some four thousand men and women of all ages had joined Cornwallis's army by the summer of 1781. This was far less than the thirty thousand Jefferson claimed fled to the British, though Ewald may not have included large numbers of slaves who died within weeks of fleeing their plantations.[40]

How did Jefferson reconcile the flight of his slaves to the British with his advocacy of universal freedom? He wrote at the time that the British abducted them, implying that the slaves had no desire to be freed, but it is more accurate to say that Jefferson's slaves were willingly abducted, knowing that freedom would be theirs. The twenty-three slaves who fled from Jefferson's three plantations in what were apparently premeditated flights included Black Sal with her three young children, along with Harry, Barnaby, and Robin, adult males, and a boy named Will from Monticello; two men and two women from Elk Hill in Cumberland County; and Hannibal and his wife and six children, along with another couple and an old woman, from Willis Creek. Perhaps Jefferson took solace in the fact that only a minority of his slaves decamped to the British. But it must have been sobering that nearly half of the escaped slaves were women, for it was unusual in this era for women to escape from their masters. In a bitter conclusion to his two-year service as governor, Monticello became the prize of Tarleton and his green-coated dragoons on June 3, 1781, just one day before his term expired.[41]

After Jefferson left office, the Virginia assembly conducted an inquiry into his flight to the interior as Tarleton's army advanced. Though he was absolved of blame, Jefferson later confessed that he was so emotionally wounded that his spirit could "only be cured by the all healing grave." His personal difficulties notwithstanding, prospects for the American side brightened when the Continental Army, replenished from the north and steadied by Nathanael Greene's sturdy generalship, won a notable victory at Cowpens. By fall, with the arrival of the French army and navy, Cornwallis's seven thousand men, who had relentlessly scourged the Virginia countryside, now found themselves pinned down at Yorktown on the James River peninsula. Surrounding the British, the American and French troops besieged the enemy for three weeks. Victory for the Americans came on October 19, 1781, when Cornwallis surrendered his army.

The American victory was a disaster for the rebellious slaves, most of whom had tasted freedom only briefly. With hunger and smallpox stalking the British fortifications, Cornwallis had expelled several thousand black auxiliaries from the British encampments. Hessian officer Johann Ewald wrote bitterly that "we had used them to good advantage and set them free, and now, with fear and trembling, they had to face the reward of their cruel masters." Cornwallis could hardly have done differently. With surrender imminent, he knew that every former slave in his camp would be returned to his or her master, so by thrusting them out of the British fortifications they had at least a small chance of hiding in the woods and escaping to a more distant place. Fleeing into the countryside, most of them were swept away by a new wave of smallpox. Jefferson estimated that smallpox claimed 90 percent of Virginia's escaped slaves as the war wound down, and many of his slaves were among them.[42]

After the great victory at Yorktown, the Americans shifted their effort southward. Still in South Carolina amid fetid swamps, Kościuszko and Hull learned that Cornwallis had surrendered his army to the Franco-American encircling army. But that did not end the work of the Polish military engineer and his orderly. The British still held three important seaports in the South—Wilmington, North Carolina; Charleston, South Carolina; and Savannah, Georgia. With his army receiving reinforcements from Pennsylvania, Maryland, and Delaware, General Greene began clearing the South Carolinian interior of British units. By December, he was closing in on Charleston.

The prospects for a decisive move to end slavery brightened momentarily in South Carolina as the war neared its end. Almost two years before, John Laurens had proposed freeing hundreds of slaves to augment the depleted American forces. Now he reintroduced this proposal to reinforce General Greene's army with "a well chosen corps of black levies." Greene firmly endorsed the plan, arguing that South Carolina and Georgia would not have been pillaged and overrun with British and Loyalist forces if they had earlier raised black troops with promises of freedom. Greene's own experience with black soldiers left him with no doubt "that they would make good soldiers," and, he argued, the state "has it not in its power to give sufficient reinforcements without incorporating them."[43]

Laurens's proposal gained force when Congress urged South Carolina to raise two battalions of black troops to help Greene oust the British. Laurens tried to sweeten his plan by proposing that twenty-five hundred black troops could be seized from confiscated Loyalist estates, thus not touching the chattel property of a single Patriot. Though it gained support in the South Carolina legislature, the plan ultimately failed. Aedanus Burke, Laurens's fellow legislator, identified the crux of planter resistance: they believed that northerners secretly hoped for a general emancipation after the war, and that enlisting slaves as soldiers with promises of freedom would abet this dismantling of the Lower South's slave regime. Frightened at this prospect, Carolinian legislators scotched Laurens and Greene's proposal, willing to prolong the internecine slaughter rather than agree to a pacified but potentially slaveless society.[44]

Though unwilling to free slaves to defeat the British, South Carolina's legislators were agreeable in February 1782 to assigning four hundred slaves confiscated from Loyalist estates as wagoners, tree cutters, and servants for the officers in Greene's army. Greene insisted that these men be clothed at the public expense and "allowed the same wages granted by Congress to the Soldiers of the Continental army" because "unless the Negroes have an interest in their servitude . . . they will be of little benefit and by no means to be depended on."

Thus Nathanael Greene and his still underprovisioned army soldiered on. Not yet devastated by the surrender of Cornwallis's army at Yorktown, British forces in the Lower South continued to hold Charleston and Savannah and used Hessian contingents to strike inland. Greene's plaintive description of the army tells us what Kościuszko and Hull witnessed in the last year of the war. From his headquarters near Charleston, Greene described his situation: "We are remote from support and supplies of every kind. No large bodies of militia can be hastily called together here, nor can supplies of any kind be had, but with the greatest difficulty. We have 300 men now without arms, and twice that number so naked as to be unfit for any duty but in cases of desperation. Not a rag of clothing has arrived to us this winter. Indeed our prospects are really deplorable. It is true we get meat and rice, but no rum, or spirits. Men and officers without pay in this situation cannot be kept in temper long."[45]

Near the end of hostilities, Kościuszko received his first command as a line officer leading troops into battle, and he promptly used African Americans to good advantage. The death of his comrade-in-arms John Laurens provided the opportunity to test his mettle in combat. In late August 1782, leading fifty infantrymen against a British foraging party outside of Charleston, where the Americans were besieging the British, Laurens had marched into an ambush near Combahee Ferry. There he died on the battlefield. Five days later, always attentive to black Americans, Kościuszko importuned General Greene to distribute some of Laurens's clothing to the South Carolinian's black servants. "They are naked," he wrote; "they want shirts and jackets [and] breeches, and their skin can bear as well as ours good things." Kościuszko now took up an advanced post about six miles closer to Charleston than Greene's main encampment on the Ashley River. As the British prepared to evacuate Charleston, Kościuszko relied heavily on black spies and couriers to provide information on the British positions.[46]

In organizing an assault in October 1782 to root out the British light horse, black troops, and Loyalist militiamen on James Island, where Fort Johnston covered the approaches to Charleston, Kościuszko again turned to an African American. Knowing the island and all its fords, Prince, formerly a South Carolina slave, led the way. After capturing sixty horses from the British, Kościuszko marched his unit back to the mainland. A month later, they returned to Fort Johnston to fire the last shots of the eight-year revolutionary war. With fifty-seven men, some of whom "had no blankets, some without shoes, and [a] great many . . . that are little boys not fit to carry arms," Kościuszko reached the island at two AM and engaged the British just after sunrise. His own report of the firefight makes it clear that Kościuszko's troops were overwhelmed by the superior British force, which included former slaves from New York who had gained their freedom by joining the British. Many years later, a South Carolina historian related that Kościuszko, in the thick of the battle, barely escaped death when "a very young and gallant volunteer who had joined the expedition" killed a British dragoon "in the act of cutting him down."[47]

Retreating to the mainland with his coat pierced by four musket balls, Kościuszko, along with Agrippa Hull, now awaited the British evacuation of Charleston. This occurred on December 14, 1782. With General Anthony Wayne leading the triumphant American troops into Charleston, Kościuszko and his detachment fell into line—Hull, no doubt, at the Polish hero's side. The retaking of Charleston was remembered in historical accounts for noisy celebrations and an effusion of gratitude by the townspeople, but in reality the still bedraggled American force, as one Pennsylvanian officer recorded in his diary, "experienced a most shameful neglect by the public," which refused their "liberators" firewood and provisions to the extent that for six days the American soldiers lived on short rations.[48]

Kościuszko and Hull must have been pained to see the British in Charleston decide which of the former slaves to take with them and which to return to their American masters. In the last two weeks of October 1782, the Polish engineer and his orderly watched a flotilla of British ships sail out of the harbor with some 1,300 troops, 1,900 American Loyalists, and 1,700 blacks. The final British contingent left on December 14, 1782.[49]

The officer and his orderly remained in Charleston over the winter of 1782–83 at the American encampment on James Island. The long-suffering remnants of Greene's Southern army finally received what they had not enjoyed through two years of Southern battles: adequate food, rum, clothes, shoes, and even some of their back pay. When word arrived in April 1783 that a preliminary agreement had been reached in Paris to end the war, it was time for Kościuszko and Hull to think about the future, though the Pole and his long-serving black attendant tarried in Charleston until June.

As the nation approached a peacetime footing, Greene praised Kościuszko's engineering skills, stamina, steadfastness, and cool indifference to danger. "Among the most useful and agreeable of my companions in arms," wrote Nathanael Greene, "was Colonel Kościuszko. Nothing could exceed his zeal for the public service, nor in the prosecution of various objects that presented themselves in our small but active warfare. . . . [He was] one, in a word, whom no pleasure could seduce, no labor fatigue, and no danger deter."[50]

Agrippa Hull's experience changed him from a callow youth to a hardened veteran of the Revolution. He had marched with Kościuszko for thousands of miles, often shoeless, through some of the roughest and most dangerous terrain in North America. Many years later, when Stockbridge's first historian gathered her thoughts about Grippy from the tales she heard from neighbors and friends, she dwelt on how "he has no cringing servility, and certainly never thought meanly of himself" and yet how "he was perfectly free from all airs and show of consequence." The black patriot who served a longer term in the war than a vast majority of his 250,000 fellow soldiers could well afford to see himself in this light. Though unpretentious, he was proud, "feel[ing] himself every whit a man," as Electa Jones put it. Kościuszko would have agreed, and so did many of the revolutionary officers with whom Hull had interacted during the long war. The young black Stockbridgian, it was later said, was "a great favorite with all the officers of the army who knew him."[51]

Whatever the future held, Hull, Kościuszko, and Jefferson all emerged from the Revolution keenly aware that the Americans had proclaimed universal liberty. At the same time, each was conscious that one-fifth of the new nation's population remained enslaved.

3

Peace and War

TADEUSZ KOŚCIUSZKO boarded the *Christiana* in Charleston on June 7, 1783, bound for Philadelphia. He was almost surely accompanied by Agrippa Hull, for his black orderly was not discharged from the army until July 23, 1783, and it is highly unlikely that the Polish war hero would have left Grippy stranded a thousand miles from home. With General Greene's pregnant wife also aboard, the ship sailed up the Delaware River on June 14, tying up at the Philadelphia wharves amid turmoil and panic in the new nation's capital.

On the day before the *Christiana*'s arrival, hardened veterans of the Pennsylvania Line mutinied. For months the grizzled soldiers had grumbled about overdue pay, and their tempers had reached a boiling point upon hearing that Congress had ordered Washington's army to disband. Without receiving their back pay, they were to be furloughed and given paper certificates redeemable at some unspecified point in the future. When Congress ignored their angry remonstrance, the soldiers surrounded the statehouse and gave the state's president twenty minutes to answer their demands. Unsatisfied, they promised to "turn . . . an enraged soldiery on the council and do themselves justice."[1]

Congress and Pennsylvania's leaders debated over who might rescue the dignity of the nation's infant government. It was suggested that the city's militia could drive off the soldiers, but militia officers told the politicians that this "would be imprudent"—a polite way of saying that the militiamen would just as soon shoot Congressmen as turn against their brothers. Held hostage, the Continental Congress scrambled for a way out of the impasse, surely disheartened by the sight of the thousands of citizens who gathered to witness the stand-off, crying "stand for your rights!"[2]

No doubt amazed by this spectacle, Kościuszko and Hull were among those who watched the Congress slip away shamefaced to spend the summer in the dusty village of Princeton, New Jersey, fifty miles to the north. They had hardly left when General John Paterson marched into Philadelphia, commanding hundreds of soldiers dispatched from West Point by Washington to snuff out the mutiny. It was a chance for Hull, Paterson, and Kościuszko to swap war stories and celebrate the end of the long fight against the British—and a chance to hear about Paterson's remarkable new orderly. This was Robert Shurtleff, who had been discovered, while undergoing treatment in Philadelphia for a delirious fever, to be Deborah Sampson, a young Massachusetts woman who had disguised her sex after enlisting in May 1782.[3]

Only faint traces remain that tell how Hull bade Kościuszko farewell in Philadelphia, though oral history has it that the Polish officer, finding Grippy "very useful to him and almost necessary to his comfort," begged his companion to return with him to Poland. As a token of his affection, Tadeusz gave Hull an expensive flint-lock pistol with a silver front sight and the Polish gun maker's name inlaid in gold on top of the barrel. Without Kościuszko, Hull then made his way north to New York from Philadelphia, probably traveling through Trenton, then Princeton, where he would have seen Congress trying to conduct the nation's affairs in the sleepy college town.[4]

Hull mustered out on July 23, 1783, at West Point, where he had spent so many months in 1779–80. No record exists of how he reached the Point from Philadelphia, a distance of about 160 miles, but almost certainly he made his way just as did almost all other enlisted men—by foot. A journey of more than 120 miles back to Stockbridge still awaited him.

When Hull finally reached the Berkshire hills, there was no one there to sing his praises or to write a word about the years the young black New Englander had served in the war. That would come later. His was the silent story of the many poor soldiers whose ability to withstand adversity had enabled Washington's outgunned, outprovisioned, and outtrained army to prevail against the British and their German and Indian auxiliaries. We have only a fragment to tell us of Hull's thoughts as he mustered out of the army. "The war could not last too long for him," local historian Electa Jones reported, when she was stitching together Stockbridge's first history.[5] The Revolution had thrust an obscure young black man from a backwater western Massachusetts village into daily contact with two significant officers, both closely connected to George Washington. In the seven-year scrum of war Hull had discovered himself, and for the remainder of his long life he replayed his revolutionary experiences with relish. For him the war had ended too soon, when he left the service of Kościuszko, with whom he had forged an emotional bond.

Though he left no account of mustering out and making his way to Stockbridge, Hull's experience very likely paralleled that of Joseph Plumb Martin, a Connecticut youth who was born one year after Hull in a town about thirteen miles from where Grippy grew up. Like Hull, Martin was a "long-timer"—among the tiny fraction of men who served in the Revolution for as much as six years. Mustered out at West Point just a few days before the mutiny in Philadelphia in June 1783, Martin remembered how many of the enlisted men said their good-byes as much "a band of brotherhood as Masons and, I believe, as faithful to each other." Some left "the same day that their fetters were knocked off," while others remained a few days to get their mustering-out certificates, "which they sold to procure decent clothing and money sufficient to enable them to pass with decency through the country and to appear something like themselves when they arrived among their friends" at home. Not one in twenty had a farthing to his name, reported one of their officers. They were sent home with nothing "but poverty in their pockets."[6] Many begged their way home, seeking handouts from town to town. Others made their way down the Hudson River to work in New York City on the ships preparing to evacuate the British army, along with American Loyalists and several thousand former slaves who had fought under George III's banner.

Discharged at West Point, Hull may have sold his "settlement certificate" of $80—notes bearing the signature of the superintendent of finance—in order to clothe himself decently and complete his trek back to Stockbridge. Or perhaps he held on to the certificate with his future in western Massachusetts in mind. The mustering-out process embittered Martin, who remembered that "when the country had drained the last drop of service it could screw out of the poor soldiers, they were turned adrift like old worn-out horses and nothing said about land to pasture them upon." Congress had promised each man a hundred acres of bounty land in the Northwest Territory, but "no care was taken that the soldiers should get them." Like most soldiers, Martin sold his land certificate at a sharp discount to "speculators who were driving about the country like so many evil spirits, endeavoring to pluck the last feather from the soldiers," who "were ignorant of the ways and means to obtain their bounty lands. . . . The truth was, none cared for them; the country was served, and faithfully served, and that was all that was deemed necessary. It was, soldiers, look to yourselves, we want no more of you."[7] But Hull, it seems, was less bitter than Martin. He too was promised a certificate for a hundred acres of land in the distant

West. As for a pension, Hull received nothing. Kościuszko, like all officers, was promised half pay for life, later commuted to five years' full pay. The Polish officer, as we shall see, waited many years before receiving his pension. But enlisted men were not awarded a penny until 1818, when Congress passed the first pension act to help impoverished revolutionary enlisted soldiers.[8]

Returning to Stockbridge in July 1783, Hull faced less than rosy prospects. He had come back to his hometown with military skills, travel experience, and the affection of many revolutionary war officers, but that translated poorly into postwar life for a man with empty pockets, especially one who was black. After the war Kościuszko could return to his country estate in Poland, and Jefferson could retire to Monticello. For Grippy, the return to Stockbridge promised only uncertainty.

Finding his mother widowed, blind, and nearly helpless, Hull had few choices in finding an income to support her and himself. One possibility was farming. We can imagine that Hull aspired to the ideal of the New England yeoman farmer who gained independence, free from reliance on the social and economic patronage of the wealthy. We will see how he moved by steps toward that goal. But for now, he had to bide his time. It was hardly an auspicious time to embark on such an endeavor, for even white yeomen in the region were barely eking out a living in the years following the Revolution. Having lost the war, the British barred American exports to their West Indies sugar-growing colonies, and this hit Americans hard, depriving Northern farmers and merchants of one of their best markets. Falling farm prices and a severe shortage of hard money quickly followed. Adding to this burden the Massachusetts legislature imposed heavy taxes to pay off the swollen revolutionary indebtedness and insisted that taxes be paid in hard money—something in desperately short supply. Failing to get paper money restored as legal tender, many farmers in towns such as Stockbridge faced court actions to satisfy their creditors and the tax collectors. By the time Hull reached the Berkshire hills, sheriffs were seizing farmers' animals, grain, and even their small acreage, exposing them to auction and using the proceeds—often knocked down to a fraction of their real worth—to pay taxes and creditors. The Berkshire towns were soon aboil with farmers wielding clubs and pitchforks to stop debt collection.[9]

So Hull played the only card in his hand. He was fortunate to secure a position in Sheffield, a few miles from Stockbridge, in the household of Theodore Sedgwick, a wellborn and successful thirty-eight-year-old lawyer who had just won a landmark slavery case before the Massachusetts Supreme Judicial Court.

Hull's new employer, Theodore Sedgwick, traced his lineage back to the Puritan migration of the 1630s. By Theodore's birth in 1746, the Sedgwicks were successful farmers, enough so to send their son to Yale College. From this promising start in life, he studied law in Great Barrington and then established a practice in Sheffield. By 1773, he was supporting the protests against England. But Sedgwick was a cautious revolutionary, as firm in opposing the egalitarian reforms pushed forward by western Massachusetts radicals as he was in contesting British policies. During the Revolution he did brief military service and then profited handsomely as a supplier of military stores.

More fond of order and hierarchy than of equality, Sedgwick feared the upstart Berkshire hills yeomen—the "shoeless ones," he called them—who pursued social leveling and claimed political entitlements. By war's end, the stern, tall lawyer had become a leading western Massachusetts conservative. Townsmen elected him to the legislature, but many resented his defense of Loyalists, whose land had been confiscated to punish their disloyalty to the American cause.[10]

Why Sedgwick took up the case of two slaves in 1781 is uncertain. Bett and Brom labored for John Ashley, the wealthiest man in Sheffield, indeed in all of Berkshire County. Nothing with profit attached to it escaped his notice. Acquiring vast acreage, Ashley built a general store, saw and grist mills, and an iron forge. Almost as a matter of course he held important offices—judge of the Berkshire

County Court, militia officer, and representative in the Massachusetts legislature. With much to lose in the aftermath of war, Ashley
had become a reluctant revolutionary, suspected of loyalism by
many and hated by some because of it.[11]

Out of the turmoil of the American Revolution came conflicts between Ashley and his slaves. Bett's parents were African-born and
had seen their baby girl given as a wedding present to John Ashley's
new wife. Growing up and toiling in the Ashley household, Bett had
married just before the American Revolution and had then lost her
husband, who fell on a revolutionary battlefield. Her grief for her
mate melded with public discussion of unalienable rights and the
glorious cause of Americans fighting and dying for their freedom.
She voiced her new beliefs plainly while waiting on Colonel Ashley's
table, stating that "she never heard but that all people were born
free and equal, and she thought long about it, and resolved she
would try whether she did not come in among them." The matter
simmered for a time, then resurfaced in a domestic dispute in early
1781, between Bett's sister, Brom, and Colonel Ashley's hot-tem-
pered wife, later called "the shrew untameable." Bett threw herself
into the fray, stepping between her sister and the angry woman, who
swung a heated kitchen fire shovel during the dispute. Bett received
the blow on her arm, "the scar of which she bore to the day of her
death." Outraged, she stalked from the house and refused to return.
When Ashley appealed to the local court for the recovery of his
slave, Bett called upon Theodore Sedgwick to ask if Massachusetts's
new constitution with its declaration of rights stating that "all men
are born free and equal" did not apply to her. Where, asked Sedgwick, did she get such an idea? She replied that the "Bill o' Rights
said all were born free and equal and that, as she was not a dumb
beast, she was certainly one of the nation."[12]

In postrevolutionary Massachusetts, as in New Jersey, New
York, and Connecticut, brutal or deceitful masters were on the defensive as growing calls for abolition in the Northern states made

judges more amenable to black claims of freedom or for relief from cruelty. Sedgwick took Bett's case, arguing before the Berkshire County Court of Common Pleas that Bett and Brom should not be considered slaves for life, for the declaration of rights that introduced the state's 1780 constitution made no exception to the principle that all humans were born free and equal. A white jury found for Brom and Bett. The Massachusetts Supreme Judicial Court was prepared to hear the case on appeal in October 1781, but Ashley withdrew his case. He bowed to the gathering sentiment that slavery was morally bankrupt and knew that an all-white jury, in a parallel high court freedom suit, had just ruled that the slave Quock Walker, who also lived in western Massachusetts, was a free man. The jury was persuaded by the argument of Walker's lawyer, who made the courtroom tremble with his eloquence: "This Quock is our brother. We all had one common origin, descended from the same kind of flesh, had the same breath of life. . . . Is it not a law of nature that all men are equal and free? Is not the laws of nature the laws of God? Is not the law of God, then, against slavery?"[13]

The jury decisions in the cases of Walker and Bett and Brom presumed that slavery was incompatible with the state's Declaration of Rights. Yet the two decisions did not unequivocally abolish slavery or force masters to free their slaves immediately. Those still enslaved could take their cases to court if they could find the means and hope that juries would favor them as individual litigants. Yet a decade later, Jeremy Belknap, a Boston minister deeply committed to abolitionism, judged that the two cases delivered "a mortal wound to slavery" in Massachusetts. That indeed was the case, for by the first federal census of 1790, slavery was virtually dead in the Bay State.

After the trial, Bett came to the Sedgwick household as a free waged servant, serving as cook, nurse, housekeeper, and, as the Sedgwick children testified many years afterward, their moral compass. Several years later, Hull came to serve as butler and handyman. At the beginning of a lifelong friendship with Hull, Bett renamed herself Elizabeth Freeman, thereby announcing her free status.[14]

Even as a free man—and one gratified that slavery had been sent on the road to extinction in Massachusetts—Agrippa Hull had to fashion a secure position in a world of shifting status and long-held prejudices. While court decisions were dismantling lifelong bondage in Massachusetts, slavery still cast a lunar shadow over all blacks, regardless of status. Many rural masters simply ignored the court rulings against permanent bondage and felt entitled to extract long-term service from people of color. Masters sold, traded, and willed years of obligation for nominally free people; still advertised for runaway slaves; and bound free people of color to long-term indentures. Unscrupulous masters sold black people with short terms of service to the Southern states, where they became permanent chattel. Kidnappers roamed the region, especially because slavery was still legal just a few miles away in New York, where slavery was not abolished until 1799. Living adjacent to the New York border, Hull had to realize that a determined kidnapper could seize him and whisk him to a slave state in just a few hours. Thus, regardless of whether born free or enslaved, black New Englanders had to fight against constraints set in place by whites who believed in the immutable inferiority of African-descended people.[15]

Hull's position of service in the powerful Sedgwick family partially shielded him from the economic insecurities that haunted most northern African Americans and put him a notch above Sheffield's few dozen free blacks, almost all of whom were landless wage laborers. His revolutionary experiences followed him as if a good spirit had lit on his shoulder. Only months after he joined the Sedgwick household, word spread that the magnetic Lafayette was returning to America after an absence of three years for a grand tour of the states. In August 1784, Sedgwick took Hull to New York City to greet the famous Lafayette, whom Hull had met at Valley Forge in the winter of 1777–78 and again in 1778 in Albany, when

Kościuszko and Lafayette were both part of the planned invasion of Canada. The meeting must have been an emotional and affirming experience for Hull.[16] That the French hero of the American Revolution, fêted at every town on his itinerary, would spare a few moments to grasp the hand of the humble, young black New Englander, and exchange memories of the long war for independence, must have gratified Hull enormously.

Hull and Lafayette found comity over a key, mutual interest. The Frenchman was intensely interested in the emancipation of American slaves, "one of his three hobby-horses," as he told James Madison at the time. Commitment to this cause had grown in Lafayette after witnessing African American bravery and steadfastness in the years of revolutionary struggle. In 1784, near the end of his American tour, he voiced his passionate antislavery views when he met with Virginia legislators in Richmond. In an emotional address, carefully phrased to make his point but not give offense, he stated his hope that Virginia would "continue to give to the world unquestionable proofs of her philanthropy and her regard to the liberties of all mankind." A day later, Lafayette met with James Armistead, the slave assigned to him and the man who had played a key role as a spy in the climactic Yorktown victory. Shocked that Armistead was still enslaved, Lafayette wrote a testimonial that convinced the Virginia legislature to free Armistead, who then renamed himself James Armistead Lafayette.[17]

Flush with abolitionist sentiments, Lafayette dared to push his hobbyhorse to the top of American discourse. A year earlier, Lafayette had boldly proposed to Washington that the revolutionary commander join him "in purchasing a small estate where we may try to experiment to free [our] Negroes, and use them only as tenants." If Washington would join him, Lafayette proposed, "such an example as yours might render it a general practice," leading, perhaps, to the abolition of slavery in America and even in the West Indies. Far from dismissing this breathtaking proposal, Washington expressed interest: "I shall be happy to join in so laudable a work," he wrote to his surrogate son. After returning to the United States in 1784, Lafayette spent more than a week with Washington, where the two discussed the matter extensively.[18]

Though Lafayette was probably too discreet to mention this initiative to Hull, the black revolutionary veteran surely noticed Lafayette's antislavery enthusiasm. Like others in Massachusetts, Hull knew that despite the cases of Bett and Quock Walker, many in the state were still enslaved. Hull's circumspect temperament kept him from stepping forward publicly on this issue, but he knew all too well the unfulfilled promise of the American Revolution to liberate half a million slaves. Lafayette's fervor for emancipation probably reinforced Hull's self-confidence to pursue his own dreams.

Hull pursued his hope for personal independence by increments. In August 1784, just before meeting with Lafayette, Grippy had taken a nearly unprecedented step for a young black New Englander. For nine pounds (the equivalent of several months' wages) he had purchased a small triangular piece of land in Stockbridge, situated next to Konkapot Brook, named for the Christianized Stockbridge Indian John Konkapot, who had died in 1765 after holding several town offices. It is unclear how Hull had accumulated nine pounds only a year after his discharge from the army; possibly he had tucked away, and only now redeemed, the certificates he had received in lieu of back pay.[19]

Though his purchase was only half an acre, it was land of his own—and land fronting on Berkshire County's main north-south road. For generations in New England, acquiring freehold property was treasured as the foundation of independence. But many white veterans returning from the war were too poor to purchase even a small plot of land. In addition, this land had special significance. Hull had served with Abraham Konkapot, son of John Konkapot, in Captain John Chadwick's company in the Massachusetts Line.

They had been together at Valley Forge, an experience that melded soldiers together with a special bond.

Hull took a further step toward full manliness a year after his first land purchase by wedding Jane Darby, a young black woman from nearby Lenox. Like Elizabeth Freeman, she had fled an abusive master. Taking refuge in Stockbridge, she appealed to Theodore Sedgwick for assistance in gaining her freedom from her owner, known only in documents as "Mr. Ingersoll," who sought to seize his chattel property. After Sedgwick convinced Ingersoll to release Jane, she and Agrippa "agreed to tread life's path in company." A religious woman, Darby was known, as Stockbridge's first historian put it, as "a woman of excellent character and made a profession of her faith in Christ."[20]

In 1785, Sedgwick moved to Stockbridge, and Hull and his wife followed him there, only to find themselves in the eye of a storm. The postwar economic dislocation, triggered by Britain's closure of its West Indies markets and worsened by legislative attempts to retire the war debt with drastic tax collections that bore unequally on small farmers, flared into a full-scale insurrection. Its reluctant leader, Daniel Shays, had enlisted as a private in the revolutionary war and worked his way up to the rank of officer. A plainspoken farmer, Shays was one of hundreds of farmers who burned at the sight of the red flags placed by sheriffs on farmhouses signaling an auction to satisfy unpaid taxes and small debts. These were the farmers who had defeated Burgoyne and Cornwallis, who had returned home to difficult lives, and who now brimmed over with bitterness as lawyers, creditors, and process servers began stripping them of their only means of livelihood. One of the few revolutionary army enlisted men who had achieved officer status, Shays had great appeal to the impoverished farmers who made up the rebels.

Determined to close the courts that ordered their property sold at auction, the Shaysites recruited hundreds of hard-luck men from Berkshire and other Massachusetts counties. Only a few miles from where Agrippa Hull lived, they forcibly closed the court at Great Barrington in September 1786 and freed imprisoned debtors. James Bowdoin, the governor of Massachusetts, immediately called out the state's militia to protect the court. Commanded by Hull's old leader, General John Paterson, the militia quickly arrived to disperse the insurgent farmers. However, most of the militia, farmers themselves, defected to join the rebels, thus convincing the Berkshire court judges to suspend court actions until the farmers' grievances could be redressed. Among these judges was William Whiting, the senior justice on the court that had declared Bett and Brom free a few years before.[21]

In January 1787, with the insurgency spreading, Governor James Bowdoin commissioned a private army to march west and put the rebels down. With former revolutionary general Benjamin Lincoln at their head, the expedition fortified the Springfield federal arsenal. Marching through deep snow and intending to seize weapons at the arsenal, the Shaysites were repelled by Lincoln's artillery on January 25, 1787. Four Shaysites died, and dozens fell wounded, leaving the snow crimson-covered, while the remainder of the rebels fled the scene.

Agrippa Hull heard of the Springfield rout the next day and knew that still-determined Shaysites were gathering in West Stockbridge. Most of the Shaysites were small farmers like himself. Yet when he had to make a decision regarding loyalty, personal issues controlled Hull's politics. He must have had mixed feelings when Sedgwick, his employer, gathered mounted volunteers to scatter the rebels. Circumstances forced a choice as small contingents of Shaysites harassed the elite of the frontier towns. Tramping through the snow-blanketed Berkshire highlands in late February 1787 and promising death to merchants and lawyers, the roughly dressed farmers chose Stockbridge as their first target in what became the final stage and bloodiest encounter of Shays's Rebellion. Led by Perez Hamlin, another former revolutionary officer who had come home a poor man at the end of the war, the rebels swept down on Stockbridge on February 26. Moving door to door, they took prisoners, including the son of Silas Pepoon, a revolutionary officer and retailer, and Timothy Edwards, son of Jonathan Edwards, a prospering retailer.[22]

Their next quarry was Theodore Sedgwick himself. Hated by many as one of Berkshire County's busiest lawyers and a man known to profit handsomely by collecting legal fees while representing creditors pursuing the indebted, Sedgwick was especially choice game. He had recently built a fine mansion, which contrasted sharply with the plight of the impoverished. Disappointed not to find Sedgwick at home, the incensed farmers confronted Elizabeth Freeman, by this time known as Mumbet (for her motherly role in the Sedgwick family). In a story told for many years, Mumbet allowed them to search the house and "run their bayonets under the beds and into the darkest corners to find Judge Sedgwick." Not finding him, they looked for valuable silver plate. After they searched Mumbet's room and asked what was in her floor chest, she replied, "Oh you had better search that old nigger's chest . . . as you call me." In this way, she shamed them and saved the silver she had hidden there.[23] Faced down, the Shaysites satisfied themselves with trashing Sedgwick's silk stockings, ruffled shirts, and "parlor costumes," emblems of his wealth and status, and then decamped.

Before leaving Stockbridge, Hamlin's troop took thirty-two hostages and headed south along the county road, passing Agrippa Hull's house on their way to Great Barrington, only a short distance from the New York border, where they intended to take refuge. Now Hull had to make a difficult choice. As soon as Hamlin's men left town, militia captain Silas Pepoon called out the village militia. Would Hull respond? He could prove his mettle by mustering on the side of law and order, or he could sit out the affray in sympathy for the debt-ridden farmers. Like everyone else in the Berkshire hills, Grippy knew that Hamlin had fought bravely as part of General

Greene's southern army in 1780–82. Yet Hull's debt of gratitude to Sedgwick for extricating his wife-to-be from detested bondage surely weighed heavily, and he knew that General Paterson, whom he had served in the Continental Army, was playing a key role in trying to quell Shays's Rebellion.

At least for now, Hull's politics were personal. In a fractured economy and time of great unrest, patronage was precious, and a secure place in the service of an important local dignitary was hardly to be sniffed at. So Hull made his decision. Fifty-two men turned out for duty on February 27; Hull waited a few more days. But on March 3 he was among fourteen additional men who signed up to put down the rebellion.

Hull may well have carried the pistol Kościuszko had given him four years before. He never had use for it, however, because Sheffield militiamen, led by Colonel John Ashley Jr., the son of Mumbet's former owner, had tracked down Hamlin's troop and engaged them on February 27 in a pitched battle on a back road from Sheffield to South Egremont. The Shaysites suffered thirty casualties before General Paterson arrived to mop up. Taking scores of Shaysites prisoner, Paterson and Ashley brought the insurgency to a close. Hull remained on duty for eight days, receiving two shillings a day for his service. Sedgwick later represented the Shaysites charged with treason. Six were sentenced in March 1787 "to be hanged by the neck until dead," but some escaped from jail and the others were pardoned by Governor Bowdoin.[24]

In the years after Shays's Rebellion, Agrippa Hull began accumulating the parcels of property that marked his identity as a yeoman farmer. He continued to serve the Sedgwick family, but his careful cash transactions recorded in the Berkshire County deed books show that he was becoming his own man. In 1789–90 he purchased two parcels to enlarge his home lot to 2.5 acres, all part of the old Stockbridge Indian township. In the deeds recording these purchases, Hull was called a "Negro man and laborer" and "yeoman," the latter signifying that he was farming the land. Also between 1789 and 1792 he purchased three parcels of land on Cherry Hill, a mile west of his homestead. By now, his properties totaled about eleven acres.[25]

White leaders of the nation had created a new constitution, the people's delegates to state conventions had ratified it, and the nation had embarked on a new era of party politics. Like most small landowners, Hull was a bystander to all of this. But it must have been a matter of great pride to Grippy that he had attained the status of a full-fledged citizen, qualified to vote in Massachusetts by dint of his accumulation of the requisite amount of property.

While Agrippa Hull edged forward in Stockbridge, Tadeusz Kościuszko was embarking upon the most dramatic and tragic years of his life. His experiences in the American Revolution and his beliefs in an egalitarian society would soon propel him to a leading role in the Polish rebellion against Russian occupiers. That revolt, named after Kościuszko, ultimately failed, but his name would become synonymous with Polish identity and dreams of national independence.

After Hull left to obtain his discharge at West Point, Kościuszko prepared for a return to Poland. But a grateful nation asked something more of him. At Congress's request, he managed a fireworks display in Philadelphia on July 4, 1783. Opening the day with church bells ringing, the celebration continued with noonday firing of cannons and an evening musical procession with a "Triumphal Car" displaying portraits of Washington, General Horatio Gates, and the French Admiral Rochambeau. White-clad boys and girls carrying torches added an aura of youth befitting the new nation.[26]

This patriotic spectacle did not bring Kościuszko closer to a paycheck, however. It would be many months before Congress voted Kościuszko $12,280 plus interest payable at 6 percent from January

1, 1784—to be paid at some point in the future—and five hundred acres of land in the Northwest Territory. Though Congress refused to promote him to the generalship he coveted, Kościuszko could take solace in his inclusion seven months before in the Society of Cincinnati, formed to commemorate the contribution of military officers in the Revolution and to create an honorary officer society. Given a set of pistols and a sword inscribed with the nation's gratitude, Kościuszko accompanied Washington on the march down the Bowery in New York City on Evacuation Day, November 25, 1783. He was present at Fraunces Tavern when Washington made his famous speech saying adieu to his officers.[27]

In one last sentimental flourish, Kościuszko visited Nathanael Greene and his wife in Newport, Rhode Island, in March 1784. His affection for his commanding officer must have been mixed with disappointment upon learning that Greene, the former Quaker from Rhode Island, had decided to become a Southern planter. After accepting plantations of about ten thousand acres in Georgia and South Carolina as gifts from their legislatures for his wartime service, Greene had purchased hundreds of slaves from confiscated Loyalist estates. The fighting Quaker who had pushed hard for South Carolina and Georgia to offer freedom for those slaves willing to defend their states had, in an extraordinary reversal, joined the Lower South's slaveocracy. Criticized by Warner Mifflin, a leading Quaker abolitionist, Greene rationalized that he would manage his rice plantations humanely and hoped to devise a plan for freeing his slaves and hiring them to work on the land to which they were attached.[28] But Greene's decision to move his family to the South and tie his future to the life of a slaveowning planter was hardly what Kościuszko hoped for as he departed America.

Kościuszko left the United States from New York on July 15, 1784, aboard the *Courier de l'Europe* bound for L'Orient, France. Accompanying him was "Negro John," an African American who would stay with Kościuszko for the next twelve years. To this day,

Negro John remains largely hidden from history, though Polish and American newspapers would later refer to him as Kościuszko's "inseparable companion."[29] Also on the ship was Colonel David Humphreys, formerly an aide-de-camp to Washington, now headed to France to serve as secretary to the American commission charged with negotiating commercial treaties for the new nation. Humphreys reported back to George Washington that he and Kościuszko landed in France on August 8, 1784, embarking at once for Paris in a carriage.

Arriving in Paris just a few days ahead of Kościuszko was Thomas Jefferson, now the American minister replacing John Jay in the powerful triumvirate that also included John Adams and Benjamin Franklin charged by Congress to negotiate treaties of friendship and commerce with the French. Accompanied by his daughter Martha (known as Patsy) and his valued slave James Hemings, the half brother of his deceased wife, Jefferson set up at a fashionable boardinghouse to accommodate his retinue and receive visiting Americans and other friends of liberty. Kościuszko was prominent among those who called at the boardinghouse, where he had the opportunity to meet with French sons of the Enlightenment and Americans who had come to Paris after the war.[30]

By mid-September 1784 Kościuszko returned home to Poland after an absence of nine years. Having heard from a countryman that Poland was in desperate straits, Kościuszko girded himself for the worst. Still awaiting payment for nearly eight years' worth of American military service, he faced great difficulties in Siechnowicze, his family home. His brother Joseph had barely avoided financial ruin, and the family estate was in dire conditions. With the Polish army at low ebb, Kościuszko could not find employment there either. Instead, he had to assume the role of a small Polish landlord in order to salvage the family property and honor.[31]

For four fallow years, while Agrippa Hull was positioning himself in remote Stockbridge, Kościuszko lived quietly as a country landowner, imitating the legendary Cincinnatus by turning from the sword to the plow. With the labor of many serfs, he crafted his own eating utensils, cultivated a well-stocked garden and a grove of fruit trees, worked on new seed combinations for his farm, and constructed a maze along a hillock above his simple home. He further amused himself corresponding with a nearby sister and receiving friends from their country homes. Southern founding fathers such as Washington and Jefferson might have envied Kościuszko's withdrawal to his rural retreat—a quietude they yearned for—but down-at-the-heels Siechnowicze was no Monticello or Mount Vernon. All the while, as his correspondence indicates, Kościuszko dreamed of returning to America to participate in the new nation's youthful exuberance.[32]

While in seclusion, Kościuszko strived to maintain contact with his American friends. After receiving no letters for two years—communication between remote regions of Poland and the United States was painfully slow and unreliable, and some of Kościuszko's correspondence may have been lost—he wrote Nathanael Greene in January 1786, pining for a commission in the American army and imploring Greene to intercede for him. After learning that Greene had died, Kościuszko drew a portrait of him from memory, ordered a number of engravings struck, and sent them to friends in America and Europe. With his estate producing little income, he wrote to remind the American Congress in September 1787 that for three years he had not received any principal or even interest on his back pay. This complaint produced one year's interest of about $700 that temporarily eased matters for him in Poland.[33]

While Kościuszko tended his farm, reformist proposals and political upheaval propelled him once more to buckle on the sword of freedom. During his years in America, Enlightenment thought had spread across Europe to Poland, stimulating calls for reform never before heard there. Chief among them were calls for a stronger, more effective legislature, expanded political freedom for ordinary Poles, and even some murmuring, later to become louder, about freeing the serfs. Discussions about the Sejm had circulated for decades, but the other calls for reform were new, indicative of the wide influence of Enlightenment and American revolutionary principles. In 1785 reformer Stanislaw Staszic called for the abolition of the liberum veto, widely seen as the main source of Poland's ills; for a hereditary rather than elected monarchy; and for industrial development, a larger army, and the emancipation of the serfs. Three years later, as Kościuszko began to emerge from his rustic refuge, Hugo Kollàtaj, who had previously reformed the University of Krąkow, called for many of the same changes in his Several Anonymous Letters (1788–89). Kollàtaj also argued for shoring up the Polish army to strengthen the nation. Compared to its rivals, the Polish military was impoverished, starved by the nobility's unwillingness to support the military and preference for shirking their duties: they would show up only on ceremonial occasions and absent themselves from drill and instruction. While other nations had curtailed use of the cavalry, armed horsemen accounted for over a third of the Polish army—as if medieval days still reigned. The common soldier received miserable pay and often resorted to plunder to survive.[34]

When a new assembly of the Sejm met in Warsaw in October 1788, Kościuszko's mind was fired with thoughts about a better future for Poland and the role he might play in it. Like all reform-minded Poles, he watched the deliberations of the Sejm closely. With reform in the air, the Sejm divided into three factions. On the right were Republicans, dominated by conservative magnates and their impoverished gentry clientele who favored ties with Russia, which garrisoned thousands of troops in Poland and stayed vigilant for signs of any increased monarchical power that might threaten its grip on the nation. The king and his followers, influenced by Phillip Mazzei, Jefferson's old friend and neighbor in Virginia, took a moderate stance. Mazzei believed strongly in the republican virtues of the American Revolution and had become the Polish king's agent in Paris in 1788. Especially eager to escape the satellite role assigned him by Czarina Catherine of Russia, the king admired the American Revolution and wished to implement some of its ideals, yet he realized that too much reform would irritate the Russian bear and invite repression. On the left were the Patriots, who subscribed to the reform agenda pushed by Staszic and Kollàtaj. Attracting support from the Prussians to offset the Russian menace, the radicals made inflammatory anti-Russian speeches and convinced the king to induce Empress Catherine to withdraw Russian troops, needed in any event for the Russian war against Turkey that was now in progress.[35]

Reformers in the Sejm understood they were standing at the brink of "revolution on a worldwide scale"—one that promised global upheaval the likes of which had not been seen since the Protestant Reformation. After an initial year in which little was accomplished, the Sejm, later to be known as the Four Years Diet because it lasted for so long, began to move forward. In the second year of the Diet, just three months after the Declaration of the Rights of Man in August 1789, which brought the exploding French Revolution into the consciousness of the entire Western world, spokesmen for 141 Polish towns signed an Act of Union in Warsaw requesting representation in the Diet for the town-based burghers. The measure shocked the gentry, who feared losing power to middle-class town merchants and shopkeepers, upstart lawyers, and even peasants rising against their masters.[36]

Quickly, legislative debate ignited calls for revolution within Poland and patriotic resistance against the nation's occupiers. In 1790 the Diet excluded landless nobles from representation and considered giving burghers representation. In 1791, just as Americans applauded the changes brewing in Poland, the nation became the stage for international quarrels over the French Revolution. Russia and Prussia, desperate to protect monarchism in Europe, once again threatened to further partition Poland and squelch reform there. Inside Poland, in April 1791, Julian Ursyn Niemcewicz, Kościuszko's classmate in the cadet school and now a deputy in the

Diet, made an electrifying speech before the Diet that demonstrated how the American and French revolutions had affected Polish thought. Applauding Washington and Franklin, both of whom, he noted, came from obscure origins, Niemcewicz argued that the gentry could not defend Poland or themselves without uniting with the burghers. Offering the burghers a political voice and giving them the right to buy "noble" land outside the towns promised to produce a stronger Poland that could attract "swarms of immigrants from foreign regions."[37]

Reformers in the Diet, realizing that the dominant Russians were distracted by the Russo-Turkish War, solidified these reforms by adopting the Constitution of the Third of May in 1791. Supported by King Stanislaus and endorsed by the radical Kollàtaj and leading gentry such as Prince Karol Stanislaw Radziwill and Ignacy Potocki, the constitution proclaimed Poland a constitutional monarchy of gentry and bourgeoisie. Amounting to a coup d'état, it incorporated a panoply of changes. The Polish constitution made the monarchy hereditary and allowed for a much stronger chief executive. By abolishing the liberum veto, it eroded the power of the upper nobility. Reflecting Charles de Secondat, Baron de Montesquieu's treatises and the American Constitution, the Polish constitution established separate executive, legislative, and judicial branches of government. For the first time, city burghers gained new freedoms, such as the ability to create town governments by vote, serve in local offices, receive commissions in the army (except in the cavalry, which would remain the nobles' domain), and even enter the ranks of the nobility. While the constitution recognized Roman Catholicism as the official church, other faiths were promised toleration.

The Polish constitution of 1791 did not, however, free the serfs—though it did ameliorate their condition. Taking the serfs under its protection, the state proclaimed them as "the most bountiful source of national riches," while it took authority over contractual arrangements between peasants and gentry so that serfs could take their abusive masters to court. Of supreme importance, the constitution guaranteed that contracts between noblemen and serfs were alterable only by mutual consent. In a significant adaptation of the "free soil" position then circulating among European intellectuals regarding slavery and serfs, the constitution declared that any immigrant, including a runaway serf, was declared legally free upon his or her arrival in Poland.[38]

However imperfect, the constitution of May 3, 1791, brought about changes in the Polish polity that would have been unimaginable only a few years before. Only the world's second written constitution (after the American), it excited reformers throughout the Western world. To many observers concerned by the radical developments in France, the Polish constitution offered a more palatable model for change. Thomas Paine, in France at the time, even considered applying for Polish citizenship. Holland's *Leiden Gazette* exclaimed that "if there are any miracles in this century, one has happened in Poland." Americans followed the events in Poland with enthusiasm and awe. In Philadelphia, the *Gazette of the United States* called it "a most wonderful revolution . . . in favor of the rights of man," all the more so because it was "begun without violence or tumult." Boston's *Columbian Centinel*, forgetting that millions of serfs were not yet free, enthused that "a nation of Freemen has been born in a day."[39]

As reformers hammered out new constitutional relationships on the anvil of Poland's historic miseries, Kościuszko was eager to get back into the action. His opportunity arose with the army's expansion, and a number of influential people, including his old love, Princess Lubomirska, wrote the king on his behalf, recommending him for a prominent military commission. King Stanislaus was enthusiastic about appointing him to a generalship, based upon Kościuszko's experiences in America. Members of the Sejm also dwelled on his personal virtues. One member enthused that "if [Kościuszko] knew how to shed his blood for a foreign country, he undoubtedly will not spare it for his own." Kościuszko appeared at the Diet in 1789, and on October 1, the legislative body commissioned him a major general in the Polish army.[40]

Recommissioned, Kościuszko seemed initially satisfied with the new reforms. Writing to Major Elnathan Haskell, an American revolutionary veteran from Massachusetts, he enthused that "we are upon the means to be respectables [sic] abroad" by creating the rule of law and destroying forever a "*Monarchique Pouvoir* [monarchical government]." For now, Kościuszko kept his boldest ideas private, though he was already planning a Polish army based upon the American model. The new army would level social differences—rich and poor, landed and landless—so all would serve as equals united to reclaim their country. Kościuszko's long association with Agrippa Hull and later with the faithful Negro John no doubt bolstered his convictions that ordinary men, once given a sense of equality, were as patriotic and brave in battle as any of their countrymen. "We must all unite for one purpose: to free our country from the domination of foreigners," wrote Kościuszko, as he prepared for battle. "Even the most unimportant and least instructed can contribute to the universal good." His was a dream of liberated serfs in a unified Polish nation.[41]

With a division of four thousand soldiers, the reenergized Kościuszko took up his first assignment at Wloclawwel, then Ludlin, and finally Polonne. Using lessons sharpened during the American Revolution, he regarded the soldiers and peasants as his brothers and countrymen united against a common foe. Training them by example, Kościuszko visited their huts and shared the food, shelter, and deprivations of his foot soldiers. One contemporary recalled that Kościuszko slept on the bare ground like the foot soldiers under his command and refused a good supper if his soldiers went hungry, much as he had in his fifty months with Agrippa Hull. In the process, he narrowed the distance between officers and enlisted men that had prevailed in the American army, where an officer fraternizing with ordinary men of the line often faced court-martial.[42] His humor was contagious, and his speeches were short. A student of Washington, suffused with American democratic ideals, he matured into the magnetic Polish leader who to this day has captivated the nation's imagination.

Polish political reforms and preparation for a war to liberate the nation from external occupiers ultimately enraged Czarina Catherine and spawned a countermovement to overturn the new constitution. Polish gentry clients of Russia, resentful of their lost powers under the new constitution, conspired against it, while the empress, who vowed to "fight Jacobinism and beat it in Poland," moved to obstruct the reforms that threatened Russia's stranglehold on Poland. In league with each other, they formed a new Confederation of Targowica in April 1792. Quickly, the czarina's forces mounted a juggernaut offensive of over a hundred thousand troops to invade Poland. In a major confrontation, Kościuszko's division of five thousand men battled a Russian force three times its size at the pivotal battle at Dubienka. Using engineering skills honed in America, Kościuszko built a shielding defense of high palisades above the river Bug that frustrated the Russian advance and allowed the Polish army to withdraw with minimal casualties, compared to Russian losses of three thousand dead and wounded. Even though it ended in retreat, Poles regarded the battle as a heroic exploit against the superior Russian forces.[43]

Despite the courage of Kościuszko and his forces, however, King Stanislaus considered further resistance futile. Forced to humble himself, he confessed that he had been "seduced by new and bold maxims." Annulling the new constitution, he accepted the conservative faction's government. Kościuszko, now recognized as a capable commander and ardent patriot, tendered his resignation to protest the collapse of the reform government. The king rejected his resignation—Kościuszko was a national hero—and gave Kościuszko the Order of Virtuti Militari (an award created in 1792 to honor military virtue). It was a bittersweet honor for Kościuszko, since the reforms he cared about so passionately had been swept away almost overnight.

Readers of American newspapers followed the fast-moving Polish developments first with optimism, then with despair. Even in remote Stockbridge, Agrippa Hull could follow the ill-starred hopes of Kościuszko in the *Western Star*. Hull must surely have joined other Americans in saluting the Constitution of the Third of May for its union of nobles and the people, certain that Poland had dodged the failure of the nobility in France to accommodate the common people, which had led to their annihilation. But now American newspapers dolefully reported the alliance of alienated gentry with the ferocious Russian attackers that led to the Confederation of Targowica and the ensuing Russian repression of Poland.[44]

Attempts to placate the Russian ruler proved fruitless. King Stanislaus's repudiation of the Constitution of the Third of May and his acceptance of the conservative Targowica government opened Poland to further dismemberment by the Russians, Prussians, and Austrians. Even the pro-Russian Targowicans were shocked in January 1793, when the Prussian and Russian governments amputated huge sections of Poland for a second time, reducing the nation's population, its land size, and the reach of its autonomous government by two-thirds. Agreements between Prussia and Russia brought further appropriations of Polish territory. By the summer of 1792, nearly thirty thousand Russian troops were stationed permanently in Poland with over seven thousand in Warsaw alone.[45]

In America and Europe, disheartened supporters of reform in Poland looked to Kościuszko for leadership. But his home country was now too dangerous for him. His life imperiled, he planned to leave with other dissenters to seek exile in Leipzig or Dresden. After a brief stay in the remaining portion of independent Poland, he headed west, determined to return to America, his "second country to which I have acquired a right by fighting for her independence."

Despairing of change in his native country, he vowed to convince the Americans to support the establishment of a stable, free, and responsible government in Poland.[46]

Traveling in exile under the assumed name of Mr. Beida ("misery" in Polish), Kościuszko found little succor in Europe. The Austrians gave him twelve hours to leave their country, and Russian agents tracked him through Saxony. A coalition of Polish leaders in exile delegated Kościuszko to seek help from the French revolutionary government, much as the Americans had done a decade and a half before.

Kościuszko arrived in Paris in January 1793 on the day King Louis XVI was executed and the rule of the Jacobins' Reign of Terror began. Counting on his stature as a "Citizen of France," an honor given him by the French Assembly in August 1792, Kościuszko expected that French revolutionaries would help his butchered nation. He received nothing but promises. The French, in truth, were bargaining recognition of the latest Polish partition for their own advantage. He spent a miserable summer in Paris, where the political mood grew increasingly hostile and suspicious of outsiders. The promise of some support from the French government evaporated once the French became distracted by their war with England.[47]

Frustrated with the worsening political situation in Paris, Kościuszko left Paris for Italy early in 1794, ostensibly to visit his friend there, the poet-reformer Julian Niemcewicz, but in fact to meet with fellow conspirators who were plotting an uprising against the Russians and the compromised Polish monarchy.

These meetings did not bode well. Though an idealist in his hopes for Poland, Kościuszko became adept at judging the sincerity of Poland's so-called friends and became more realistic about the massive power arrayed against his nation. He worried that Phillip Mazzei, now the emissary of the Polish king in Italy, would inform the king and the Russians of his intentions. Even more worrisome were the limited chances that the plot would succeed against such staggering odds. Though exiled conspirators begged him to assume command of the planned insurgency, Kościuszko knew that the cause was hopeless until they addressed the issue of emancipating the serfs, since raising the hundred thousand troops he deemed necessary for any chance of success was impossible without recruiting serfs who would gain their freedom by joining the cause. In early 1794 he announced that "I shall not fight for the gentry alone." Rather, he insisted, "I desire the freedom of the entire nation and only for it will I risk my life."[48]

Hard upon this announcement came the news in March 1794 that the Russians were determined to demobilize the remnant Polish army in order to squelch any Polish resistance. Meanwhile, the Russians unmasked part of the conspiracy. In what may have been a diversionary tactic, Kościuszko announced shortly afterward that he was departing for America to pursue the land claims and pension that were owed him. Eager to free his own peasants, but unable to do so in exile, Kościuszko ordered a reduction of their forced labor.[49]

Whether Kościuszko really intended to go to the United States cannot be determined, but what is sure is that events soon pressed him into action in his homeland. When the Russians announced the reduction of the Polish army in March 1794, Polish brigadier general Antoni Józef Madlínski refused to disband his regiment and withdrew into the Prussian-held Polish territories. While rumors of a new partition of Poland swirled around European capitals, Madlínski quickly attracted support and marched back into Russian-controlled territory to battle the occupying troops.

On March 23, 1794, as Madlínski distracted the Russians, Kościuszko slipped back into Kraków, where he publicly accepted the role of commander-in-chief of the insurrection. He pledged to restore Poland's government by evicting the occupying forces of Russia and Prussia, and he swore to pursue the goal of universal freedom for all Poles. Kościuszko's Act of Insurrection, promulgated on March 24, 1794, became the Polish equivalent of the Declaration of Independence and the French Declaration of the Rights of Man. It blamed the occupiers for reducing Poland's citizens to a condition of "slavery" and called for a universal struggle of "freedom, integrity, and independence," slogans found on all seals of the rebellion and on all documents he thereafter signed.[50]

With King Stanislaus keeping to the sidelines, Kościuszko, now a national hero, used his newly won prestige and the exigencies of the situation to initiate reforms. He ordered the army to provide chapels for Orthodox, Muslim, and Jewish worship, thus proclaiming equal rights for all faiths. He also pushed for a unified educational system and linguistic conformity, both seen as requisite for a true nation that had been plagued by provincialism and religious fanaticism. Kościuszko had to mask some of his radical ideals so as not to alienate the nobility and higher clergy. But even when tactical considerations forced accommodation, he held hopes for abolishing royal power and emancipating the serfs; this aligned him with the program of the Polish radicals.[51]

In rallying Polish nationalism behind his Act of Insurrection, Kościuszko indicted Empress Catherine and the Russian forces for cannibalizing his nation, appealed to other nations to help Poland gain its independence, and denounced those traitors who had assisted the enemy. In the third part of the Declaration he proposed an interim constitution with shared legislative and executive power, though all military decisions were reserved for himself until the day that Poland achieved its independence. After that, the nation would need to create a permanent constitution. His declaration differed from Jefferson's famous "life, liberty and the pursuit of happiness" by using "life, security, and property," which better fit the needs of the occupied nation and expressed his desire to extend reforms beyond the parochial interests of the landed gentry.

His imagination still fired by the American ideals of social and political equality, but mindful of how radical reform in France had plunged the country into a reign of terror, Kościuszko confronted a delicate situation. To gain manpower for his armies, he had to extend liberty to the serfs and offer some incentives for the allegiance of the urban working classes. But how could he accomplish this without alienating the gentry, who were thoroughly disillusioned with their Russian occupiers but unwilling to move beyond the reforms embodied in the Constitution of the Third of May? Neither a political theorist nor an adroit statesman experienced in brokering compromises, Kościuszko was caught between the moderate followers of the king, who sought simply to rid Poland of the invaders and restore the 1792 constitution, and the radical patriots with whom he most closely identified—intellectuals, professionals, burghers, and landless gentry—who extolled Jacobin ideals and dreamed of emancipating the serfs.[52]

Kościuszko made clear his emerging radicalism in his famous Manifesto of Polaniec of May 7, 1794. It was a brave effort to deal with the accumulated weight of history that had rendered Poland so vulnerable to the powers surrounding it. It tried to marry the problem of serfdom with the need to raise a citizen-soldier army, roughly the same problem in the American Revolution, where some leaders had been eager to recruit slaves who could be induced to fight bravely if promised their freedom. Concluding that Polish independence could never be achieved unless the serfs were given reason to fight for it, he called for their freedom—but with conditions. "Every peasant is free in his person," pronounced the Manifesto, "and may live where he pleases." Yet the Manifesto, while reducing days of labor to be performed for their landlords and promising protection under the law, still maintained partial labor service and denied serfs the instant right to leave the land to which they were attached. Nevertheless, Kościuszko's embrace of the peasantry, though conditional, went beyond any comparable actions toward slaves in the United States, where legislative or judicial emancipation took place only in the Northern states—and very gradually in most of them. Yet the Manifesto, judged historian R. R. Palmer, "lacked the ringing appeal of true revolutionary declarations, . . . too calculated and practical to fire anyone with a passion for combat and sacrifice, too tepid to ignite any mass upheaval."[53]

In proclaiming his Act of Insurrection and calling for the emancipation of the serfs in his manifesto, Kościuszko openly defied the Russian monarch. As the Russian juggernaut prepared to suppress the new Polish army, Kościuszko became the commander of Polish forces and second to the king in title only. His name became synonymous with the rebellion, known ever since as the Kościuszko Insurrection. His humility, icy courage, tireless efforts, and matchless military skills inspired many. Yet without igniting a mass upheaval, Kościuszko faced highly unfavorable odds, even greater than those the Americans confronted in taking on the English military machine in the revolutionary war. Using his American revolutionary experience, he planned battles carefully, using terrain to his advantage and demonstrating an inspiring fearlessness. "The enthusiasm he generates in camp and throughout the nation is incredible," wrote one fellow insurrectionist who was with Kościuszko at Kraķow.[54]

Despite revolutionary ideals and fervor, Kościuszko could muster but fifteen thousand troops, many of them armed only with scythes to face the fully armed, well-trained Prussians and Russians. Only in a few localities did peasants answer the call to arms, nothing akin to the state militias and the Continental Army that prosecuted the American Revolution or the French citizen army then engaged in war to throw back the counterrevolutionary armies of Austria, Prussia, and Russia. Most peasants, wary of the threats of their noble masters if they left the land, stayed at home, but those who joined Kościuszko served bravely. Even though his army was badly undermanned, Kościuszko managed to best the Russians at Raclawice, just outside Kraķow. Donning peasant garb, he led 320 peasant scythemen on April 4, 1794, in a spectacular assault on the enemy artillery that sent the Russians reeling in retreat. Two weeks later, from April 19 to April 22, a mass of citizens joined the Polish troops in assaulting the Russian occupying forces in Warsaw, Vilna, and Gdańsk, forcing the enemy to withdraw.

Kościuszko, said to have donned a peasant coat, honors the capture of Russian artillery by Polish scythemen as the cannon are brought into Kraķow three days after the battle. Later generations of Poles remembered Kościuszko's victory in literature, art, and music as one of the finest feats of Polish valor and patriotism. Michal Stachowicz, *Kraķow Marketplace After the Battle of Raclawice*, Polish Army Museum, Warsaw.

But these victories were fleeting. A battle on June 6, 1794, at Szczekociny cost the Polish army over two thousand dead and wounded, including a slightly wounded Kościuszko. The war then turned to the defense of Warsaw. The Battle of Warsaw began on July 14 and lasted until September 6. In preparation for the battle, Kościuszko had ordered the city's fortifications constructed well in advance and had supervised much of the work himself. Now the Russo-Prussian forces, over forty thousand strong with 250 cannon, battered the city walls. The Polish army was far weaker, consisting of only twenty-five thousand troops equipped with 140 pieces of artillery.

Kościuszko repeatedly led his forces, including a Jewish battalion, into combat in the most dangerous situations. As the assault on Warsaw dragged on, the Russian forces tired and moved to confront

Polish forces elsewhere. Hoping that he could prevent the retreating Russians from joining fresh troops sent by Empress Catherine and expecting support from another sizable contingent of Polish forces, Kościuszko attempted to cut off the Russians, much as he had done at Saratoga two decades before. Placing regiments of nobles on both wings, Kościuszko took command of the center, leading serfs and raw conscripts forward.

But when the promised support did not arrive in time, the Russians quickly seized the initiative and overwhelmed Kościuszko. The formidable Russian army killed over half of the outgunned Polish forces and captured two thousand survivors, many of them badly wounded. Among those ensnared was Kościuszko himself. Amid the din of Russian artillery and cavalry, Kościuszko's horse fell, trapping him beneath the dying carcass. Cossacks pounced on him, slashing and stabbing him with sabers and spears. Only after they realized his identity did the attackers spare him and bring him unconscious to the headquarters of the Russian general.[55]

Within weeks, the insurrection collapsed. Reoccupying Warsaw, the Russians slaughtered six thousand civilians. They carted Kościuszko across Poland in a wheelbarrow to show his fellow citizens the extent of his defeat and terrible wounds. His old friend and compatriot Niemcewicz, himself a captive, described the maimed Kościuszko as a man half dead. "His head and body, covered with blood," he wrote, "contrasted in a dreadful manner with the livid paleness of his face. He had on his head a large wound from a sword and three on his back above his loins from the thrust of a pike. He could scarcely breathe." As the wheelbarrow procession passed within twenty miles of the home of his old love, Princess Ludwika sent gifts of clothing, food, and books for the wounded leader and his soldiers.

The tortuous journey through Poland lasted from October 13 to December 10, after the Russian czarina ordered Kościuszko and Niemcewicz imprisoned in the Petropavlovsk Fortress on the banks of the Neva River in St. Petersburg. Throughout this period Russia plundered and sacked Poland and ravaged its women. "As we advanced," Niemcewicz later recounted, "the booty increased; towns, villages, and particularly the country seats of the nobility were laid waste, plundered and destroyed." A few months later, Catherine instructed that Kościuszko, his wounds still untreated, be moved to the Grigorii Orlov Palace, where an English physician began to minister to him.[56]

After deporting King Stanislaus, Poland's conquerors divided the remainder of the nation, removing it from the map of Europe as if it had never existed. In the Third Partition of 1795, Russia took the eastern provinces, Prussia gained Warsaw, and Austria devoured the remainder, including Krakow and the surrounding region. Even the name "Poland" disappeared so far as the Austrians, Russians, and Prussians were concerned. Poland, as an independent nation, would not reemerge until the end of World War I. Some three thousand Poles languished in Russian prisons, and the door to freedom through which the serfs had had some promise of passing slammed shut.

While the Russians paraded Kościuszko like a pet animal en route to St. Petersburg, Americans reacted to the unfolding events with horror. American newspapers had followed each turn of the Kościuszko Insurrection, recounting the David and Goliath-like battles that reminded Americans of their own struggle against the vastly stronger British army. Like other Americans, Stockbridge villagers, Agrippa Hull doubtless among them, stayed alert to the events in Poland and to Kościuszko's leadership and dreadful capture through local newspaper coverage. From Stockbridge's newspaper, Agrippa learned of Kościuszko's gallantry at Maciejowice in October 1794 in "the battle that determined the fate of Poland." With the nobles falling back, Hull read, "the center maintained its ground under the auspicious valor of the general."

In a Stockbridge July 4 oration in 1795, Barnabas Bidwell, a lawyer and budding Jeffersonian leader, celebrated the Pole's unyielding battle for freedom. Mixing memory of the American Revolution with denunciations of the Russians who stamped out freedom in Europe, Bidwell compared Kościuszko with Washington: "Some of you who compose this audience knew that gallant soldier [Kościuszko], that champion of liberty, that practical friend to the rights of man." Among the few patriot veterans living in Stockbridge, Hull must have felt that Bidwell was addressing him directly.

Grippy's eyes must have moistened when he heard Bidwell continue: "He was your companion in arms, your brother in those perilous days 'which tried men's souls.' You can testify to what zeal he fought the battles of our country by your side, how ardently he aspired to promote the emancipation of the oppressed in all quarters of the world." But, sadly, Bidwell told the Stockbridgians, the "scene is reversed." Then in a moment of prescience, he hoped that the Polish hero of two continents could escape the Russian dungeon and "revisit these shores, where rejoicing millions [would] remember his services and would gladly reward them."[57]

Imprisoned and dreadfully maimed, Kościuszko did not know of American grief about his plight or their celebration of his heroism, for no word of this was allowed to reach him. Only a cook and his faithful valet, Negro John, remained at his side in the Petropavlovsk Fortress. Agrippa Hull's heart must have sunk when Stockbridge's *Western Star* reported on November 24, 1795, that Kościuszko had died in prison. "It is said that even the Empress of Russia could not, without shedding tears, hear of the death of this man, whose courage rendered him worthy of a better fate." But six months later Hull would read that his revered officer was still alive and that Empress Catherine, apparently concerned about turning Kościuszko into a martyr, ordered that he serve life imprisonment at the Grigorii Orlov Palace but receive continued medical treatment and improved general conditions. Characteristically, Kościuszko sent a portion of his daily food to other Polish prisoners.[58]

Though his wounds slowly began to heal, Kościuszko remained unable to walk. He was sickened by the demise of his country and the utter demolition of the reformist initiatives he had launched. And surely he must have wondered if he would ever again experience life outside of his prison cell.

During Kościuszko's years of travail in Poland and Russia, Jefferson was suffering agonies of his own. In 1782, his thirty-three-year-old wife, weakened by six pregnancies in ten years (with but three surviving children), sank into a terminal illness after the birth of Lucy, the Jeffersons' second daughter of that name. The amiable and graceful Martha slipped away on September 6, 1782, with Jefferson at her side. Legend among the domestic family and the Monticello slave community held that Martha made her husband promise never to marry again because she feared a stepmother might mistreat her daughters. The widower Jefferson suffered an inconsolable grief that made his peers worry about his sanity. Allegedly, Jefferson would faint at the sight of his two daughters. He gradually recovered enough to take lengthy nocturnal horse rides, accompanied by his daughter Patsy, to alleviate his grief.[59]

Eventually Jefferson returned to public service as a Virginia delegate to the Congress in Philadelphia and Annapolis in 1783-84. There, in a burst of energy, he chaired important committees and wrote key reports, including one for reforming the coinage system that adopted the dollar, replacing the English pound and shilling.

Jefferson also turned his talents and hopes for fulfilling the promise of the American Revolution to a proposed major revision of the 1776 Virginia constitution. With all eyes upon him, he ventured one of the boldest steps toward abolishing slavery he ever took in his long career. Buried in his revised constitution, slated to be considered by a state convention of lawmakers, was a long section concerning civil rights, capital punishment, and a ban against torture—and then an explosive clause specifying that the legislature should not permit "the continuance of slavery beyond the generation which shall be living on the 31st day of December 1800," with "all persons born after that day being hereby declared free." Jefferson shared his constitutional draft only with James Madison, hoping that his fellow Virginian would use it to their advantage if the convention actually convened. The plan remained a secret between the two for the time being; the convention did not meet for another five years.[60]

With such antislavery sentiments in mind, Jefferson turned to the momentous matter of settling the vast lands beyond the Appalachian Mountains that the states had agreed to cede to the national government. The war over, land-hungry Americans were pouring through the mountain gaps into valleys watered by the Ohio, Kanawha, Cumberland, and Kentucky rivers. This migration demanded an orderly plan to both settle these western lands and secure them from their Indian possessors; it also provided the chance to limit the spread of slavery. Chairing the committee charged to draft a plan, Jefferson deftly constructed the Ordinance of 1784, with a protocol for admitting new states on an equal basis with the original ones as soon as their population reached the number in the least populous of the original states.

Adding to this plan, Jefferson proposed what Kościuszko, only weeks from departing for Europe, must have heartily endorsed—the end of slavery and servitude in the western lands by 1800. Supported by northerners Timothy Pickering of Massachusetts and David Howell of Rhode Island, the sixth article specified "that after the year 1800 ... there shall be neither slavery nor involuntary servitude" in the trans-Appalachian national domain. This bold stroke was consistent with his draft of a new Virginia constitution and kept faith with the revolutionary principle of universal, unalienable rights. Here was the best possibility for the new nation to extend its "empire of liberty" and set the practice of slavery on the road to extinction.

Voting by state, the congressional delegates were almost evenly split. But for the sickness that kept an antislavery New Jersey delegate confined to his bed, the mandate to extinguish slavery in the western lands would have been carried. "Thus we see the fate of millions unborn hanging on the tongue of one man," Jefferson wrote later, "and heaven was silent in that awful moment."

His attempt to resolve the troubling paradox of American freedom built on the backs of hundreds of thousands of slaves narrowly failed, though if passed it would still have been but a limited blow against slavery. Even if the clause had passed, it would have left slaveowners sixteen years to settle into what soon became Kentucky and Tennessee. Once there, masters could organize politically to remove the clause. Nonetheless, in passing this legislation, Congress would have taken a stand on slavery. Jefferson appears to have sincerely wanted this, for his America of the future depended on white yeoman farmers to anchor a free republic that would not, he believed, survive the slave-based plantation system of agriculture.[61]

The failure of Jefferson's brave attempt to prevent slavery from moving west with a flood of land-hungry Americans wounded him deeply. He never forgot the refusal of every fellow Virginia delegate to support him. In fact, among all the Southern delegates, only Hugh Williamson from North Carolina backed his clause to limit the spread of slavery. Sharply rebuffed by all but a few Southerners, he never again would participate as an elected representative in any legislative matter regarding slavery.

If the Southern delegates failed to support Jefferson, his cautious antislavery maneuvers found resonance in the North. Some states had already moved to end slavery, and others, except New York and New Jersey, began to follow suit. Capping this surge of antislavery sentiment, the Continental Congress in 1787 passed the Northwest

Ordinance, which banned the entry of slaves into states being created north of the Ohio River. South of the river, slavery was implicitly sanctioned. Expanding America was now to be half-slave, half-free.

Throughout the early 1780s, Jefferson's fertile mind had been churning on slavery and the character of African Americans. Already he had been penning some extraordinarily frank comments on the state of his thinking, set down in a manuscript he hoped at first would never be published. His *Notes on the State of Virginia* is of signal importance, for within its pages are hints of how Jefferson would make decisions regarding his relations with Tadeusz Kościuszko many years later.

Notes on the State of Virginia stemmed from twenty-two queries sent to influential members of the Congress in 1780 by François Barbé de Marbois, a French government official, about the state of the fledgling American confederation. Jefferson first composed his responses in November of that year, just before British raids led by Benedict Arnold and Banastre Tarleton forced a halt to this enterprise. Jefferson picked up his manuscript again in 1781 and continued to write it even during his wife's final suffering. He worked on *Notes* for the next few years, intending it to be read by a select group of friends.

Jefferson never meant for *Notes* to be published in a more limited edition. To this end, before departing for Europe in 1784, he attempted to publish *Notes* in Philadelphia. But time was short and the costs high, so Jefferson took the manuscript with him to France. There he revised it and printed two hundred copies in May 1785—the authorship was not indicated—with an appendix that included his draft of his constitution for Virginia. It was not intended for general publication, but he presented copies to Franklin, John Adams, James Madison, James Monroe, Lafayette, and other friends.

Once it was published in Paris, printers issued their own versions (which obliged Jefferson in 1787 to acknowledge his authorship in a London edition). Everywhere the small book became famous for its extraordinary evocation of Virginia's geography and natural history—descriptions of rivers, mountains, and flora and fauna—and for Jefferson's deep thinking about American law, politics, and social institutions. However, his insights about slavery and the capabilities of Africans as he observed them in America almost immediately drew fire.[62]

In *Notes* Jefferson was particularly concerned about the effect of slavery on white Americans and seemed to be troubled only incidentally about the plight of the slaves themselves. Unlike many of his Virginia friends, who believed that ownership of slaves was necessary for a gentleman, Jefferson opined that slavery fostered only brutality, false pride, and tyrannical impulses. Slavery, he wrote, produced "a perpetual exercise of the most boisterous passions, the most unremitting despotism on the one part and degrading submission on the other." Thinking perhaps of his own daughters, he continued, "Our children see this, and learn to imitate it; . . . the parent storms, the child looks on, catches the lineaments of wrath, puts on the same airs in the circle of smaller slaves, gives a loose to his worst of passions, and thus nursed, educated, and daily exercised in tyranny, cannot but be stamped by it with odious peculiarities." With personalities shaped by slaveowning, "the liberties of a nation" could never be secure. Agreeing with his friend George Mason, who had argued just before the Revolution that it was impossible for "our future legislators and rulers" to maintain republican virtues when they were "habituated from . . . infancy to trample upon the rights of human nature," Jefferson minced no words about how statesmen would be viewed if they allowed half of society to be despots and the other half to be internal enemies.[63]

The immediate responses to Jefferson's comments on slavery were highly positive. John Adams wrote that the passages on the corrosiveness of slavery were "worth diamonds." James Monroe pushed for general circulation of the book but deferred to Jefferson on keeping the publication private. French intellectuals seized upon his attack on slavery, while generally ignoring Jefferson's speculations about innate black inferiority.

Jefferson became internationally prominent after he arrived in Paris in August 1784 bearing Congress's commission as minister to France. With his oldest daughter, Patsy, at his side, he would spend the next five years there. Attending him was his nineteen-year-old enslaved servant, James Hemings, whose mother had been the mulatto mistress of Martha Jefferson's father. Taking his slaves into France, where he was aware that enslaved blacks were obtaining their freedom by petitioning the government, Jefferson never notified French officials about James or his sister Sally Hemings, who arrived later. As he advised a fellow American slaveholder anxious about bringing chattel property into France, the best procedure was to remain quiet and hope the slave would not learn of his or her rights.[64]

Even if James Hemings did not hear of French opposition to slavery, which seems unlikely, as Paris was the home of many free black servants, his master could not escape conversations about abolition that were coursing through the French capital. As did Benjamin Franklin (who had been the American minister since late 1776), Jefferson loved the vibrant, egalitarian, optimistic intellectual scene. This set Jefferson apart from John Adams, who hated the charged intellectual atmosphere in Paris and had soured on the virtue and judgment of the people at large. The French philosophes, who celebrated Franklin as the man who had "seized fire from the heavens and the scepter from tyrants," heralded the sunny Jefferson for his authorship of foundational political documents. Never far from the mind of the philosophes were slavery and the necessity of abolishing it if the Enlightenment project was ever to succeed.

Jefferson fell in with the French reformers, meeting with French intellectuals of the day, including François-Jean de Beauvoir, Marquis de Chastellux; Marie Jean Antoine Nicolas de Caritat, Marquis de Condorcet; Georges-Louis Leclerc, Comte de Buffon; François

Alexandre Frédéric, Duc de la Rochefoucauld-Liancourt; Constantin François Chassebœuf, Comte de Volney; Abbé Raynal, and Abbé Henri Grégoire. Renewing the relationship they had established during the American Revolution, Lafayette became one of Jefferson's closest and most important friends in Paris. Years later, Jefferson remembered that Lafayette, already an honorary citizen of several American states and cities, "was my most powerful auxiliary and advocate" and the man who paved the way for negotiating commercial and diplomatic treaties.

Lafayette was afire with new ideas for abolishing slavery. Fresh from two weeks with Washington at Mount Vernon, Lafayette could hardly have withheld from Jefferson his plans to enlist Washington in a precedent-setting venture in which both would free their slaves and resettle them as free farmers in French Guiana. Nor would Lafayette have withheld from Jefferson what he wrote to John Adams, that "in the cause of my black brethren, I feel myself warmly interested and most decidedly side, so far as respects them, against the white part of mankind." Lafayette lamented that Americans were still involved in the slave trade, which he regarded as a deep stain on America's reputation, earned with blood and sacrifice in the American Revolution.[65]

At Lafayette's home Jefferson communed with other leaders of the Enlightenment from whom he could draw reinforcement for his antislavery sentiments. Most important among them were Abbé Raynal, a fierce campaigner against slavery, and the Marquis de Condorcet, a founder of the antislavery Société des Amis des Noirs. Both men had profoundly influenced Kościuszko during his stay in Paris in the early 1770s.

Dubbed the "snowy volcano" for his calm exterior that concealed passionate views, the Marquis de Condorcet had made the abolition of slavery and the equal rights of women the priorities of his reform agenda. As early as 1776 he had referred to slavery as a "horrible violation of human rights," and in 1781 he had written a widely circulated treatise denouncing slavery as a criminal act.

In a second edition of his treatise in 1788, Condorcet had proposed a plan that deeply influenced Lafayette: once emancipated, blacks could become free wage laborers. Slaveowners, wrote Condorcet, deserved no compensation for emancipation because in effect they were only relinquishing stolen property. Jefferson purchased two copies of this tract when it was republished in Paris and began translating it into English. One sentence must have made him reflect on the popularity of slavery in his native Virginia: even if "the human race unanimously voted approval [of slavery], the crime would remain a crime."[66]

Meanwhile, Jefferson became attuned to provocative new ideas about the abolition of slavery wafting over the English Channel. Among the English radicals who were sharpening their pens against slavery in the late 1780s were Thomas Clarkson, Granville Sharpe, and William Wilberforce. Clarkson's "Essay on Slavery and Commerce in the Human Species" had stirred reformers in 1786, spurring attempts by Sharpe and Wilberforce to end the slave trade and ameliorate—if not dismantle—slavery. The fiercely determined Sharpe was also concerned with the fate of poor blacks in England, some of them African American veterans of the British army in America who had fallen on hard times in the English capital. Sharpe worked out a plan with Afro-Britons in 1786 by which they would leave London and settle on Africa's west coast at a new colony named Sierra Leone. That the English had no title to this land bothered nobody except the Mende people who lived there, and this would soon cause trouble. By 1791 Sharpe's scheme to populate Sierra Leone enticed over a thousand Black Loyalists to leave their miserable conditions in Nova Scotia. Word of all this probably heartened Jefferson, who had already stated that free descendants of Africans would be better off returning to the African homeland.[67]

The influence of French and English abolitionists on Jefferson in Paris was palpable. Prizing his inclusion among the intelligentsia, relishing their admiration of his *Notes*, and far from his Virginia plantations, he found no discomfort in aligning himself with a circle of cosmopolitan intellectuals who were decidedly antislavery and prepared to do something about it.

Amid such stirring conversations about a transatlantic movement to make the "cause of liberty" the cause of all humankind, Jefferson had to consider what effect his impassioned antislavery prose in *Notes on the State of Virginia* would have at home. Worries that his comments would offend his fellow slave masters were the primary reason why he did not want to set his thoughts before the public. His attack on slavery and the emancipation clause in the draft of a constitution for Virginia, he wrote friends on both sides of the Atlantic, "are . . . the parts which I do not wish to have been public" because "they might produce an irritation which would indispose the people toward the two great objects I have in view, that is the emancipation of their slaves and the settlement of their [Virginia] constitution on a firmer and more permanent basis."[68]

Jefferson was telling his friends that the time was not right for floating an emancipation scheme, yet he was simultaneously telling the English abolitionist Richard Price that the time *was* right. Price had written Jefferson in 1785 after reading *Notes*; he lamented that the Americans "who have been struggling so earnestly to save themselves from slavery are very ready to enslave others." This mortified "the friends of liberty and humanity in Europe," Price admonished. They were now appalled at the prospect that the legacy of the American Revolution would turn out to be "a new scene of aristocratic tyranny and human debasement."

Eager to redeem the American reputation, Jefferson replied that in the Northern states "you may find here and there an opponent to your doctrine [of ending slavery] as you may find here and there a robber and a murderer, but in no greater number." Southward of the Chesapeake, he continued, most would oppose all emancipationist schemes. But in seaboard Virginia, he assured Price, "with some degree of certainty, . . . the bulk of the people will approve it in theory, and it will find a respectable minority ready to adopt it in practice, a minority which for weight and worth of character preponderates against the greater number who have not the courage to divest their families of a property which however keeps their consciences inquiet." Marylanders, he explained, were not as ready "to begin the redress of this enormity," but here too the "spectacle of justice in conflict with avarice and oppression" was tilting toward abolitionism because of "the influx into office of young men grown and growing up" who "have sucked in the principles of liberty as it were with their mother's milk."[69]

Unburdening himself in this way, Jefferson implied that leading men of conscience who wanted to abolish slavery, supported by "the bulk of the people," needed only courage to place the "weight and worth of [their] character" behind an emancipation scheme. Yet Jefferson was not ready to step forward. Part of his reluctance was concern about his political future, and linked to this was the fear of offending friends and fellow planters ready to charge him with betraying his class. He had learned early in 1786 that the Virginia legislature had taken up the revised constitution he had drafted in 1783 and had scornfully rejected a petition calling for a general manumission of Virginia's slaves. This, Madison reported to Washington, "was rejected without dissent, but not without an avowed patronage of its principle by sundry respectable members." Those sympathetic to Jefferson's proposal, which would have freed all slaves born after the passage of the law once they reached adulthood, held back the measure, reasoning that since the legislature had rejected the petition for a general emancipation, they would scorn and revile proponents of such a weighty attempt to change the course of Virginia's history—and that of the nation.[70]

The defeat of his gradual emancipation plan in Virginia was much on Jefferson's mind in 1786. He learned of the setback while he mingled with French intellectuals who yearned to see America wash its hands of slavery and bring its laws into conformity with its revolutionary principles. Pressing him hard was Jean Nicolas Démeunier, the young French thinker and devotee of Abbé Raynal, who was preparing a long essay on the United States for Condorcet's revised *Encyclopédie méthodique*. Why, asked Démeunier in a series of queries to Jefferson, had Virginia passed a revised legal code without some promise of emancipation for the slaves? Eager to save Virginia from opprobrious comments in a book that was sure to reach an international audience, Jefferson waffled in his reply to Démeunier. Though he and the abolition-minded George Wythe were unable to participate in the debate, he said, "men of virtue" were not lacking to press cogent arguments for ending slavery. And yet, Jefferson continued, "they saw that the moment of doing it with success was not yet arrived, and that an unsuccessful effort, as too often happens, would only rivet still closer the chains of bondage, and retard the moment of delivery to this oppressed description of men." It cannot be known whether Jefferson was dissimulating with Démeunier's article in mind or actually describing his own ideas.[71]

His disgust with slavery unmitigated, Jefferson scourged the man who "inflicts on his fellow men a bondage, one hour of which is fraught with more misery than ages of that which he rose in rebellion to oppose." But then Jefferson retreated to a position that would soon steer the course he maintained for the next four decades of his life. If he and his friends could not do what they knew must be done, they must patiently await God's intervention, that is, "the workings of an overruling providence." When the slaves' "groans shall have involved heaven itself in darkness," he assured Démeunier, "doubtless a god of justice will awaken to their distress, and by diffusing light and liberality among their oppressors, or at length by his exterminating thunder," slavery would come to an end. Caught between his friends in the "empire of reason" and his fellow planters in the Upper South who might punish him politically if he advocated practical steps toward abolition, Jefferson looked for divine intervention to solve what the Enlightenment taught was humanity's work.[72]

Jefferson labored under another fear, which was rooted not in politics but in the psyche. This was his fear of free black people—an anxiety bound up with his strong suspicion of inborn black inferiority. He had spelled this out in his *Notes on the State of Virginia*, in which he claimed he had never known a single African who could paint a picture, compose music, form an eloquent thought, or discover a truth. Casting aside the widely held belief that such apparent inferiority was the result of being held perpetually in slavery, in which blacks were denied education and the opportunity to develop their abilities, Jefferson wrote that "it is not their condition . . . but nature, which has produced this distinction" that made them "inferior to the whites in the endowments both of body and mind." Jefferson concluded that blacks' memories were equal to whites', but in terms of their reasoning faculties, "one could scarcely be found capable of tracing and comprehending the investigation of Euclid," and in imagination "they are dull tasteless, and anomalous." Painting and sculpture were far beyond their innate talent.

Jefferson responded icily to African Americans who showed unique talents. Unlike Washington, who had courteously responded to a poem and letter sent to him by Boston's heralded young black poetess, Phillis Wheatley, Jefferson denigrated her as a poet, calling her compositions "below the dignity of criticism." One historian calls these comments "the veritable fountainhead of American racism," while providing "the moral foundations of proslavery ideology." Merrill Peterson, Jefferson's distinguished biographer, concludes that these indictments of black inferiority were the "product of frivolous and tortuous reasoning, or preconception, prejudice, ignorance, contradiction, and bewildering confusion of principles." Yet beyond bewilderment and confusion lurked Jefferson's deep instinct for maintaining his Old Dominion class allegiance.[73]

Calibrating his inner compass, which bound him to the slaveocracy he declared noxious, were frightening changes occurring in Virginia. Ever the student of new data, he read with alarm that the free black population of Virginia had grown from 2,000 in 1782 to 12,766 in 1790, the result of many planters freeing their slaves. For Jefferson, this signaled the coming of a nightmarish future. In his *Notes* he claimed that racial mixture would elevate blacks, but that once freed, inherently inferior black men would seek white partners and thus corrupt the white race through mixture. In his mind, this would sweep away his dream of a nation of independent, virtuous, forward-looking white yeoman farmers.

Jefferson borrowed from history to make his point. A Roman slave, once free, could mix with his betters "without staining the blood of his master," as he put it in his *Notes*. But that was because Roman slaves were white. For white Virginians, the risk of racial degradation was too great. Theorizing that Africans were "originally a distinct race" and unalterably inferior, he concluded that the best solution was to colonize freed slaves in "such a place as the circumstances of the time should render most proper," there to be equipped with tools, seeds, domestic animals, and weapons. America should ensure their protection and declare them a free and independent people, but they could not be fellow citizens, and none should be allowed to stay among white people, even if they were of mixed blood. In 1779 he had backed up this opinion by proposing a law to the Virginia legislature that would require expulsion from the state of any white woman bearing a mixed-race child.[74]

Jefferson's heart as well as his head may have played a role in his shifting views on race. Although his late wife had reputedly demanded he never remarry, Jefferson was only in his mid-forties and indeed highly eligible for a good match. Among his known flirtations in Paris with married women, the most notable was with the twenty-seven-year-old Maria Cosway, the wife of Richard Cosway, the foppish English portrait painter (and the peddler of pornographic snuffbox paintings). Dissatisfied with her London life and unhappy with her vain and pompous husband, Maria abruptly left England and soon landed in Paris in 1786. After she met Jefferson, the two became almost inseparable. Jefferson's head-over-heels infatuation with the languorous young Cosway was certainly the most emotional and ensnaring of his life. His famous parting letter to Cosway about "My Head and My Heart" tells us of his craving for love and how powerfully Maria promised to supply this need. In other letters, however, retreating from emotional commitment, Jefferson contrasted the domestic virtue of American women with the "empty bustle" of their Parisian counterparts. In one passage he set down one of the rules he followed in both private and public affairs: "The art of life is the art of avoiding pain."[75]

Romantic trysts with Maria Cosway did not allow Jefferson to forget the painful subject of slavery. Working in the London home of Richard and Maria Cosway was black abolitionist writer Ottobah Cugoano. Enslaved at age thirteen in West Africa in 1770, Cugoano had gained his freedom in England in 1772, was baptized at St. James's Church the next year, and had entered the service of Richard Cosway in about 1784. By this time he was a leader of London's Committee for the Relief of the Black Poor and a friend of the reformer Scipione Piattoli, advisor to Poland's King Stanislaw and drafter of the Third of May Constitution. One of the Africans who gained literacy and put it to use, the twenty-six-year-old black Londoner was working on *Thoughts and Sentiments on the Evil and Wicked Traffic of the Slavery and Commerce of the Human Species* at just the time Maria Cosway was consorting with Jefferson in Paris. Cugoano's *Thoughts and Sentiments* came off the press in 1787, one of the first antislavery pamphlets to flow from the pen of an African-born ex-slave and the most radical of a spate of such pamphlets. A friend of Olaudah Equiano and Thomas Clarkson, Cugoano became part of the growing international campaign to end the slave trade and slavery.[76]

Did Jefferson read Cugoano's *Thoughts and Sentiments* while playing cat-and-mouse with the wife of Cugoano's master? Jefferson could have read either the first edition of 1787 or a French translation published in Paris the next year. The Cosways certainly knew of the publication, for it was extraordinary for a person serving in the household of the court painter to publish a book on a touchy subject. Maria Cosway was fascinated with music, art, and Jefferson, so she may have found the muscular attack on slavery by her servant an inconvenient topic of discussion with her paramour. But Jefferson's head, if not his heart, must have caught the poignancy that the woman who had captured his heart was also the mistress of the household in which the black man who served there had gained a public platform in London through his attack on slavery.

The year 1788 seems to have marked a turn in Jefferson's thinking, though only briefly, about his role as slave master. With Cugoano's attack on slavery circulating widely, Jefferson's friend Brissot de Warville took the lead in founding the Société des Amis des Noirs as a political lobby to end France's involvement in slavery and the slave trade. Lafayette, Condorcet, and others quickly joined to implore the Master of Monticello to add his name to the lobby. Dodging behind diplomatic protocol, Jefferson argued that he could not join for fear of charges that he was meddling in French politics (though he soon became involved in the intricate politics of the French Revolution). Yet Jefferson was still caught up in the vibrant salon discussions that typically turned from gardens, literature, science, and philosophy to the universal rights of humankind.

News from home must have given Jefferson further pause about his doubts regarding the feasibility of emancipation. In May 1788 he received a letter from Edward Bancroft asking his views on an experiment in Virginia where Joseph Mayo, a Quaker, had freed his two hundred slaves and then hired them as tenant farmers. Undeterred by fragmentary reports that the Quaker experiment had not gone well (perhaps because freed slaves without title to their own property would not work hard), Jefferson seized upon the idea to formulate his own plan to replace his slave labor force. He vowed that "I am decided on my . . . return to America to . . . import as many Germans as I have grown slaves." In an astounding change of position, he said he would allot fifty acres to each family, with slaves and Germans intermingled, and "place all on the footing of the Metayers [landowners] of Europe." Now promised freedom, the children of former slaves would be trained "in habits of property and foresight, and I have no doubt," he wrote, "they will be good citizens." From the produce they harvested, he would retain only "a moderate portion of it as may be a just equivalent for the use of the lands they labor and the stocks and other necessary advances." Jefferson's plan to intermingle freed slaves and German immigrants on his Virginia land sharply reversed the conviction he had firmly expressed in his *Notes*. There he had argued that emancipated slaves must be sent to some distant land because admixing with whites would never work peacefully.[77]

Is it possible that he had changed his mind not only because of his glowing friendship with his Enlightenment friends in Paris but also because of a warmth that was developing, at just this moment, with another beautiful young woman in his own Paris household? Hard on the heels of ending his rapturous relationship with Maria Cosway, Jefferson filled the hole in his heart by initiating an intimate liaison with his enslaved servant Sally Hemings. It was a shadowy, surreptitious bond that has made Jefferson's later inaction on the problem of slavery all the more difficult to fathom.

Sally Hemings had crossed the Atlantic with Polly, Jefferson's youngest daughter, in the summer of 1787. Thirty years his junior and later described by another Jefferson slave as "mighty near white" and "with straight hair down her back," the fourteen-year-old Sally was the daughter of Betty Hemings, the slave mistress of Colonel John Wayles, Jefferson's father-in-law. Betty Hemings birthed fourteen children, six of them with the colonel. When Wayles died in 1773, the Hemings children became Jefferson's property. Sally was the half sister of Jefferson's deceased wife and therefore his sister-in-law and the aunt of his daughters; Sally's brothers, including James, Jefferson's valued chef, were Martha Wayles Jefferson's half brothers and Jefferson's brothers-in-law. Despite these blood ties, the Hemingses remained enslaved, though all of them but "Dashing Sally," as she was known at Monticello, would be freed later in Jefferson's lifetime or after his death, the only such manumissions he made. The Hemingses were favored slaves and worked in and around the house rather than toiling in the fields. Almost part of the family, Betty and Sally Hemings attended to Martha Jefferson in her last illness, and James Hemings became Jefferson's faithful servant in Paris.[78]

Soon after her arrival in Paris in 1788, Sally Hemings became Jefferson's mistress. In a city filled with loveliness, Sally's beauty shone, enhanced all the more by Jefferson's extravagant outlays of money to dress her with finery. It was typical for slave masters in Virginia to dress their domestic slaves shabbily, but in Paris this was not de rigueur, for it made the master look stingy. Jefferson's expenditures on Sally's wardrobe, in all likelihood, also owed something to the deep emotional reactions that the beautiful teenager aroused in the lonely widower.

In Paris (and later in America), Jefferson conducted his relationship with Sally Hemings in a kind of shadow world. He could mask his feelings toward Sally in public, while delighting in the liaison in private. For Sally, the relationship also had advantages. It elevated her status and allowed her to live, however secretly, as Jefferson's common-law wife. She and her brother James were also able to extract wages from their master in Paris. Knowing that slaves brought to France were free under French law enacted during the French Revolution, they apparently obliged the patriarch to treat them almost as if they were French servants.

When Jefferson made plans for returning to America, Sally Hemings was many months pregnant. Undoubtedly anxious about returning to lifelong servitude, she wanted to remain in France. But Jefferson convinced her to return to Monticello, promising he would free any of her children when they reached age twenty-one. Once in Virginia, Sally remained his chambermaid lover for many years, with three conceptions occurring during Jefferson's presidency. In a relationship suffused with unequal power, Jefferson never acknowledged his paternity of the resulting children. In the enclosed world of Monticello, Jefferson masked his emotions, showing no affection toward Sally's children, but effusive love for Martha's. It was a mask he wore for many years.[79]

Jefferson's return to the United States occurred late in 1789, with the French Revolution in full force. Returning with him were his daughters; Sally Hemings, big with child; and her brother James, now equipped with an education and experience as a French chef. On the voyage back, Jefferson arranged the rooms on the ship so that he and Sally would not be far apart. Jefferson promised James his freedom once he had trained another person to be a "good cook," but seven years passed before James won his release from slavery. Accompanied by eighty-six large crates of oil paintings, sculptures, formal chairs, full-length mirrors, marble-topped tables, and other emblems of the genteel life, Jefferson returned to Monticello to resume his role as slave master.

Five years among abolitionist friends of the Enlightenment seemed to have made little impact on the repatriated Jefferson. He showed no interest in the abolition societies that were forming around the country, nor did he show any signs of ambivalence about the slaves at his own Virginia plantations. Having sold off thirty-one slaves in 1785 to satisfy creditors, Jefferson owned about 150 people upon returning to his country. He sold other slaves in 1791, 1792, and 1793 to pay off more debts, some inherited from his father-in-law and others incurred during shopping sprees in France.

During this time, he freed only two of his slaves, both of them brothers of Sally Hemings. In 1794 Jefferson allowed Robert Hemings to purchase his freedom, and two years later he grudgingly honored his agreement with James Hemings.[80]

Awaiting Jefferson was President George Washington's request that he serve as secretary of state. Reluctantly accepting the position, Jefferson plunged into a sea of domestic and international issues—and into a renewed debate over his charges in his *Notes* of black innate inferiority. During his four-year tenure in charge of foreign relations, he faced repeated opportunities to nurture the growing abolition movement and to reconsider his speculations about black inborn deficiencies. But in each case Jefferson retreated from his earlier abolitionist stance while refusing to back away from his doctrine of racial inferiority.

Jefferson had hardly settled into his quarters in New York City in March 1790 when a sulfurous debate over slavery interrupted critical deliberations on Secretary of the Treasury Alexander Hamilton's plan for the funding and assumption of the revolutionary war debt by the federal government. A month before, the Pennsylvania Abolition Society and several other groups of Northern Quakers had petitioned Congress to assert its power to extend the blessings of liberty "without distinction of color, to all descriptions of people"— a polite way of calling for an abolition of slavery. As Jefferson traveled to New York, acrimonious debate over these petitions occupied a full day, with representatives from South Carolina and Georgia trying to take the petitions off the table. However, many Southerners joined Northerners by voting 43 to 11 to establish a committee to consider them.

As the issue of slavery and its fate preoccupied the legislators of the young nation, Jefferson must have felt that he was walking into the nightmare he had described to French philosophers. He arrived five days after Congress debated the committee report, which in the main condemned slavery and held out the idea that

Congress might exercise the power of emancipation after 1808. That in itself infuriated deep Southerners. One observer of the debate believed the report created "as great an uproar . . . amongst the slave-holders as St. Paul's preaching did among the silversmiths at Ephesus." In the end, support for the report evaporated as Northern congressmen, eager to gain the votes of Southern representatives for Hamilton's funding and assumption scheme, gave up on the report. One of those Northerners was Theodore Sedgwick, who found the antislavery petitions an irritating delay to the debate over funding and assumption.[81]

Jefferson's return to the United States also ignited controversy over his statements about black inferiority that he had expressed in his *Notes on Virginia*. Even before his return, his ruminations that black people's intellect was inferior to that of whites had incited antislavery advocates. Gilbert Imlay, a Continental Army Kentuckian who had roamed the nation's western frontiers and mingled with people of many genetic crossings, scorned Jefferson's ideas. In a book on travels on the western American frontier, published first in London in 1792 and then in New York the next year, he put it baldly: "It is certain" that blacks and whites "are essentially the same in shape and intellect."[82] Other antislavery stalwarts, including Benjamin Franklin, argued that slavery, not genetic inheritance, held down black intellectual development. Meanwhile, newspaper editors began to cite examples of black achievement that implicitly challenged Jefferson's unenlightened speculations about irredeemable black inferiority, while African Americans pointed to blacks' accomplishments, refuting Jefferson's theories. Two of them attracted notice so great that Jefferson fell on the defensive.

Thomas Fuller, an aged, illiterate Virginia slave known as the "African Calculator," had stunned the nation in 1790, when reports of his spectacular mental abilities appeared in newspapers largely in the Northeast. When asked to calculate the number of seconds a man has lived after seventy years, seventeen days, and twelve hours, he reflected briefly and then answered 2,210,500,800 seconds. After his white interlocutors charged him with a small error, he stunned them by pointing out that they had forgotten to account for leap years. Fuller topped off the performance by answering without pencil or paper the question of how many sows a farmer would have if he started with six, each sow had six female pigs in the first year, "and they all increased in the same proportion to the end of eight years." After brief reflection, he produced the correct answer of 34,588,806. Philadelphia's *General Advertiser*, read by all government officials in Philadelphia, opined that if average opportunities had come Fuller's way, "neither the Royal Society of London, the Academy of Sciences at Paris, nor even a Newton himself, need have been ashamed to acknowledge him as a brother in science." Jefferson's views notwithstanding, Fuller amply demonstrated "the genius, capacity and talents of our ill fated black brethren" and should shame those who "supposed [the] inferiority of their intellectual faculties; sentiments as ill founded in fact as they are inhuman in their tendency."[83]

Jefferson showed no signs of changing his mind about black inferiority after learning of the African Calculator's death in 1791, but a year later he had to confront a live African American who was all too ready to challenge the author of the Declaration of Independence about his views on black inferiority. Benjamin Banneker, a free black man from Maryland who was adept at mathematical puzzles, the construction of clocks, surveying, and astronomy, published an almanac in 1791 that took many Americans by storm. The almanac compiled useful data on weather, agriculture, medicine, and astronomy and was peppered with proverbs, folk wisdom, poems, jokes, and much more. But at the core of the almanac was the ephemeris, a complicated set of astronomical computations that established the positions of the sun, moon, and planets for each year. From these calculations, which required the knowledge of spherical trigonometry, one could chart lunar and solar eclipses, the rising and setting of the sun and moon, and the cycle of tides. It was an extraordinary scientific feat for a man with little formal education.

David Rittenhouse, considered America's finest astronomer, hailed the Marylander's achievements as proof of the equality of blacks once freed from bondage. In a pointed dig at Jefferson, the Baltimore printer of Benjamin Banneker's *Pennsylvania, Delaware, Maryland and Virginia Almanack and Ephemeris* prefaced the book with the advice that it "must be considered an extraordinary effort of genius" by a man "who, by this specimen of ingenuity, evinces, to demonstration, that mental powers and endowments are not the exclusive excellence of white people, but that the rays of science may alike illumine the minds of men of every clime . . . particularly those whom tyrant-custom hath too long taught us to depreciate as a race inferior in intellectual capacity."[84]

When Banneker sent him a manuscript copy of the almanac, Jefferson responded that "no body wishes more than I do to see such proofs as you exhibit." But Jefferson was only willing to grant just so much credit. Nearly twenty years later, after Banneker had become almost a household word, Jefferson still withheld full praise. "We know he had spherical trigonometry enough to make almanacs," he wrote, "but not without the suspicion of aid from Ellicot, who was his neighbor and friend." Jefferson went on to say, "I have a long letter from Banneker, which shows him to have had a mind of very common stature indeed."[85]

The long letter from Banneker (which still rankled Jefferson after his presidency) had become an embarrassment in 1792, when the letter was published in Philadelphia for every member of the nation's federal government to read. In it, Banneker had implored Jefferson to rethink his views about African inferiority and had chided him for continuing to hold slaves at Monticello and his other plantations. Never had such a letter from a poor black man been directed to such a celebrated and wealthy white man. "I apprehend you will embrace every opportunity to eradicate that train of absurd and false ideas and opinions which so generally prevail with respect to us," Banneker had written, "and that your sentiments are concurrent with mine, which are that one universal father hath given being to us all and that he hath not only made us all of one flesh but that he hath also without partiality afforded us all the same sensations, and endowed us all with the same faculties." Reminding Jefferson of his oft-quoted words in the preamble of the Declaration of Independence that "all men are created equal and that they are endowed by their creator with certain unalienable rights," Banneker had rebuked Jefferson for turning away from the time when he "clearly saw into the injustice of a state of slavery." But now, he continued, "how pitiable is it to reflect" that "you should at the same time counteract his mercies, in detaining by fraud and violence so numerous a part of my brethren under groaning captivity and cruel oppression." Should not Jefferson "be found guilty of that most criminal act, which you professedly detested in others?"[86] Jefferson's reply was brief. Saying not a word about his ownership of slaves, he simply acknowledged receipt of the manuscript almanac about to be published and noted that he was sending it to the secretary of the Academy of Sciences in Paris.

Banneker's challenge to Jefferson's notion of innate black inferiority—an idea that became an important weapon in the arsenal of proslavery ideologues—discomfited the secretary of state. But he felt no discomfort in the position he assumed on the world-shaking slave rebellion in the Caribbean that had ignited in 1791 just as Banneker's almanac went to press. Here was the first moment when Jefferson had an opportunity, as statesman and policymaker, to do what he had once said he so fervently desired—to hasten the end of slavery.

In August 1791 slave rebellion broke out in the French colony of Saint Domingue (to be called Haiti), touching off a movement for national liberation that lasted twice as long as the American Revolution and ended two centuries of plantation labor, which had swallowed up the lives of several hundred thousand slaves.[87] An extension of the French Revolution's quest for universal liberty and equality, the Haitian Revolution terrified American slaveowners, who feared that the spark of black liberation would jump the water from the Caribbean island to the North American mainland. When self-liberated slaves overran the main seaport of Le Cap Français, burning and killing those in their way, thousands of panicked French planters and merchants fled the island. Most sought refuge in American coastal cities.

Many Americans, especially black Americans, applauded the black rebellion because it had the potential to inspire slaves in the South to break their chains or convince Southerners that they must begin a program of gradual emancipation lest a Haiti-like firestorm envelop them. Many white Americans also supported the struggle of enslaved Haitians to seize their freedom. As one Pennsylvania newspaper essayist put it, "It would be inconsistent on the part of a free nation to take measures against a people who had availed themselves of the only means they had to throw off the yoke of the most atrocious slavery; if one treats the insurrection of the Negroes as rebellion, what name can be given to that insurrection of Americans which secured their independence?"

In principle, Jefferson should have welcomed the rebellion for the very same reason. He had been an ardent supporter of the French Revolution, of course, and in his first public words after arriving in America in 1790 to a welcoming assemblage at Alexandria, Virginia, he proudly spoke to the "animating thought that, while we are securing the rights of ourselves and our posterity, we are pointing out the way to struggling nations who wish, like us, to emerge from their tyrannies also. Heaven help their struggles, and lead them, as it has done us."[88]

Jefferson responded to the crisis by pressing Lafayette to work for a negotiated settlement with the rebelling slaves. If they retreated to the mountains and stopped their efforts to overthrow the entire slave system, they would be guaranteed their safety. Jefferson had solid reasons for taking no further action. His first concern as secretary of state was to preserve his nation's valuable commercial relations with Saint Domingue. And as the nation's diplomatic leader, he could do little to aid the freedom-minded slaves while maintaining favorable relations with France's government. It was a delicate proposition inasmuch as France was in the throes of a massive revolution with constantly shifting regimes.

In his private writings, however, Jefferson demonstrated no empathy toward the rebellious slaves, no sign that he was inspired by their uprising. Instead, his sympathies lay with the colonial sugar and coffee planters—though nobody doubted the planters' antipathy to the principles of the French Revolution that Jefferson so ardently supported. His heart bled for the French planters driven from the island, he wrote his friend James Monroe: "Never was so deep a tragedy presented to the feelings of man," he wrote, disregarding the feelings of several million enslaved Africans and free black people in the Americas. Yet Jefferson believed that the ejection of the whites by rebelling slaves would occur sooner or later throughout the West Indies, and then the unstoppable black insurgency would spread to the United States. "It is high time," he wrote Monroe, "we should foresee the bloody scenes which our children certainly, and possibly ourselves, . . . have to wade through, and try to avert them."[89]

And so Jefferson did not celebrate in August 1793, when the Jacobin commissioner in Haiti declared a general emancipation. Nor did he celebrate, a short time later, when the revolutionary government in Paris decreed universal emancipation in all French colonies. Instead, Jefferson turned his effort to provide relief for those fleeing slaveowners who had reached America, including many who had arrived with slaves in tow and possessed of a fierce antipathy to the revolutionary government in Paris that Jefferson applauded.

While black insurrectionists reduced le Cap Français to ashes in a firestorm of violence in mid-1793, Jefferson was contemplating the Fugitive Slave Act, which Congress had passed just a few months before. Like the maelstrom in Saint Domingue, it heightened his growing uneasiness about slavery. Agrippa Hull's employer, Theodore Sedgwick, helped draft the bill in the House of Representatives to strengthen the hand of Southern slaveowners pursuing runaway slaves, most of whom followed the North Star across the Mason-Dixon Line and many of whom reached the nation's capital in Philadelphia. The Senate debated a revised bill at length, and Congress put it before President Washington for his signature in February 1793. Seen as strengthening the hand of the slaveocracy because it allowed claimants of fleeing slaves to seize their putative property without a court warrant, the act encountered little resistance from the budding Jeffersonian party that was coalescing to oppose Federalist maneuvers to increase the power of the federal government.[90]

By this time Jefferson's growing rancor with Alexander Hamilton and conservatives who seemed to control President Washington had made him the putative head of an embryonic opposition political party. But Jefferson begrudgingly held his office only until the end of 1793. Then he retired. Retreating to his Olympian perch at Monticello, he remained there for more than three years, intent on quitting politics altogether. "My farm, my family and my books call me to them irresistibly," he wrote as he departed Philadelphia. His withdrawal from the public realm allowed him to cast off his potential to influence the nation on the subject of slavery. But he could neither dissociate himself from slavery nor drive from his mind worries about how the infection of black rebellion might reach American shores.

Jefferson's return to Monticello thrust him back full-time into his role as slave master. For three rustic years, he trafficked in slaves, buying some, selling others, all the while hearing of slave unrest and free black protest in various parts of the country. While Kościuszko languished in prison, Jefferson received disturbing reports at his Monticello aerie of blacks torching the urban centers of America in Baltimore, New Haven, Waterford, Boston, New London, Charlotte, Williamsburg, and Norfolk. He continued to wrestle with the paradox of American liberty and American slavery, not knowing that in his return to public life he would cross paths unexpectedly with Poland's maimed hero.[91]

4

❧❈❧

Struggles for Liberty

WHEN HE RETIRED as secretary of state in late 1793, Jefferson said he would never again leave Monticello for public life. But three years at his pastoral idyll did nothing to repair his precarious finances, nor did it satisfy his nagging ambition to play on a larger stage. With Washington announcing his retirement after two terms as president, Jefferson succumbed to the pleas of his friend James Madison and others to run as Washington's successor. In 1796, John Adams won the election narrowly, and Jefferson became vice president.

Arriving in Philadelphia for Adams's inauguration as president in March 1797, Jefferson was greeted by a boisterous crowd lifting a banner emblazoned "Jefferson the Friend of the People." An artillery company fired sixteen rounds from twelve-pound cannons to cap the reception. But while Jefferson was a friend of the people, he was less than a friend to President Adams. Adams represented conservative Federalism, while those embracing liberal visions of Republicanism coalesced around Jefferson.

Two days after the inauguration, Jefferson and Adams parted company. Earlier, Adams asked Jefferson to enlist Madison to become the American minister to France. But strolling together down

Market Street, Adams informed Jefferson that he had dropped the matter because of objections to Madison that had been raised by prominent Federalists. The two men then took leave of each other to go to their separate lodgings. "He never after that said one word to me on the subject," wrote Jefferson, "or ever consulted me as to any measures of the government." From that moment, Jefferson was removed from any influence on the executive branch of the government, as Adams depended mostly on advice from the conservative wing of the Federalist Party. Jefferson had anticipated this outcome; even before the inauguration he had written that "a more tranquil and unoffending station could not have been found for men," but he took satisfaction that "it will give me philosophic evenings in the winter and rural days in the summer [at Monticello]."[1]

Jefferson's sojourn in Philadelphia was sweetened somewhat by his election on March 10, 1797, as president of the American Philosophical Society, the nation's scientific and intellectual nerve center. It was a frequent meeting place for overseas visitors and the intellectual elite, putting Jefferson in close contact with dedicated abolitionists. At the first meeting that Jefferson presided over, in March 1797, the abolitionist Enlightenment leader Comte de Volney sat on his right, and England's eminent chemist and philosopher Joseph Priestley, another foe of slavery, sat on his left. That he lived in the foremost abolitionist city in the nation was all the more apparent when Philadelphia's black leaders helped four free black migrants from North Carolina petition Congress to revoke the detested 1793 Fugitive Slave Act—a law that allowed Southern body snatchers, without a court warrant, to seize free men alleged to be slaves. Jefferson never commented on the petition, publicly or privately, but he may not have been sorry that Congress took no action on the petition.[2]

Jefferson and his friends at the Philosophical Society soon learned that Empress Catherine II had died in Russia. Shortly thereafter, news arrived that her successor, Czar Paul I, had freed Kościuszko and granted him an estate with fifteen hundred peasants

Negro John, who accompanied Kościuszko to Europe in 1783, is shown at the left next to a chair with Kościuszko's cloak and hat. It was after this visit that Kościuszko and his servants were released from prison. Gaugain worked from a painting by Aleksander Orlowski, which has been lost for many years. Engraving of Czar Paul I visiting Kościuszko in St. Petersburg (1801), by T. Gaugain, from a painting by Aleksander Orlowski, National Museum, Warsaw.

attached to the land.[3] Like most Americans, Jefferson rejoiced at the news that the imprisoned Pole's agony was nearly over. Little did Jefferson know that his life and Kościuszko's were about to become entwined in one of the most remarkable relationships of the revolutionary era.

The full story of Kościuszko's release, filtering into American newspapers, heightened anticipation of the Polish hero's return to America, where he had fought for "the glorious cause." Through the press, Jefferson could read details of how Kościuszko, along with his friend and secretary, Julian Niemcewicz, and many other Poles, had remained imprisoned until November 1796, when Czar Paul I visited Kościuszko and arranged for their release. Kościuszko had courageously refused his own freedom unless every Pole in the czar's prisons, including some ten thousand of them rotting away in Siberia, was pardoned. In exchange, he offered an oath of allegiance to the Russian czar. It was a painful acknowledgement of the failed revolution Kościuszko had led a few years earlier. When Czar Paul offered Kościuszko his own sword, the magnanimous gesture of one nobleman to another, the Pole replied, "What need have I of a sword since I have no longer a country to defend?"[4]

Americans devoured reports that the czar had granted Kościuszko permission to travel across Europe and on to America. In taverns and ceremonial dinners, American patriots raised glasses to the valiant Pole. The Society of Cincinnati in Boston, for example, hailed Kościuszko as "an electrick spark of French fire to the people of Poland." Pictures of Kościuszko went on sale in American cities, as Americans began to install Kościuszko in a pantheon already occupied by Washington, Jefferson, Franklin, and Lafayette.[5]

Leaving Russia on December 19, 1796, Kościuszko, Niemcewicz, a Polish officer named Libiszewski (whose job was to carry Kościuszko from bed to carriage and back again), the faithful servant Negro John, and a Russian officer assigned to accompany them traveled first through Finland and the Aband Islands to Sweden. Everywhere they went, locals turned out to greet Kościuszko, the "man who so bravely defended his dying country." Amid this stream of visitors, the Russian minister in Stockholm visited Kościuszko every day, sending reports back to Russia about his health.

Their arrival in Stockholm marked the end of Negro John's lengthy service to Kościuszko. Why he stayed behind is unknown, but it is possible that the black American, having lived in Europe for thirteen years, did not wish to return to the United States.[6] Whatever the explanation, Kościuszko ventured forth for the first time in twenty years without a black American at his side. During the final two decades of his life he would never again share company with a black aide such as Agrippa Hull or Negro John; nonetheless, he preserved a special place in his heart for the blacks who had served him so well.

By reading Philadelphia's newspapers, Jefferson could follow Kościuszko's entourage as they left Stockholm for the ancient university town of Gothenburg and then London, where they arrived on May 29. Londoners saluted the British Crown's former opponent as a hero, in spite of the Tory government's official stance in favor of the Third Partition of Poland. Leading liberals, including William Wilberforce and Charles James Fox, the dramatist Richard Sheridan, prominent aristocrats such as the Duchess of Devonshire, and a wide assortment of other notables visited Kościuszko to pay their respects. British physicians declared his severe headaches the result of a blunt sword wound that had severed a nerve on the back of his head and concluded that a pike wound in the sciatic nerve near his hip had caused the paralysis in his legs. But they assured Kościuszko that ample rest would cure his wounds and enable him to walk.[7]

Though intent on returning to America, Kościuszko did not give up his dream of leading a movement to regain Poland's freedom. He had heard that a Polish Legion was forming in Italy, but he remained aloof, fearful of jeopardizing the newly wrought agreement freeing thousands of Polish prisoners in Russia, many of whom were still making their way home. He convinced himself that somehow a return to America would lead to a brighter future for Poland.

Having departed Bristol aboard the *Adriana* in June 1797, after a storm-tossed, two-month passage Kościuszko and his companions reached Philadelphia on August 17. There Kościuszko found a nation awaiting him with open arms. As the *Adriana* neared the dock, its sailors cried three times, "Long Live Kościuszko!" Philadelphians echoed with three more cheers as they watched the powerful Libiszewski carry Kościuszko ashore.[8] Jefferson, however, was not among the crowd welcoming him back to America. He had left Philadelphia in early July after Congress recessed and would not return to the federal capital for another five months.

For all of this rapturous welcome, Kościuszko had entered a young nation deeply divided by the French Revolution. Though

Little more than a decade after the American Revolution, British citizens, high and low, celebrated the brave Kościuszko as the living embodiment of liberal concepts of freedom. This image portrays Kościuszko recuperating from severe wounds to his back, stomach, and head. The best physicians in London examined and treated his injuries. Benjamin West, *Kościuszko Blessed in London* (1797), Allen Memorial Art Museum, Oberlin College.

France had been the indispensable ally of the American Revolution, the violent spasms of the French Revolution alarmed many Americans. Much of the nation continued to feel deep gratitude toward the French, applauding the revolutionary principles of liberty, fraternity, and equality. But Federalists and their supporters, appalled at the radical direction the French Revolution had taken, instead supported the once-hated English and hoped for their defeat of the advancing revolutionary French armies. President Adams, lacking the commanding presence of George Washington and unable to stifle the factionalism that emerged late in Washington's presidency, especially over the pro-British Jay Treaty of 1795, struggled to lead a bitterly divided country. The opposition, coalescing around Vice President Jefferson, sought peace with the French and charged that the Federalists, regarding any dissent as treasonous, were fast becoming tyrants. In the summer of 1797 Jefferson accepted the leadership of the Democratic-Republican Party, a status that left him all the more ostracized by the Adams administration, of which he was ostensibly a member.

Arriving as an emblem of the Revolution's past glory, with his wartime reputation now burnished by his courageous battle against Empress Catherine, Kościuszko convinced most Americans that a true republican was in their midst. However, Federalist newspaper publisher Peter Porcupine (William Cobbett) attempted to quell such adulation. Wielding his acidic pen, Cobbett reminded Americans that while in England Kościuszko had accepted a ceremonial sword from General Banastre Tarleton, hated English general during the Revolution and now spokesman for Liverpool slave merchants who were trying to stifle parliamentary debates on ending the slave trade. No evidence survives to indicate that Kościuszko was conflicted about taking the sword from a former enemy, but Cobbett's article alerted him that not all Americans welcomed him or viewed him with undiluted love.[9]

After the mass welcome, Kościuszko and Niemcewicz moved into cramped quarters on South Fourth Street in Philadelphia, just a few blocks from Richard Allen's Mother Bethel Church. But the stay was brief, for the Polish contingent arrived amid a plague. A yellow fever epidemic, echoing the devastating scourge four years before that had killed thousands, was again gripping the city. At first, Dr. Benjamin Rush, who began treating Kościuszko's injuries, believed that the fever was in decline. But a week later, with authorities barricading the streets to quarantine the infected areas and thirty-six thousand residents pouring out of the city, Rush convinced Kościuszko to leave.

Invited to visit Generals Anthony Walton White and Horatio Gates, his old revolutionary officer friends, Kościuszko and his party headed northward by carriage. Passing through small farms and villages, they arrived on August 31 in New Brunswick, New Jersey, where they visited General White, who had fared poorly in speculative ventures in Georgia. Now he owned little more than a farm and some slaves.[10]

Kościuszko, openly antislavery, surely had mixed feelings about progress toward ending slavery in New Jersey. In the state's Quaker-dominated southern counties, slavery was all but dead, and in north-eastern towns, where Episcopalians, Quakers, and Presbyterians were influential, about 650 blacks had gained freedom and secured small landholdings. Yet Kościuszko could see that opponents of slavery had a long haul ahead of them. In Monmouth, Middlesex, and Essex counties, through which Kościuszko and Niemcewicz passed, over 4,500 people remained in bondage. In Bergen and Somerset counties, both dominated by people of Dutch extraction, another 4,000 blacks worked as slaves. Debate over slavery in the state legislature waxed and waned with the prospects for gradual emancipation seeming dim seventeen years after neighboring Pennsylvania had passed its famous gradual abolition act. All the accoutrements of slavery, including a thriving internal slave trade, repressive laws, and active pursuit of runaway slaves, remained much as they had existed in the colonial period. We can imagine that Kościuszko chafed at hearing White speak of plans to purchase more slaves.[11]

Kościuszko and Niemcewicz found similar successes and failures in the state of New York, their next destination. Journeying north to New York City to meet Horatio Gates, Kościuszko found that his old mentor had prospered from the sale of land given him by Congress, had remarried into more money, and then moved from Virginia with his new bride to a farm just north of Manhattan. No doubt to his delight, Kościuszko learned that before leaving his Virginia plantation, Gates had freed his slaves. At Gates's house, Kościuszko had the opportunity to meet several black people whom the general had freed and then hired to manage his farm while serving as cook and house servant.[12]

But even more delightful was Kościuszko's reunion with Agrippa Hull, who had traveled from Stockbridge to greet the man he had served so dutifully for more than four years of war. No records survive to indicate what the two men discussed after thirteen years apart, but we can imagine that Kościuszko told Hull about his attempts to free Poland's serfs, about his long imprisonment, about his lengthy journey across Europe and the Atlantic, and about Negro John. And Hull had his own stories to tell—about marriage, the birth of his children, and his modest success in Stockbridge, all of which would have reaffirmed Kościuszko's faith in black Americans.[13]

New York City, with its diversity, vibrancy, and embrace of republican values, enchanted Kościuszko and Niemcewicz. Yet slavery and African American life still retained much of the character that Kościuszko witnessed when he had last visited the city in 1784. In fact, New York's slave population continued to grow during the 1790s, while shrinking almost everywhere else in the North. Nevertheless, many white New Yorkers were working to end human bondage. In 1785, Alexander Hamilton, while still a slaveowner, had formed the New York Manumission Society, which included the kind of political, military, and social leaders with whom Kościuszko was likely to consort. The Society's members guarded the precious manumission papers of free blacks and defended them in court and in the streets against slave catchers, who whisked unwary blacks off to bondage in the South or the West Indies. With the election of Manumission Society member John Jay as governor of the state the year before Kościuszko arrived, the impulse toward a gradual emancipation had quickened.[14]

Emancipation, however, was a mixed blessing for black Manhattanites, as throughout much of the country. As Kościuszko almost certainly observed, many free blacks who had negotiated their freedom with their owners continued to work in their households because there were few if any alternatives. Still, Kościuszko would have seen evidence that black New Yorkers were developing a sturdy community.

At John Street Methodist Church, where Peter Williams, a black revolutionary war veteran, was sexton, black Methodists had established a separate congregation with their own ministers. The African Free School, sponsored by Episcopalians and Quakers, educated black youths to become black clerics and activists. Free black artisans and property owners were common in New York City, as were free blacks who announced their liberty by taking on names like Thomas Paine, Royal Cromwell, and New Year Evans. Also notable was that many free blacks in New York had connections with black Haitians whose masters had freed them upon reaching New York and who told inspiring stories about the black rebellion launched to create the hemisphere's first black republic.[15]

Taking leave of New York, Kościuszko and his friends ferried back across the Hudson River to New Jersey, where they whiled their time away with revolutionary officer friends until mid-November. By then, the fever had subsided sufficiently in Philadelphia to allow for Kościuszko's safe return. Aided by Dr. Rush, Niemcewicz found inexpensive second-story lodgings for Kościuszko at the busy corner of Pine and South Third streets. Then, like a personal guide, the reform-minded Rush explained the changes that had occurred in America during Kościuszko's long absence. Treating the Pole's lingering injuries, Rush frequently refreshed himself "from the toils of the day by passing an hour with [Kościuszko] every evening."[16]

Though not fully recovered from his wounds, Kościuszko quickened to the abolitionist tremors of the "walking city," where face-to-face encounters with diverse city dwellers were common. He would have encountered many like-minded liberals, including leaders of the Pennsylvania Abolition Society, which was energetically encouraging free black enterprise and education, lobbying state and federal governments to end slavery, and gaining freedom for as many slaves as possible. Every day James Forten, a celebrated revolutionary veteran and successful black sail maker, strolled past Kościuszko's door. Directly across the street lived Absalom Jones, who had gained respect as the founder and minister of St. Thomas's African Methodist Episcopal Church. A few blocks away stood Richard Allen's African Methodist Church. Both recently established sanctuaries were now thronged on Sundays by hardworking black congregants, who were launching schools, mutual aid societies, and literary groups. Here in a city where the abolitionist spirit prevailed, Kościuszko could see growing black self-confidence, a great thirst for education, and the blossoming of black talent—all concrete evidence that, given an opportunity, black Americans were worthy of citizenship.

Squeezed into his cramped second-story rooms, Kościuszko entertained a stream of visitors. Congressmen, revolutionary war veterans, publishers, the famous Mohawk chief Joseph Brant, and Louis Philippe, the future king of France, paid their respects. The French consul, Philippe André Joseph de Létombe, was also a frequent guest. Among the special visitors was Michikinikwa (Little Turtle), the chief of the Miami Indians. When he came to pay homage, Little Turtle gave Kościuszko a decorated tomahawk. In the spirit of Indian reciprocity, the Pole gave the Indian chief a pair of glasses. Donning them, Little Turtle exclaimed, "You have given me new eyes."[17]

But above all others, the most constant visitor was Vice President Jefferson, who had arrived in Philadelphia about four weeks after Kościuszko had returned to the city. Thus began a momentous relationship with the Polish hero that would lead toward the Virginian's most puzzling and tragic decision of his life.

In the company of Kościuszko, Jefferson was primed for a spirited discussion about liberty and slavery. Only weeks before he returned to the federal capital, Jefferson had read a newly published general emancipation plan sent to Monticello in August 1797 by his friend

St. George Tucker. As a William and Mary law professor in 1790, Tucker had admonished his students that the United States could never fulfill its destiny of leading the world's nations toward freedom while clasping the viper of slavery to its bosom. Tucker, who had married into the land- and slave-rich Bland-Randolph family, had led a Virginia militia unit in the war and fought alongside Lafayette. Tucker had thought hard about how some of his family's slaves had fled to the British during that harrowing year of 1781, when British commanders Banastre Tarleton and Benedict Arnold had plundered Virginia. He also knew that many Virginians were currently wallowing in debt as their slaves worked land-exhausted tobacco plantations unprofitably. Heightening his misgivings about slavery was a slave mutiny at the plantation of one of his in-laws in 1787. Tucker had not taken immediate action, but thoughts about ending slavery had filled his mind for years.[18]

By 1793, Tucker was becoming an abolitionist leader. Two developments in particular propelled him to action. One was the stunning data revealed by the first federal census in 1790 that the number of slaves in Virginia had increased by a third since 1782. Instead of withering after Virginia halted slave imports in 1774, as many had expected, the slave population had grown through natural increase. Virginia's future was clearly not to be the yeoman farmers' republic that Jefferson had once dreamed of, but rather a contorted state of slaveholding republicans, whips in hand, exercising dominion over a growing mass of slaves.

Tucker's abolitionist sentiments were consolidated also by the spiraling black rebellion on Saint Domingue, which he feared would touch off a sister insurrection in the American South. "The calamities which have lately spread like a contagion through the West India islands," Tucker wrote a Massachusetts friend, "afford a solemn warning to us of the dangerous predicament in which we stand." Tucker's evolving antislavery stance combined a dread of slave rebellion, worries about Virginia's escalating planter debts, and a belief that slavery degraded all who touched it. His ultimate plan to free and colonize African Americans outside the South fit well with antislavery ideology being expressed on both sides of the Atlantic.[19]

In 1796 Tucker took pen in hand to lay out his thoughts. In constructing his "Dissertation on Slavery with a Proposal for the Gradual Abolition of It," he seems to have had Jefferson in mind. He had visited Jefferson at Monticello as he was finishing his long essay, and he knew that leadership was a crucial element in ending slavery. He began his pamphlet with the words of Montesquieu, one of Jefferson's Enlightenment heroes: "Slavery not only violates the laws of Nature, and of civil society, it also wounds the best forms of Government; in a Democracy, where all men are equal, slavery is contrary to the spirit of the Constitution." Then Tucker drove home the point that had been made repeatedly in recent years: "Whilst America hath been the land of promise to Europeans, and their descendants, it hath been the vale of death to millions of the wretched sons of Africa. The genial light of liberty, which hath here shone with unrivalled lustre on the former, hath yielded no comfort to the later, but to them hath proved a pillar of darkness." Tucker argued further that while the men of '76 might be excused for dealing with slavery "during the convulsions of a revolution," now, in a state of "constitutional health and vigour," it was time to remove the stigma of slavery in order to uphold "the principles of our government and of that revolution upon which it is founded."[20] Failure to do so, when slavery was poisoning the new republic to its roots, was a national disgrace.

Tucker set forth in his tract a plan for abolition that took into account the two main obstacles that were keeping the peculiar institution in place on American soil: the huge economic investment of slaveholders in their chattel property and the ingrained belief among whites that black Americans could never be absorbed in white society on an equal footing. To surmount the first obstacle, he copied Pennsylvania's gradual abolition act of 1780. Rather than proposing the freeing of any living slave, he offered a nearly cost-free plan in which female slaves would gain freedom only after reaching the age of twenty-eight—freedom thereby descending through the mother. This would allow their owners to recapture their investment while costing the state or federal government not a dime for purchasing the freedom of living slaves. Further to stroke the pocketbooks of slaveowners, Tucker stipulated that even the children of these black women scheduled for freedom would gain their freedom only at their twenty-eighth birthday. In theory, then, a woman born of a slave mother in 1800 would be free in 1828; if she bore a child just before her release from bondage, that child would be free in 1856.

To counter the second obstacle, Tucker offered a harsh proposal that paralleled Jefferson's ideas about the fate of free black people in America. By spreading abolition over half a century, blacks could acquire skills and behavioral traits that would make them more acceptable to whites. Even so, he suspected that many white Virginians would balk at even a semblance of equal rights for freed slaves, so they were to be excluded from most civil rights, including suffrage and the right to hold office, own land, keep arms, marry a white person, or serve as witness or juror in cases involving whites. Given legal freedom but kept in social bondage, freed slaves, he predicted, would migrate voluntarily to uninhabited western lands or to the Spanish territories in Florida and Louisiana, where under autocratic governments they might find what the liberty-loving Americans would not provide.

Tucker's plan was highly conservative by Northern standards. Though New York and New Jersey—the largest slave states above the Mason-Dixon Line—were still debating the end of slavery, none of the explicit plans afoot proposed to expel free blacks. Other Northern states from Pennsylvania to Massachusetts had already legislated the gradual emancipation of slaves with no provisos for colonization. And Tucker's scheme was filled with unusually punitive clauses designed to make Virginia unwelcome to freed blacks.

Tucker's abolition plan rolled off the press of Philadelphia's immigrant printer Mathew Carey in September 1796 under the eyes of the national government. From Williamsburg, Tucker dispatched copies to Jefferson, Madison, and Monroe, reminding Jefferson that he had inscribed the pamphlet to Virginia's legislature and relating that some delegates believed his abolition plan might do considerable good.

In his reply Jefferson endorsed Tucker's doctrines of universal liberty and agreed about the danger of the black rebellion in Saint Domingue precipitating further rebellions within the United States. Subscribing to Tucker's belief that freed slaves must somehow be induced, if not forced, to relocate elsewhere, he penned memorable words that have often found their way into history books: "The sooner we put some plan under way, the greater hope there is that it may be permitted to proceed peaceably to its ultimate effect. But if something is not done, and soon done, we shall be the murderers of our own children. . . . The revolutionary storm now sweeping the globe will be upon us, and happy if we make timely provision to give it an easy passage over our land. . . . Every day's delay lessens the time we may take for emancipation."[21]

While Jefferson pondered Tucker's plan, the unexpected death of Tucker's stepson, Richard Randolph, produced a stunning bequest that must have given Jefferson pause. Only in his mid-twenties, Randolph had died while his stepfather was completing his "Dissertation on Slavery." His will provided for the emancipation of all the slaves he had unhappily inherited from his father, John Randolph, who was Jefferson's cousin. Mentored by George Wythe and deeply influenced by his stepfather, Richard Randolph had penned his will the year before, at age twenty-five. Filled with castigations of slaveowners who "exercised the most lawless and monstrous tyranny" over African people "in contradiction to their own declaration of rights," it begged for his slaves' "forgiveness" for his participation in the "infamous practice of usurping the rights of our fellow creatures, equally entitled with ourselves to the enjoyment of liberty and happiness." To ensure that the emancipated slaves had a chance to enjoy their freedom, Randolph provided four hundred acres of land to hold as their own. Randolph's widow, Judith, strived to follow her husband's wishes but was stymied by debt. Some slaves were sold to satisfy creditors, and others were mortgaged for years. While only five slaves gained freedom, the example set by his cousin could not have been lost on the Master of Monticello.[22]

It was with Tucker's abolition plan and Randolph's astounding will fresh in mind that Jefferson reached Philadelphia on about December 12, 1797. Shortly after his arrival, Jefferson met with Kościuszko, who was eager to renew his friendship with the nation's vice president. And Jefferson had plenty of time to see the Pole, since President Adams assigned very few duties to his second in command. Jefferson complained to his daughter several weeks after arriving about "passing my time so uselessly when it could have been so importantly employed at home." Two months later he described "the dreary scene where envy, hatred, malice, revenge, and all the worse passions of men are marshaled to make one another as miserable as possible."[23]

Virtually an outcast in the Adams administration, Jefferson took comfort in the warmth of a growing friendship with Kościuszko. The two men were nearly the same age, but they made an unlikely pair: Kościuszko was a man of action and Jefferson a man of thought. Yet they developed a curiously close relationship. What attracted Kościuszko and Jefferson to each other?[24] On the face of it, the cerebral Jefferson, with his flowing pen and wide-ranging mind given to majestic abstractions, was an unlikely match for the down-to-earth and linguistically clumsy Kościuszko, who tended to focus on matters practical and immediate. Perhaps the key to the deep-running emotions that ran between them was their shared ideas about human improvement and a belief that individual virtue in the nation's service was indispensable in any republic. Abhorring the increasingly bitter factional politics of the late 1790s, Jefferson seems

Kościuszko's romantic picture of his bosom friend Jefferson, completed during their intense, soul-searching talks in Philadelphia, was derided by Jefferson's family. The image features Kościuszko's favored method of uptilted nose. President Franklin D. Roosevelt hung the portrait on the wall of the Oval Office while he devised plans for the Jefferson Memorial from 1934 until its dedication on April 13, 1943, the bicentennial of Jefferson's birth. Kościuszko's watercolor painting of Jefferson, Yale University Art Gallery.

to have found in Kościuszko a selflessness and strength of character that were in short supply in the new nation. In Jefferson, Kościuszko found the embodiment of reason and enlightened thinking.

As their relationship ripened, Kościuszko bestowed gifts upon the vice president: a Swedish coin that Jefferson later donated to the Philosophical Society and an amusing profile that the Pole drew of Jefferson with a tilted head and upturned nose. Jefferson also accepted two other gifts from Kościuszko—a fur collar he long prized and a bearskin coat given to the Pole by Czar Paul.[25]

Only scraps of evidence survive to tell us what Kościuszko and Jefferson discussed in their many hours together. But who can doubt that they would have explored issues and concerns dear to both of them? Among these were Franco-American relations and the possibility of international support for a restoration of the Polish nation,

Jefferson wore this fur collar, a 1798 gift from Kościuszko, for many years and chose it for this classic portrait, symbolically indicating his emotional ties with "the purest son of liberty." Rembrandt Peale, portrait of Jefferson wearing a fur collar, 1805. From Presidential File, Prints and Photographs, Library of Congress.

of supreme importance to Kościuszko. Both knew, however, that Napoleon's rise in France and the truce he signed in 1797 with Austria struck a heavy blow against Kościuszko's hopes that the French government might assist as midwife to a reborn Poland. And in light of what was about to transpire between them, it is almost certain that Jefferson and Kościuszko also discussed the burning issue of this age of democratic revolutions: the promise of liberty for all and the need to end the scourge of slavery that continued to besmirch the young nation. This is all the more likely because by the time Kościuszko and Jefferson had reached Philadelphia, St. George Tucker's "Dissertation on Slavery" had animated public discourse. "All our men of mind rejoice in its appearance," Tucker heard from Mathew Carey, "as a strong proof of the advancement of a great and fundamental truth, in spite of the opposition from inveterate prejudice, and interest still stronger than prejudice."[26]

What Kościuszko expressed to Jefferson, as their friendship ripened, can be inferred from the words the *Paris Moniteur* put in the Pole's mouth just before he reached Philadelphia. In an appreciation of "General Kosciusko" that was soon reprinted in American newspapers, a Paris journalist remarked that "Kosciusko speaks but little, like all men who feel and think much." But on the forge of the American, French, and Polish revolutions in which he had figured so importantly, he had hammered out his polestar principle: "to begin first by making men of slaves, and to form afterwards citizens of men." Such "fruits of long and profound meditation" were "not a wild torrent of systems of innovation, but they constitute a system of reform, planned with wisdom and measured with prudent gradations." Here, then, was the ideological core of what Kościuszko brought to America upon his return. "If Kosciusko be a leveller," wrote the *Moniteur*, "(which, by the bye, every revolutionist who exerts himself for the benefit of humanity ought to be) he is a leveller that levels with the rule and the compass; he wishes to level, as it were, in order to raise all to the same height, but not to trample every thing under foot; he wishes to level rights, but not fortunes; he knows that a fortune, obtained by lawful means, is the just right of its possessor, and that the rest have no claim to it; he wishes to level men, but he deems it impossible to level knowledge and talents."[27]

These thoughts jibed so neatly with those of Jefferson that it is no wonder that they spent so many evenings together in Philadelphia. As Jefferson informed Horatio Gates, one of Kościuszko's most valued revolutionary compatriots, he saw the Pole often "with great pleasure mixed with commiseration" (a reference to Kościuszko's broken body and perhaps to the broken body of Poland). Kościuszko, he declared, was "as pure a son of liberty as I have ever known, and of that liberty which is to go to all, and not to the few or the rich alone."[28]

How does one explain this exalted encomium? As an internationally famous Enlightenment saloniste and founding father, Jefferson might have reserved such compliments for Washington, Madison, Thomas Paine, Adams. Or, if he had in mind the fate of

millions of enslaved Africans in the Americas, he might have bestowed the laurel on brave souls such as Abbé Raynal, Condorcet,
Comte de Volney, Thomas Clarkson, William Wilberforce, Anthony
Benezet, George Wythe, St. George Tucker, or even Benjamin Banneker of Maryland or Richard Allen of Philadelphia—all of whom
were storming the ramparts of the international slave trade and the
execrable institution of slavery. But in his private letter to the aging
Gates, Jefferson had no reason to gild the lily. Surely it was a heartfelt compliment revealing that Kościuszko had touched him in a special way. When he referred to Kościuszko's insistence on "liberty for
all," was Jefferson thinking about not only European serfs but some
six hundred thousand slaves in the United States and countless others in the Americas? Nothing in Jefferson's letters to many correspondents in this period yields another word about this unabashed
affection and admiration for Kościuszko. But clearly their friendship
transcended mere emotion; as Jefferson's letter indicated, it was a
meeting of minds as well. How this special bond had developed
would soon become apparent.

Their friendship was facilitated by their outsider status in the
Adams administration. While Jefferson and Kościuszko saw each
other frequently—neither found much comfort in consorting with
Federalist administration figures whose anti-French animus was
growing more virulent—the Pole kept abreast of political developments in Europe. Members of the Polish émigré community in Paris
and even the French government sent invitations to Kościuszko, urging him to return to Paris, now the center of Polish hopes for revival. J. H. Dombroski, one of the heroes of the Kościuszko-led
rebellion of 1794, had organized a Polish Legion and recruited six
thousand refugees living in France, Venice, and the Ottoman Empire
to carry war and revolution to Eastern Europe in order to evict the
Russians. Kościuszko knew that the tiny army could not traverse
half of Europe unmolested and that whoever survived such a trek
would have little chance facing the vast Russian army. While he con-

templated these utopian schemes, Kościuszko also considered retirement to a farmer's life in New York or in Virginia, where Jefferson promised to help pave the way.

Meanwhile, Kościuszko also pursued one of his objectives in returning to America: procuring the back pay and land warrants that were still owed him. Congress at last voted to make good Kościuszko's back pay with interest for a total of $18,912, a large sum at the time. Additionally, they awarded him a land warrant for five hundred acres in Ohio.[29]

That much accomplished, Kościuszko turned back to the tangled problem of restoring the shattered Polish nation. His hopes depended on French help in rescuing the Polish people from the jaws of their predatory neighbors. Here he ran afoul of American politics: Federalists were determined to stop any private dealings with the French revolutionary government, particularly by an émigré such as him, and indeed were demanding a complete break with revolutionary France. Hoping for friendly Franco-American relations to enable him to lobby for his agenda to revive Poland, Kościuszko had to have been dismayed by the rise of anti-French feeling in the United States that had led to the brink of war. After attempts at neutrality had failed, the Adams administration had aligned themselves with the English, suspended diplomatic relations with France, and prepared for war with the French.

In early 1798, Kościuszko's American mission suffered another blow, this time irreparable, when Congress began debates that would result in passage of the notorious Alien and Sedition Acts. Upon enactment, the laws would allow the president to expel without a hearing any alien he deemed "dangerous to the peace and safety of the United States." Noncitizens who failed to leave faced imprisonment for up to three years and would be barred permanently from gaining American citizenship. For visitors such as Kościuszko, who were immersed in the uncertain waters of international diplomacy, debate on such laws potentially meant a return to prison. Knowing that

Kościuszko might be considered a Jacobin and an enemy of the United States, Jefferson urged his friend to go to France to help heal the breach with America. Hoping that such negotiations might also benefit Poland, Kościuszko quickly agreed to go.[30]

Huddling frequently with Kościuszko and talking late into the night, Jefferson arranged the Pole's departure. To ensure secrecy, Jefferson secured a passport for the Pole under the name of "Thomas Kanberg, a native of the north of Europe, (perhaps of Germany)." In issuing the passport, Jefferson claimed he had known Kanberg for over a decade and stated that Kanberg was innocent of any political intentions and simply a man traveling first to Lisbon strictly for personal reasons. Kościuszko and Jefferson exchanged frequent notes about the wording of the passport and about the planned mission.[31]

Kościuszko now had to deal with his suddenly large financial assets awarded by Congress. Securing cash from his pension money to pay for his passage, he then drew on his approved back pay for drafts from Amsterdam banks for use in Europe. On Jefferson's advice, he retained John Barnes, the vice president's Philadelphia-based private banker, to invest his remaining American assets. Jefferson wrote up the agreement, and Virginia's Congressman, John Dawson, signed it as a witness.

As Kościuszko prepared to undertake his dangerous return across an ocean patrolled by hostile English and French navies, armed only with his reputation and Jefferson's good wishes, an important matter remained—how to provide for the disposal of his assets in America in the event of his death. His decisions were quick and firm. First, he gave Jefferson power of attorney in a carefully drawn document written entirely in Jefferson's hand. Then he proceeded to the will. "Whenever you will have a time in the daytime for a quarter of hour," he scribbled to Jefferson, "I beg you would grant me to finish what I have begone [begun]." Aware that Kościuszko was composing his will, Jefferson obliged.[32]

Working together, the two men created a document that could have potentially shaken American society if both sides had lived up to their assumed roles. No description survives of how they arrived at the terms of the will, for neither ever commented on it in correspondence with friends or with each other. But the will has survived in original form. Kościuszko wrote the initial draft in his splintered English and then rewrote it, apparently with Jefferson's help. In Philadelphia, John Barnes and John Dawson witnessed the document on April 20, 1798. Kościuszko's first version deserves full quotation.

> I beg Mr. Jefferson that in the case I should die without will or testament he should bye out of my money So many Negroes and free them, that the restante [remaining] sums should be Sufficient to give them aducation and provide for ther maintenance, that is to say each should know before, the duty of a Cytyzen in the free Government, that he must defend his country against foreign as well as internal Enemies who would wish to change the Constitution for the worst to inslave them by degree afterwards, to have good and human heart Sensible for the Sufferings of others, each must be married and have 100 Ackres of land, wyth instruments, Cattle for tillage and know how to manage and Gouvern it well as well to know [how to] behave to neyboughs [neighbors], always wyth Kindnes and ready to help them to them selves, frugal to ther Children give good aducation. I mean as to the heart and the duty to ther Country, in gratitude to me to make themselves happy as possible. T. Kościuszko.[33]

In this unconventional but emotional will, Kościuszko expressed the convictions and commitments that made him such an admirable man for black Americans such as Agrippa Hull and Negro John. Drawing on his long-standing belief that the downtrodden could prosper—peasants as well as slaves—if given their freedom under favorable conditions, he wished to ensure that Jefferson would not throw liberated slaves into the hurly-burly of life to compete without skills in the ruthless marketplace of capitalism. His assets gained in the service of promoting universal liberty were to be used wisely so that those receiving freedom would have the means to succeed: an education, land, livestock, farming equipment, and traits to carry them and their children through life—frugality, kindness toward neighbors, and willingness to defend their country "against foreign as well as internal enemies" who would gladly refasten their chains. Such requirements fit the European antislavery strategies of Condorcet and Lafayette that Kościuszko had applied to his own life and to his hopes for Poland.

Three days later, Jefferson helped Kościuszko create a second and final draft of the will. Spelling and syntax were improved. But more importantly, Kościuszko introduced a change of immense significance. Rather than the vague reference in the original version to use his legacy to free "so many Negroes," he now specified that "I do hereby declare and direct that should I make no other testamentary disposition of my property in the United States. I hereby authorise my friend Thomas Jefferson to employ the whole thereof in purchasing Negroes from among his own or any others."[34] In a stroke, Jefferson's slaves had become the favored beneficiary of Kościuszko's benevolence.

Kościuszko surely made this crucial change with Jefferson's consent, for otherwise Jefferson would not have pledged his fidelity to his friend's wishes in the many years ahead. Mentioned only in passing by Jefferson scholars, participation in the writing of the will was in fact Jefferson's most dramatic step toward implementing his emancipationist impulse at Monticello. Knowing of Kościuszko's uncertain health, Jefferson had pledged to the truest son of liberty he had ever met that he was willing, if not eager, to free many of his slaves toiling on his beloved hilltop plantation in Albemarle County.[35] By this voluntary pact with Kościuszko and by his agreement to serve as the executor of an estate in which the beneficiaries were to be slaves who would be educated and remain in the United States, Jefferson had made a momentous personal decision.

Part of that decision may well be explained by Jefferson's private life at this time. Long before, while still in Paris, he had agreed to free the children born of his relationship with Sally Hemings. Kościuszko's will offered an opportunity in the future to free his daughter Harriet, now not quite three, and the newborn Beverley, a son born just ten days before Jefferson witnessed Kościuszko's signing of the will. Perhaps he was also thinking of the words of his friend St. George Tucker that he had read just a few months before: "Will not our posterity curse the days of their nativity with all the anguish of Job? Will not they execrate the memory of their ancestors, who, having it in their power to avert evil, have, like their first parents, entailed a curse upon all future generations?" We can never know. But clearly Jefferson was freely participating in an honor-bound pact with a close friend. Kościuszko had always made plain that he disagreed with the Virginian's feelings about black incapacity and that he was passionately committed to seeing slaves unshackled, educated, and put on the road to full citizens' rights. So determined was the Pole that he put in escrow the largest sum of money he would ever obtain, negotiable assets that he had earned during the American Revolution.

It is striking that Kościuszko believed that leaving his sizable estate to Jefferson was the best use of his fortune. The departing Pole could easily have transferred his assets to Europe to use for any political purpose or personal need. But his short sojourn in the mid-Atlantic states, and his reunions with old revolutionary friends, Agrippa Hull included, had ultimately inspired him to give Jefferson the opportunity to lead the nation in freeing some of his own slaves. It is even possible that Jefferson told Kościuszko about Richard Randolph's will. Whatever the case, Kościuszko's will stands as a singular act of antislavery sentiment and one that he undoubtedly believed might serve as a precedent for others to follow. Writing a will that he hoped would help end slavery in America was Kościuszko's last act on American soil. It must have pleased him that Jefferson had taken a step consistent with one of the least quoted passages of Notes on the State of Virginia—that "the spirit of the [slave] master is abating, that of the slave rising from the dust, his condition mollifying, the way I hope repairing, under the auspices of heaven, for a total emancipation."

Placing a high value on friendship, Jefferson endorsed Kościuszko's scheme wholeheartedly. For Jefferson, a promise at any time was a serious matter, but given freely under these conditions, it was to be held sacred. Promises were not civil law, but they represented a higher code of personal honor. In honor-bound Southern society, trust was axiomatic. Even to question another person's honor publicly was to invite a challenge to a duel.[36] Very likely Kościuszko's passionate belief in human liberty pushed Jefferson to agree to a plan whereby in the future he would quit the very slave system that he professed to hate. All the better, Kościuszko's will did not demand immediate action and left Jefferson an escape clause with its proviso that he could "purchase Negroes from among his own or any others and giving them liberty in my name." The choice would be his, whenever Kościuszko died.

To seal the bond as the moment of his departure neared, Kościuszko gave Jefferson more presents: a valuable sable fur that the Pole had received from Czar Paul I and Benjamin West's watercolor The Fright of Astyanax. Showing his continuing warmth for his Polish friend, for many years Jefferson wrapped the fur around his collar, and it has come down to us through the well-known portraits of him by Rembrandt Peale and Thomas Sully. Likewise, he hung the West watercolor in his parlor at Monticello.[37]

On the evening of May 4, 1798, Niemcewicz was dumbfounded to learn that Kościuszko was leaving that night for France. Pressed by the astonished Niemcewicz, Kościuszko revealed nothing of his plans. Niemcewicz begged to go with him, but Kościuszko told him it would be impossible. Largely recovered from his disabilities, Kościuszko departed before dawn in a carriage, accompanied by Jefferson, on the road south from Philadelphia. Later, Niemcewicz learned that the carriage had gone to New Castle, Delaware, where a ship awaited.[38] For the second and last time, the Polish revolutionary had sailed east from American shores.

While Jefferson guarded the secrecy of Kościuszko's whereabouts, Niemcewicz journeyed south in a bitter mood. He reached Georgetown on May 21, 1798, where he met Washington at the retired president's granddaughter's house. As Niemcewicz feared, Washington—who knew nothing of the Pole's hasty departure from America—immediately asked after Kościuszko. "My embarrassment and confusion were extreme," Niemcewicz recorded in his journal. "The first word that I said to this great man was a lie" in order to hide this "needlessly mysterious flight." Nor did Niemcewicz reveal that his friend was on his way across the Atlantic when he visited Washington at Mount Vernon. News of Kościuszko's secretive departure was only made public in September, when copies of the *Moniteur* reached America with word of the Pole's arrival in Paris on June 28.[39]

By this time, Jefferson had returned to Monticello. From there, he kept in touch with Kościuszko by letter, reporting on the Pole's financial investments and the auction of most of Kościuszko's household goods left in Philadelphia. Later, Jefferson reported that he had received the patent for Kościuszko's tract of five hundred acres surveyed along the Scioto River in what is today the city of Columbus, Ohio's capital.[40]

Nearly four weeks after returning to Monticello, in May 1798, Jefferson sent Kościuszko a moving letter, carried to France by the Comte de Volney. In it Jefferson expressed his "effusion of friendship" and "my warmest towards you, which no time will alter." With Kościuszko's remarkable will still fresh in mind, Jefferson assured him that "your principles and dispositions were made to be honored, revered, and loved, true to a single object, the freedom and happiness of man."[41]

If Jefferson meant to revere Kościuszko's "principles and dispositions," he must have been challenged when a letter arrived three
weeks after Jefferson sent his "effusions of friendship." The letter
came from William Short, a figure of special importance to him.
Born into the Virginia aristocracy and a family friend of Jefferson's,
Short was James Monroe's classmate at William and Mary, where
he imbibed abolitionist ideas. Jefferson had taken William Short to
Paris as his secretary in 1784, and there he had bonded so firmly
with him that he soon called Short "his adoptive son."

When Jefferson returned to the United States in 1789, he left
Short in Paris as chargé d'affaires. By this time Short had begun an
affair with the wife of the aristocratic reformer Duc de la Rochefoucauld-Liancourt. Short's relationship with the Rochefoucaulds was
not only romantic. Unlike Jefferson, Short had joined Rochefou-
cauld, Lafayette, and other Enlightenment figures in the French abolitionist society, the Société des Amis des Noirs. Short's immersion in
this circle was very much in keeping with the abolitionist politics he
had developed in Virginia. Indeed, he had given up his slaves prior
to leaving Virginia with Jefferson.[42]

Short's abolitionist fervor in Paris was stoked by accounts of European travelers who had explored West Africa and were amazed to
find there "a city larger than London." For Short, such reports indicated the existence of an advanced civilization. Understanding this
to prove false the charges that black Americans were innately inferior, the drumbeat claim used to defend slavery, Short foresaw "the
restoration of the rights of citizenship of those blacks who inhabit
the U.S." This, he supposed, would lead toward racial blending, because whites and blacks would rest on a more equal footing.

With this lead-in, Short took aim at Jefferson's dark broodings in
Notes on Virginia. Would the mixing of people of different colors be
such a great evil, he asked? If so, he reasoned, it is "certainly less [an
evil] than keeping 700,000 people and their descendants in perpetual
slavery" and better than "having that number of free people living in

the same country and separated from the rest of the community by a marked and impassable line." Warming to his message, he proposed that racial intermixture would produce people of "the middle ground between their present color and the black." Short argued that this would populate the land with those who would be not as dark as some inhabitants of Spain. Short had lived there for several years and learned that color had nothing to do with intelligence or a life of honest labor.

This much staked out, Short challenged Jefferson to enter the public discussion about how to end American slavery. Echoing Jefferson's own pronouncement in his *Notes* that history would execrate statesmen who permitted "one-half the citizens . . . to trample on the rights of the other [half]," Short called on his mentor to step forth as a "statesman, the philosopher, [and] philanthrope" to help end slavery. Sounding very much as if he had read Tucker's "Dissertation on Slavery," and referring ominously to the slave rebellion in Saint Domingue, Short reasoned that emancipation would have to proceed by stages as slaveowners began to build a different labor system while preparing their slaves for life as free people. Short all but begged Jefferson to take the lead. "Let the enlightened and virtuous citizens, who toil for public instruction," he implored, "turn the public mind towards this subject and endeavour to demonstrate that the owners of slaves would gain in point of interest by the change."

Moving from general principles to practical solutions, Short showed in detail how slaveholders could profit by freeing their slaves and leasing land to them. As an alternative, he proposed the Spanish system of *coartación*, whereby the slaveowner had been for many years obliged by law to give slaves one day in the week to work for wages and to allow the slave the right of self-purchase at any time, once he or she had accumulated the purchase price.[43]

Jefferson chose not to respond to his protégé's impassioned plea for action and inspired leadership on the thorny issue of abolishing slavery. He simply ignored the topic of slavery and responded instead only to Short's discussions of domestic politics and his plans to return to America. From that point on, both men avoided the topic. In a series of letters they exchanged in 1798, Jefferson graciously offered to help Short purchase a large estate near Monticello, where Short hoped to return with his beloved Rosalie, whom he described as "the future partner of my life." Short intended to establish an estate where income came from land leased to white farmers or free people of color. Jefferson supported Short in this plan but clammed up on Short's appeal to step forward on abolishing slavery.[44]

How does one explain the jarring disjuncture between Jefferson's pact with Kościuszko and his silence when confronted just weeks later by his "adoptive son" in a letter calling for his mentor to become an abolitionist leader? To be sure, Jefferson's private agreement with Kościuszko was answerable at some unknown point in the future, while Short's plea was for immediate action. Another theory is that Jefferson had already begun to make political calculations about whether more than a few allies would support him. And besides, he was embroiled in attempts to block the Alien and Sedition Acts passed on July 14, 1798, which he passionately regarded as an offense to the principles of the American Revolution. Still not regarding African Americans as fellow citizens, even those released from slavery, Jefferson seemingly chose silence on Short's plea for stalwart antislavery leadership rather than answer his protégé's call for action.

Back in Paris, hoping somehow to rescue Poland from its dismembered plight, Kościuszko found a city that had been wracked with famines and frigid winters the two previous years. Immediately, he encountered difficulty in his dealings with the French Directory. Kościuszko had some success in smoothing relations between France and the United States, but this did nothing to address the Polish situation. The Directory could be infuriatingly inconsistent in its relations with Austria, which occupied much of former Poland, and with Italy, where Poles had formed an underground army in hopes of a campaign to reclaim their country. In fact, the Directory had diverted the grand plans of General John Henry Dombroski to revitalize Poland by sending his Polish Legion to Italy to serve under the new military state imposed by Napoleon Bonaparte. After Napoleon's smashing victory there, many Poles believed he would then turn his attention to liberating Poland by going into the Crimea, in the words of a Prussian diplomat, "to support Poland and revolutionize Europe by stealing in the back door." Instead, Napoleon led his army to Egypt.[45]

Hampering Kościuszko's efforts in France on behalf of the Poles were his jagged relations with Napoleon. The soon-to-be emperor understood Kościuszko's immense symbolic importance among Poles, and shortly after returning from Egypt in 1799, he visited the Polish hero, hoping to gain his endorsement in his plans to dismantle the Russian Empire. Knowing that Russia, Prussia, and Austria had been distracted by their engulfing of Poland and could not afford to go to war against revolutionary France while leaving their rear flank vulnerable, Napoleon wanted to keep alive the dreams of the Polish émigrés while using their military services for his other campaigns. Kościuszko's endorsement would bolster Napoleon's grandiose ambitions.

But the personalities and goals of the two men clashed. Kościuszko, with his simple republican sensibilities and devotion to his nation, recoiled from the highly ambitious military genius. In the next few crowded years, major events soured their relations. In November 1799 Napoleon overthrew the Directory in a coup d'état, and Kościuszko hastily condemned him. He was again outraged when Napoleon struck a treaty in 1801 with Czar Paul to end French-Russian hostilities without any reference to the Polish state. Napoleon particularly offended Kościuszko when he sent the Polish Legions to Saint Domingue to suppress Toussaint Louverture's rebellion there, a venture that failed miserably and decimated the Polish soldiers.[46] Disgusted with Napoleon, Kościuszko lashed out at a public reception in 1801. When a French official asked the Polish hero, "Did you know, General, that the First Consul [Napoleon] spoke of you?" Kościuszko replied coldly, "I never speak of him."[47]

Despite his antipathy for Napoleon, Kościuszko persevered in his quest for a restoration of the Polish nation. In 1800, while Jefferson celebrated his election to the American presidency, Kościuszko wrote a pamphlet anonymously calling for Polish liberation. Arguing that a nation must have faith in its own strength to succeed, he counseled against depending on foreign aid. Rather, the Poles should copy the American revolutionaries by forming a Polish Congress akin to the American Continental Congress and issuing paper money to finance a fight for independence. Kościuszko's pamphlet also repeated his earlier calls for the emancipation of the serfs.[48]

Though Kościuszko's pamphlet was a plaintive appeal to Polish pride—more of a desperate call for a popular uprising than a realistic plan for action—the French government quickly suppressed the pamphlet before it could be published and promptly clapped Kościuszko under police surveillance. Now discouraged, he wrote Jefferson of plans to return to America. Though Jefferson effusively encouraged him to come back, Kościuszko, ever hopeful that some new plan to resuscitate the Polish nation might arise, decided to remain in France. Dogged by the French authorities, he moved in 1801 to the estate of Peter Joseph Zeltner, the Swiss minister to France, near Fontainebleau. Here he stayed for the next fourteen years. Despite his luxurious surroundings, Kościuszko lived simply, much as he had in his previous residences. A man without a country, he kept up a sporadic correspondence with Jefferson, most of it concerning his invested assets in the United States.

But Jefferson could spare little time to correspond with the man he had come to cherish because in 1800 he was elected president. His new role forced him to confront a multitude of daunting issues. Among these were the festering division within the country over the status of black Americans, hemispheric power diplomacy, Jefferson's personal involvement in slavery, and attacks on his ruminations about innate black inferiority. Ringing in his ears were charges leveled during the election campaign that the Master of Monticello, as John Linn, a minister in New York City, put it, had "degraded the blacks from the rank which God hath given them in the scale of being!" and had "advanced the strongest argument for their state of slavery!" Coming from a cleric in the conservative Dutch Reformed Church, such a charge placed Jefferson on the side of an emerging defense of slavery.[49]

Jefferson came into office just months after a powerful slave conspiracy in Virginia had reminded Americans of the dangers of keeping people enslaved. While Jefferson was running for the presidency, an enslaved young man who would come to be known as General Gabriel made final preparations for a frontal assault on slavery not far from Monticello. Gabriel's birth occurred just as Jefferson was composing the Declaration of Independence, and he owed his name to a midwife's prediction that he would become a bold man. Heeding this forecast, his enslaved mother and father named him Gabriel after the divine messenger who appeared to Old Testament prophets and later to the Virgin Mary.

Trained as a blacksmith, tall and muscular, Gabriel was hired out by his slave master, Thomas Prosser, to numerous employers in Richmond, Virginia, who were long on orders and short on labor. Gabriel spent many evenings in the 1790s in local taverns, where he learned about the Haitian slave revolt that began in 1791. Learning to read and write, he closely followed the black insurrection and rejoiced that, step by step, slaves were casting off their chains and rising up to dismantle the French Caribbean slave system. Learning of state decisions in the North to end slavery, he became determined that the same should happen in Virginia.

Over the sweltering summer of 1800, Gabriel prepared to pierce the heart of American slavery. Working furtively, he gathered bold men ready to lay down their lives to duplicate the success of French slaves in Haiti. Stealthily approaching as many slaves as they dared, his trusted lieutenants asked slaves and free blacks "whether they would fight the white people for their freedom." The odds against overwhelming Virginia's slave regime were huge, yet many, like a slave named Jacob, answered, "I will fight for my freedom as long as I have breath, and that is as much as any man can do." Another said simply, "I will kill or be killed." Gabriel's brother, an unofficial preacher to slaves, quickened the spirits of hesitant slaves by vowing, "I can no longer bear what I have borne."[50]

Gabriel's army of several hundred gathered after midnight on August 30, 1800. With the twenty-four-year-old leading the way, their plan was to march on Virginia's capital, capture Governor James Monroe, and hold him hostage until Virginia granted freedom to slaves and made an equitable distribution of property to self-emancipated slaves and poor whites. Gabriel targeted some whites, including his master, for execution. By counting on poor whites to join the insurrection, he hoped to avoid the prolonged and bloody conflict that had enveloped Saint Domingue for a decade.

No slave rebellion had been more carefully strategized in North America over nearly two centuries of African enslavement. Gabriel planned for one column of his freedom fighters to torch the combustible wooden warehouses in a section of Richmond, while a second column would storm the state arsenal to seize weapons. A third column would simultaneously burst into the executive mansion to take Governor Monroe hostage. But the plan unraveled when a violent nocturnal storm washed out the bridges over which Gabriel's men had planned to enter Virginia's capital. Even if nature had not conspired against the black rebels, they had been betrayed by several slaves who leaked word of the plot to white authorities. Even before a blow was struck, the insurrection fizzled out.

Shaken to their boots at the audacity of the plot, Virginia authorities hanged twenty-six of the conspirators, including Gabriel, and transported dozens to the West Indies and French Louisiana. Widespread fear of a Haiti-like outbreak soon enveloped the South. "The question now is a plain one," said one Virginian. "Shall we abolish slavery, or shall we continue it? There is no middle course to steer." Another warned that "a celestial spark" of freedom was buried in every slave and that "there have never been slaves in any country, who have not seized the first favorable opportunity to revolt."[51]

Gabriel's Rebellion, spurred by the Haitian slave insurgency, created international repercussions that Jefferson immediately faced after assuming office on March 4, 1801. While urging his friend Governor James Monroe to halt the executions, Jefferson had to make hard decisions about the nation's policy toward revolutionary Haiti. His predecessor in the White House had reopened the profitable commercial relations with Haiti's black insurgent leaders and had established consular relations there. President Adams had even given limited naval support to Toussaint Louverture, Haiti's black leader, after the British occupied the island in an effort to reinstitute slavery, motivated by fear that an independent black Haiti would bring down their slave-based Caribbean colonial system. When Adams turned over the presidency to Jefferson, the situation in Haiti was still very fluid. Louverture was not yet fully in control of the island, and black independence had not yet been declared. Nor had Napoleon, France's new dictatorial ruler, revealed his intentions— whether to continue the long struggle to snuff out the black rebellion or withdraw his decimated army from the island.[52]

As vice president, Jefferson's primary concern had been the effect the Haitian revolution might have on Southern slaves. For this reason he had opposed commercial relations with the island, knowing that along with trade goods would come black seafaring men acting as "missionaries of sedition." Jefferson wondered the same thing that most white Southerners did: if the Haitian revolutionary fervor wasn't quarantined, would the South be able to dodge another black onslaught?

Jefferson's thoughts on America's Haitian policy gained focus when the president became enraptured by the possibility of obtaining the Louisiana Territory. Spain had retroceded the territory to France in the secret Treaty of San Ildefonso, which Jefferson got wind of in May 1801. At first, distancing the United States from support of Louverture, Jefferson endorsed Napoleon's plans to send a large expedition of fifty thousand men to reconquer Haiti and crush Louverture. The plan would include British support after the French and British signed a preliminary peace treaty in October 1801. Napoleon's invasion was intended to salvage the French colonial empire in America, where Louisiana was the breadbasket providing foodstuffs to the sugar- and coffee-growing French West Indies colonies. Also, the American slave republic would gain insulation from the dreaded black revolutionary infection that continued to arrive from insurrectionist Haiti.

Jefferson's about-face occurred in 1802, after Napoleon's massive French expedition to suppress the black revolution and reinstall the slave regime convinced him that Haitian rebels, if they secured their independence, would threaten the slaveholding South less under Louverture's leadership than would reenslaved Haitians held under France's thumb. It pained Jefferson to turn against the country he had regarded as America's partner in extending the "empire of liberty" throughout the world and to embrace England and Louverture. But his hope of containing black rebellion, as well as the opportunity to vastly extend the nation's territory, was irresistible to Jefferson. Like the British, he concluded that an independent black republic in the Caribbean was less dangerous than a resuscitated French colonial empire in the Americas, particularly if that revival included New Orleans and the Louisiana Territory.

Jefferson was all the more convinced of this policy shift when French intentions to reenslave Haiti's huge black population united the internally divided island blacks. They fought with "incredible fanaticism, they laugh at death, it is the same with the women," reported General Leclerc, who led the French expeditionary army. The French army could not muster the kind of fervor that inspired those fighting to cast off slavery's chains. Weakened by yellow fever and a paucity of supplies, the French army bogged down and soon gave up on repressing the Haitian rebels. France's ardor for an empire in the Americas was a concomitant casualty.[53]

The defeat of the shattered French army convinced Jefferson that the black Haitians could never be reenslaved. And he understood that French abandonment of Haiti undercut its need of the Louisiana Territory as a colony supplying grain, wood, and draft animals. The unquenchable thirst for freedom of Haiti's half million blacks had, in effect, handed the Louisiana Territory to Jefferson on a platter. Along with this fabulous prize would come free navigation of the Mississippi River down to the Gulf of Mexico through New Orleans. Through control of this great artery of commerce, the onrushing, westward-moving yeoman farmers of Jefferson's Arcadia would find ample outlet for their exportable produce. Meanwhile, the United States doubled its territory for less than fourteen cents per acre.

Jefferson's policy toward the victorious black Haitians contained not a grain of gratitude for their decimation of the combined European armies that contributed so vitally to the acquisition of the Louisiana Territory. Nor was Jefferson interested in the aspirations of half a million self-liberated slaves to become black yeoman farmers after their destruction of the death-dealing plantation system. Jefferson refused to recognize the independent black republic and then embargoed trade with independent Haiti in 1806 in order to conciliate Napoleon. In these policies he bowed to proslavery Southern supporters—they were the main base of his political support—who feared that black Haitians had provided a model for black insurrection and self-emancipation. Nor did he speak out against South Carolina's reopening of the slave trade in 1803, which outraged much of the nation.[54]

Such policies reflected Jefferson's inertia on the slavery issue—an indifference verging on tacit support of slavery. If he had chosen to act boldly, certainly he would have been swimming against the current, but he might have effected a momentous step toward accomplishing his antislavery ideal. That Jefferson had bowed to what he regarded as the political realities faced by his administration became clear in 1805, when he explained to William Burwell, his young presidential secretary, "I have long time given up the expectation of any early provision for the extinguishment of slavery among us." If he meant by "long time" more than a year or two, Jefferson had apparently entered the presidency in 1801 with no stomach for spending his political capital on the slavery issue. Yet he still predicted that American slavery would end as it had ended in Haiti—in the spilling of blood, as "the insurrectionary spirit of the slaves" produced "dreadful scenes and sufferings," culminating in a necessity "to release them [the slaves] in their own way."[55]

Not only did Jefferson lose his earlier optimism that his own generation could end slavery in the United States, but his administration became unofficially proslavery, producing a strict slave code to be used by Congress in organizing the new Louisiana Territory. In Congress, Federalist opposition to extending the empire of slavery brought spirited debate after Pennsylvania's Quaker senator, George Logan, presented a petition to forbid slaves' importation into the Louisiana Territory. Shortly afterward, a Connecticut senator offered an amendment to the original law written to govern the territory that would have freed any slave brought into the territory by the end of his twenty-first year (the eighteenth year for females). After heated debate, the Senate rejected the amendment, but it was passed by the House, only to be rejected again by the Senate. When white settlers poured into the Louisiana Territory, they came under an unspoken federal sanction of slavery to which Jefferson consented without a murmur. Now slaves who had enjoyed the right of self-purchase under *coartación* lost that right.

Under Jefferson, Congress battened down the escape hatch from slavery.[56]

Even while Jefferson was shaping his Haitian policy and a position on governing the Louisiana Territory, his tortured relationship with slavery had taken a more personal turn. In 1802 the vituperative newspaper editor James Callender had published a story alleging that the president had engaged in a long-term sexual relationship with Sally Hemings and had fathered her children. Aware that such liaisons were common in the South, Callender added some nasty racist slang about Hemings in subsequent articles. Once the editor initiated his accusations, Jefferson's personal life became political sport. Federalist newspapers gleefully reprinted Callender's sensational accounts about Jefferson's "dusky harem" at Monticello and added essays and poetry embroidering Jefferson's love affair with Hemings. To his supporters' dismay, Jefferson remained silent. For the rest of his first term, gossip about his affair with Hemings was regular fodder for the newspapers. It was one thing to disregard the inflammatory Callender, who had managed to offend just about everyone, but given Jefferson's publicly pronounced aversion to mixed-race love, the story made him look like a hypocrite. Never refuted by Jefferson's supporters, the accusation remained dormant for some time; two centuries later it has become one of the sharpest and most commonly used points of attack on Jefferson's reputation.[57]

While Jefferson wrestled with these momentous issues, Kościuszko could only observe them from afar. Their correspondence during Jefferson's presidency kept their friendship alive, though the flow of letters between them gradually dwindled. At one point, it appeared that they might be reunited in the United States. Jefferson had assured the Pole in 1801 that "it would give me infinite pleasure to have you here a witness to our [country's] recovery and to recognize the people whom you knew during the war." Having heard of Jefferson's election victory over John Adams in the 1800 election, Kościuszko responded with warm congratulations and suggested that "under your helm I shall return to America." That did not happen, but they maintained correspondence during Jefferson's two administrations. Kościuszko's letters were generally more effusive than those of Jefferson, who took special care of what he wrote, as letters written by the president were often disclosed to prying eyes. But Jefferson did keep his friend apprised of changes in investing Kościuszko's American assets and faithfully inquired about Kościuszko's well-being.[58]

As Kościuszko sojourned near Fontainebleau with the Zeltner children, among them Thaddea, a daughter named for him, many dignitaries courted him. In 1806 Napoleon sought Kościuszko's endorsement for a planned invasion of Russia, but the Polish hero was willing to support this action only if Napoleon promised to reconstruct the Polish nation, establish a new government there modeled after England's parliamentary government, and free the Polish serfs with guarantees of title to the lands they worked. More interested in empire than reform, Napoleon curtly declined, and Kościuszko consequently withheld his support for the Russian invasion. Napoleon ridiculed Kościuszko for not accepting the "existing facts" and challenged the Poles to win their own independence.[59]

Ultimately, Jefferson could do no more about his Polish friend's failure to resuscitate Poland than Kościuszko could do to help the third American president ease his way into retirement. But they maintained their fitful correspondence. Busy winding up his presidency in 1809, Jefferson wrote Kościuszko about his longing to retire to Monticello, where "at length I hope I shall find rest and happiness among my family, my friends, my farm and books." A few days later, "like a prisoner released from his chains," Jefferson left the presidency to return home to pursue the "tranquil pursuits of science" in "an Elysium of domestic affections."[60]

Jefferson found respite from the presidency in his beloved Virginia, but he could not find refuge from his speculations about black inferiority. Awaiting him was a book by the French abolitionist and Catholic bishop Abbé Grégoire, a member of the French Enlightenment circle that had been so dear to Jefferson in the late 1780s. Grégoire's *De la Littérature des Negroes*, published in Paris in 1808, offered a refutation of Jefferson's thesis about innate black inferiority. By compiling stories of talented people of African descent, including Phillis Wheatley, Benjamin Banneker, the doctor James Derham, autobiographer and abolitionist Olaudah Equiano, mathematics prodigy Thomas Fuller, and author Ignatius Sancho, Grégoire hoped to bend the minds of people like Jefferson, who believed that people with dark skin were innately inferior.

In spite of Jefferson's prior statements on the subject, Grégoire hoped for a testimonial from Jefferson in advance of a planned English translation and publication of the book in the United States. Were the retired American president to endorse the bishop's book, it would be an acknowledgement that his earlier "suspicions" were unfounded and that the examples of talented blacks described in *De la Littérature des Negroes* demonstrated the equal intellectual endowments of blacks and whites. Jefferson's response to Grégoire indicates how his thoughts had changed since penning *Notes on Virginia*. Replying with what he called a "soft answer," Jefferson protested that his comments in *Notes* were of a personal nature and that he had even hoped for "a complete refutation of the doubts I have myself entertained on the grade of understanding allotted to [African Americans] by nature." In a polite retreat he stated that his comments only referred to blacks in Virginia. Others of African descent, he wrote, had demonstrated qualities that might place them "on an equal footing with the other colours of the human family."

Though he answered Grégoire mildly, Jefferson remained resolutely unimpressed by the bishop's celebration of black intellectual achievements. He derided Grégoire's book, calling it in a private letter a hodgepodge of fantastic tales that puffed the quality of talented blacks. Nonetheless, Grégoire found an American publisher for his book; in 1810, it was published in translation by David Bailie Warden, who had just gained Jefferson's support for a position as consul in Paris. African Americans and white abolitionists quickly seized upon its claims and for decades cited it regularly in speeches and newspaper articles as proof of black people's parity with whites.[61]

Jefferson had more on his mind than Grégoire's book. Marring his happy return in 1809 to Monticello was the unavoidable fact of his chronic indebtedness. By now his financial debt, accumulated through recurrent purchases of additional slaves and expenditures on refurbishing Monticello, was between $10,000 and $12,000. By his own description, he "sank in affliction" and felt a "thralldom of mind never before known" to him. Either he would have to humiliate himself by appealing to his Virginia planter friends for support or he would have to sell off more of his land and slaves.

But then Jefferson's financial advisor, John Barnes, came to the rescue. In February 1810 he proposed that Jefferson pay his creditors by borrowing from Kościuszko's funds. Jefferson was thrilled, likening Barnes's suggestion to "a ray of light beaming on my uneasy mind." Drawing $4,500 from Kościuszko's funds, Jefferson warded off some of his creditors and expressed confidence that his Polish friend "would be delighted with the opportunity of accommodating me."[62] In the longest letter he ever wrote to his Polish friend, Jefferson explained why he needed the money and expressed chagrin about the affair. Remembering well the provisions of Kościuszko's will and "its charitable destination," Jefferson promised that freeing his slaves "would not be at all delayed" if "any accident happen[ed] to you." Kościuszko was pleased to oblige his old friend, approving of "everything you have done with my fund."[63]

Kościuszko's blessing about the loan surely eased Jefferson's mind while giving the Master of Monticello some respite from the creditors hounding him. Yet other anxieties bore in on Jefferson.

The most pressing problem was occasioned by what has been known as the second American war for independence. The United States and England went to war in 1812 after the British navy impressed American sailors and interrupted American seaborne commerce by blockading Europe, all in the context of the Napoleonic Empire Wars (1803–15). President Madison, for his part, had decreed a trade ban with Great Britain. Thus began the War of 1812, both a conflict to end England's imperial arrogance and an American war of national expansion against the British-allied Indian nations—the Creeks in the Southeast and the Shawnee and associated tribes in the Old Northwest.

Further complicating the war, the British repeated their strategy of the revolutionary war by offering freedom to slaves willing to rise up against their masters. British officers were initially under orders not to encourage black rebellion, but they had been authorized to give freedom to any slave who voluntarily fled to enlist in their Black Corps. As in 1775, Maryland's and Virginia's enslaved people were waiting for the call and all the more ready to flock to the British after a slave uprising in eastern Virginia in the spring of 1812.[64]

Through the spring and summer of 1813, a wave of black runaways, looking for freedom, used small boats to reach the British ships. Chesapeake planters appealed to the federal government for help and compensation, while patrolling the beaches to block further escapes. Not only were the planters losing their property when the slaves fled, but they were losing tactical advantage as well. The liberated slaves offered up to the British their intelligence, labor, and piloting skills in the tricky Chesapeake Bay waters, all the while terrifying white planters, who worried about expanding slave revolts.[65]

As the tempo of the war increased in 1814, the British staged an invasion of the Chesapeake Bay with the capture of the nation's capital as their ultimate objective. As part of his strategy, British vice admiral Sir Alexander Cochrane issued a proclamation on April 2 offering sanctuary to all blacks "disposed to migrate from the

United States." Emboldened by the end of the Napoleonic Wars in
Europe and the availability of more ships, the British used former
slaves in a number of actions over the summer designed to bring the
Americans to their knees. Most notably, the Black Corps helped defeat American forces at Bladensburg, Maryland, on August 24,
1814. Hard upon this victory, the British descended on Washington,
sacking and burning the nation's capital. As one British officer reported, large numbers of the District of Columbia's black population welcomed the English and offered to serve as either soldiers or
sailors if the king's soldiers "would but give them their liberty."
When the British left the Chesapeake for the last time in September
1814, the admiral was so impressed by the valor of the slaves who
had joined his forces that he enlisted several hundred in an inte-
grated battalion. By the close of the war, with Americans fuming
over slave flight to the British, the English evacuated several thousand blacks, transporting some to Bermuda but most to Nova Scotia, the refuge of Black Loyalists three decades before.[66]

The war gave Jefferson much to contemplate. At first, he welcomed it, for, if the United States were successful, it would bolster
"the spirit of nationalism and of consequent prosperity, which
would never have resulted from a continued subordination to the
interests and influence of England." On the other hand, Jefferson
feared that financing the war would be a personal as well as nationwide misfortune. When Congress did exactly what Jefferson
feared—paying for the war by allowing a multitude of state banks
to flood the country with paper money, backed by no new taxes—
inflation and unstable property values ensued. "[By] the total annihilation in value of the produce that wed to give me subsistence and
independence," Jefferson sighed, "I shall be like Tantalus, up to the
shoulders in water, yet dying of thirst."[67]

Apart from his plantation operations suffering from the war, Jefferson was personally involved in the conflict. Most of the young
men of Albemarle County were enlisting as the British invaded the

Chesapeake Bay in the summer of 1814. Thomas Mann Randolph, Jefferson's son-in-law, was commanding a unit of six hundred militiamen to defend Richmond, and Jefferson's grandson was also bearing arms. The patriarch of Monticello vowed to do his part, if the British approached, as one of the aging "silver greys." He never had to ride to the sound of guns, but Jefferson must have been sobered by the flight of thousands of Chesapeake-area slaves to the British. Enslaved Americans were escaping to the British to secure the inalienable rights that Jefferson had promised nearly four decades before, in the Declaration of Independence.[68]

Even as the war stormed around him, Jefferson received an unsettling letter from an old protégé and friend that must have agitated his mind about slaves flocking to the British and reminded him of his pact with Kościuszko. Dated July 31, 1814, the letter came from Edward Coles, the youngest son of wealthy Virginia planters. Born in 1786, Coles had attended Hampden-Sydney College, founded in 1774 by the antislavery Presbyterian divine Samuel Stanhope Smith as an offshoot of the College of New Jersey. Hampton-Sydney imbued Coles with a healthy disrespect for established authority and with the belief that an educated citizenry had an obligation to challenge perceived wisdom. After transferring to William and Mary College in 1805, Coles fell under the tutelage of Bishop James Madison, a revolutionary war hero who taught students that the biggest obstacle posed for Americans was the institution of slavery. If the United States government would not end human bondage, then republican students must. Thus instructed, Coles would have no part of the argument that, regrettable as slavery might be, Southern planters could never find a replacement labor force. "As to the difficulty of getting rid of our slaves," Coles argued, "we could get rid of them with much less difficulty than we did the King of our forefathers."[69]

Partly inspired by his uncle, John Payne, Dolley Madison's father, who had freed his slaves in 1783, Coles grappled with the subject of

slavery for years. Convinced of its immorality, he hoped that Virginians in general would rid themselves of slaves. But if they would
not, "in direct violation of their great fundamental doctrines," as he
later wrote Jefferson, "I could not reconcile it to my conscience and
sense of propriety . . . [and] therefore determined that I would not
and could not hold my fellow man as a slave."

Just how Coles would act upon this moral commitment would
take much time. While he stewed, his family worried about their
youngest son's troubled conscience. Edward's older brother Isaac,
who had been Thomas Jefferson's secretary during his presidency
and was ready to leave Washington, recommended that Edward become President Madison's secretary. Unsure of himself, Coles at first
declined the offer, but eventually he agreed to become the president's secretarial aide, handling every letter and petition that came
across the chief executive's desk. Still implicated in slavery, it was
during this time that Coles became close to his cousin, Dolley Madison. But this closeness with the First Lady was not without tension.
Dolley's father had gone bankrupt six years after freeing his slaves
and moving to Philadelphia. Blaming his failure on his misplaced
benevolence, Dolley urged Coles to rein in his abolitionist sentiments lest he duplicate her father's mistakes.[70]

While worrying about slavery and his soul—but keeping his
thoughts about emancipating slaves relatively quiet—Coles remained Madison's secretary for six years, making excellent contacts
and dodging Dolley's plans to match him with an eligible wife. Exposure to slavery was a daily occurrence, for the nation's capital not
only was built on slave labor but was across the Anacostia River
from one of the biggest slave markets in the nation. Believing that
there was little public support for abolition, at least in the South,
Madison had decided that inaction was the best policy. Coles prod-
ded Madison on their walks around Washington, where they encountered "gangs of Negroes, some in irons, on their way to a
southern market." Showing his insouciance, Coles taunted Madison

"by congratulating him, as the Chief of our great Republic, that he was not then accompanyed by a Foreign Minister," lest such a sight humiliate the president.[71]

Coles's concern about slavery intensified during the early months of the War of 1812. Convalescing at his Virginia plantation from a mysterious illness, Coles thought hard about how he might be an instrument for cleansing the country of its deep stain. But to do this work he would need allies. Finally he decided to leave his native Virginia for the Northwest Territory, where he could then free his slaves and ensure that they would have a chance to succeed as small farmers.

It was at this moment—on July 31, 1814—that Coles took up his pen to write an impassioned letter to Jefferson. His hope was to recall Jefferson to the antislavery principles he had espoused for four decades but had retreated from in recent years. Only rarely in American history has such a young man written to an aging former president—Coles was a twenty-eight-year-old nonentity at the time, while Jefferson was sixty-eight—with such direct and passionate, if not confrontational, language.

"My object is to entreat and beseech you," wrote Coles, "to assert your knowledge and influence to devising and getting into operation some plan for the gradual emancipation of slavery." Reminding the former president of his lofty position in American history, Coles tried to rekindle Jefferson's abolitionist principles. Coles hoped that the author of the Declaration of Independence and the recent president of the nation would not step into the shadows for "the fear of failing," when the continuation of slavery continued to insult the root principles of the American Revolution. With special poignancy, Coles argued that the greatest chance of success in the work of initiating a gradual emancipation plan would come if such revolutionary leaders as Jefferson would bend their shoulders to this momentous cause. Coles appealed to Jefferson directly, asserting that the task devolved particularly on him, since he above all others was known internationally as a defender of human unalienable rights.

Asking him to consider how he would be remembered, Coles urged the former president to lend his name more vigorously to the "side of emancipation when that question shall be agitated." If Jefferson would draw upon his "irresistible influence . . . in all questions connected with the rights of man," the revered principles of his Declaration of Independence would be extended to all of America's people. In return, Jefferson's memory would be consecrated with this plea to end slavery.[72]

Almost a month passed before Jefferson responded to Coles's heartfelt letter, as it came during a month of high drama, when the British were burning Washington. Perhaps because Coles was a neighbor, friend, and former secretary to President Madison, Jefferson's response was mild. Jefferson began by enumerating the efforts he had made to abolish slavery. Then he lamented that his generation had refused to extend the principles of liberty and freedom to their bound laborers. He was, of course, choosing to ignore the fact that many of his fellow Virginians had freed their slaves, men such as John Payne, St. George Tucker, George Washington, Robert Carter, Richard Randolph, Robert Pleasants, Joseph Mayo, his former secretary William Short, William Ludwell Lee, and many others. Jefferson undoubtedly was also aware that the English political leaders William Pitt and Charles Fox had lent their great prestige to the British abolitionist movement.[73]

But any hope for abolition, Jefferson concluded, rested with younger men. "I had always hoped that the younger generation, receiving their early impressions after the flame of liberty had been kindled in every breast . . . would have sympathized with oppression wherever found, and prove their love of liberty beyond their own share of it" by calling for the end of slavery. Yet, save for Coles's solitary voice, Jefferson claimed he had met few young men sympathetic to abolition and "considered the general silence which prevails on this subject as indicating an apathy unfavorable to every hope." Subtly, he suggested that Coles was asking for assistance at the worst time—while the nation was at war—and warned that he was jeopardizing his career by such talk.[74]

Jefferson declined Coles's appeal and wearily renounced any participation in plans for ending slavery. He counseled Coles to stay in Virginia and work on gradual emancipation plans until "a phalanx is formed" to reach the desired goal. Jefferson could offer merely his prayers—"the only weapons of an old man."

In his reply to Coles, Jefferson adopted a tone of resignation that would have been unimaginable twenty-five years earlier. Jefferson had abandoned the idea, so central to the politics of a republic, that strong leaders are those who bring citizens out of indifference and immoral behavior, not by waiting for them to change their minds, but by making them see what is required for the security and integrity of the nation. In his earlier defense of the French Revolution, Jefferson had claimed that "rather than it should have failed, I would have seen half the earth desolated. Were there but an Adam and an Eve left in every country, and left free, it would be better than as it now is." But by now, in his later years, he struck a supine stance that ran against the grain of the Enlightenment friends with whom he had communed in Paris. Jefferson thereby surrendered to growing antiblack sentiment in the North and abandoned the egalitarian beliefs that had shaped the Democratic-Republican Party he had helped found and guide in the 1790s. By 1814, it seems, Jefferson had already retreated into a position that made it seem highly unlikely that he would ever fulfill his pledge to Kościuszko.

Coles was not easily put off, however. Appalled by Jefferson's refusal to make any public pronouncement, Coles sensed that Jefferson's plea that old age robbed him of the ability to do anything was merely a way of evading his moral obligations. In a subsequent letter Coles again beseeched his mentor to use the power and influence that only accrued with age. Coles knew that dedicated and uncompromising leadership could overcome the cautiousness of ambitious politicians. What was needed was Jefferson's forthright commitment.

In a comparison sure to bother Jefferson, Coles recalled that "Dr. Franklin . . . was as actively and usefully employed on as arduous duties after he had passed your age." Clearly annoyed at Jefferson's excuse, Coles asserted that he did not consider Jefferson's age as an obstacle to speaking forcefully to the nation. As for his own position, Coles maintained that if he had thought himself capable of bringing about a liberation of Virginia's enslaved people, he would happily have stayed in Virginia.[75]

Jefferson never replied to this second letter. Coles left Virginia in 1815 for a reconnaissance tour in Ohio, Illinois, and Missouri, states where he could cleanse himself of slaveholding. He would return later, but first Madison convinced Coles to go to Russia to solve a diplomatic tangle over rape charges against the Russian consul in Philadelphia. Upon his return in 1819, Coles would move with his slaves from Virginia, free them while en route down the Ohio River by raft, and establish them as free farmers when they reached Illinois.

Was Jefferson right that the time was not ripe for pushing a gradual abolition plan in Virginia? His defenders, including most of his biographers, have argued that any crusade for abolition in Virginia was bound to fail and would have rewarded its leaders only with opprobrium. To be sure, the abolitionist movement had flagged nationwide, as Northerners focused on their own economic affairs and lost the fire in their bellies on the issue of slavery. Southerners, in the period after Gabriel's plot, had clamped down on the small leeway afforded to slaves and even restricted slaveowners wishing to emancipate their slaves.

Yet inspired leadership might have made a difference in precisely such a time, for history tells us that in cases where a fundamental change has been accomplished against heavy odds, those willing to draw upon their moral and political capital have been crucial. In such instances, strong leaders have willingly embraced controversy, incurred the wrath of their opponents, and sometimes sacrificed friendship in order to achieve a goal dictated by conscience. As an enthusiastic supporter of the French Revolution, Jefferson was familiar with Georges Jacques Danton's 1793 maxim (engraved on his Paris statue): "de l'audace, et encore de l'audace, et toujours de l'audace" (audacity, and again audacity, and always audacity).[76]

Jefferson's retreat to his earlier comment that "we see the wisdom of Solon's remark, that no more good must be attempted than the nation can bear," accurately presented his state of mind but was utterly inconsistent with his former Enlightenment ideas. According to his former vision, society should not be taken for what it was, but should be worked upon, influenced, and reshaped through the efforts of the enlightened. For someone who had repeatedly influenced the hearts and minds of the American people, Jefferson's insistence that, as a man in his early seventies, he could no longer even scratch the surface of American sensibilities was at best a statement of political impotence and at worst insincere.

While Jefferson temporized on the slavery issue, Kościuszko did not let his own age prevent him from making a final attempt to restore his broken and mutilated homeland. Napoleon's refusal to come to Poland's aid, as he mounted his famous assault on Russia that he thought would seal his control of Europe, pushed Kościuszko to contemplate an alliance with the new czar, Alexander I, who had ascended the throne after the assassination of his father, Czar Paul I, in 1801. As Allied troops led by Czar Alexander occupied Paris after the Russian victory over Napoleon's winter onslaught in 1814, Kościuszko used the occasion to lobby for the restoration of Poland. The czar's response was grand but evasive. Kościuszko described in a letter to Jefferson in March 1815 how the czar sent his carriage and received the Polish hero with high honors, kissing him before the entire court. On a later occasion, Alexander led Kościuszko through a crowd, proclaiming, "Room, room; behold the great man." But such encomiums lacked weight. Kościuszko offered the czar his proposals: political amnesty for Polish political dissidents, freedom for the peasants, restoration of Poland's old borders, and a constitution similar to that of England. Kościuszko even proposed that the czar make himself king of the resurrected state. Though Czar Alexander made a general statement promising to rebuild Poland, he put off any substantive action, waiting for all the European powers to convene at the impending Congress of Vienna.[77]

Only symbolic gestures remained. As Russian and Prussian troops marched back through Europe, they came close to Kościuszko's home in Berville, near Fontainebleau. Seeing a regiment of Poles serving the czar's army about to torch a small group of homes, Kościuszko galloped on horseback in plain dress and commanded them to cease their plunder. Asked what authority he had, the aged general cried, "I am Kościuszko!" While Kościuszko lectured their officers on the dishonor of allowing such behavior, the Polish soldiers cast away their arms, fell to their knees before him, and covered their heads with road dust in a sign of repentance and respect for their national leader. It was a story that Agrippa Hull must have relished after it appeared in Stockbridge's *Berkshire Star* a year later.[78]

Kościuszko's final attempt to redeem his wounded nation came after Czartoryski, his old friend and the Russian czar's chief advisor on foreign affairs, invited him to attend the Congress of Vienna, which convened in 1815 to bring a close to the Napoleonic Wars. Ever hopeful, the Polish hero made the trip, though with difficulty, for old age and his scarred body left him with only limited mobility. There he watched with disgust as the czar bargained away Polish sovereignty in the face of opposition from England, Austria, and Prussia. Composed of England, Russia, Prussia, Austria, and a reconstituted France, the Congress strove to create political stability as it divided up Europe and restored monarchic governments as though the French Revolution had never occurred.

The European powers created the Kingdom of Poland, a tiny dependent state, smaller even than Napoleon's Duchy of Warsaw, which became a republic under the protection of Russia. Kraķow and its surrounding territories remained under control of the three major powers. Austria received Italian territories to offset the Russian gains, while Prussia received Saxony and parts of Westphalia and the Rhine province.

Angered and disgusted, Kościuszko refused an invitation to return to Poland, contending that the new entity was Polish in name only and could exist only at the whim of the czar. "I do not want to return to my country until it will be restored in its entirety with a free constitution," Kościuszko warned, and averred that the Poland created by the Congress "will in time be held in contempt, and that the Russians will treat us as their conquered subjects." Showing complete disdain for the Russian government in which he had so recently placed his hopes, Kościuszko sniffed that such a tiny population as the new Kingdom of Poland would never be able to defend itself against the "violence of the Russians." His dreams of a reborn Poland shattered, Kościuszko wrote to Jefferson that the object of European politics is "nothing else . . . but plunder."[79]

On the way back to France in 1815, just as Edward Coles was imploring Jefferson to step forward on the slavery issue, the dejected Kościuszko traveled to the Swiss canton of Soleure to visit the home of Francis Xavier Zeltner, the brother of the man who had been hosting Kościuszko at his estate near Fontainebleau since 1801. Francis Zeltner had accompanied Kościuszko to Vienna and had become an invaluable supporter. Deeply disappointed by the Congress of Vienna's butchering of Poland, spurning the czar's invitation to return to his dismembered homeland, and no longer willing to stay in France, Kościuszko accepted Zeltner's invitation to take up residence in a remote village of Switzerland.[80]

Far from the cosmopolitan centers of political and intellectual life where Jefferson and Kościuszko occupied the public stage, Agrippa Hull continued his humble life in Stockbridge, still something of a backwater in the late eighteenth and early nineteenth centuries. There, in the first decades of the nineteenth century, Hull was quietly becoming a black version of the self-sufficient white yeoman farmer that Jefferson imagined to be the future of America.

Like other Berkshire hill towns that were part of the watershed of the Housatonic River, Stockbridge grew very slowly in the late eighteenth century. Home to about 1,000 whites and 40 free African Americans at the end of the American Revolution, by the time Jefferson won the presidential election in 1800, Stockbridge numbered 1,190 whites and 71 blacks (or 5.6 percent of the population). Over the next twenty years, the population inched up to 1,377 people, including 52 free blacks, 19 fewer than twenty years earlier. Hull's Stockbridge was still a sleepy village, where life went on in modulated rhythms, in contrast to the booming commercial towns of Albany, across the New York border, and Hartford, Connecticut, a day's journey to the southeast.

Though free black Yankees like Grippy were outnumbered more than twenty to one by white Stockbridgians, their presence there—and in other Berkshire hill towns such as Sheffield, Lenox, Great Barrington, and Pittsfield—was greater than in any other rural part of Massachusetts. Most black Bay Staters in the early republic had migrated to the seaboard centers such as Boston and Salem, where they had the best chance to find jobs, marriage partners, and black community life. In 1790, outside of these port towns, less than 1 percent of the Massachusetts population was black, and as the nineteenth century unfolded, the black presence dwindled even further. By 1820 more than a third of all black Massachusetts families had gravitated to Boston and Salem. But farther west the Housatonic River valley towns had great appeal to black Yankees. While the black population of neighboring counties stagnated in the early decades of the nineteenth century, Berkshire County's African American population tripled between 1790 and 1830.

What drew black people such as Agrippa Hull to towns like Stockbridge? The beauty of the winding river valley, with its clear mountain air and upland pastures, may have counted for something, but idyllic physical surroundings were not enough to attract struggling black families. More importantly, the Berkshire County towns provided a degree of economic opportunity and social ease that encouraged African Americans to sink roots there. From before the Revolution, an antislavery spirit had coursed through the Berkshire hills, and many runaway slaves from New York had crossed the border to find refuge there. After Elizabeth (Mumbet) Freeman's and Quock Walker's freedom suits brought slavery in Massachusetts nearly to an end, Berkshire County became a magnet for freedom-minded New York slaves and also free blacks who worried about being kidnapped into slavery.[81]

As in other Northern states, opportunities in Stockbridge for men of little means, and particularly those who were dark-skinned, were limited. But the town's smallness and the absence of change were advantages for those who could carve out at least a small niche. Hull knew there was a white Stockbridge and a black Stockbridge and that he was lower-class. Yet he was still a Stockbridgian, a part of the community and indeed a valued member. For him, wealth was not the measure of the man; rather it was the regard in which the man was held. He may have wished for upward mobility, but security and respect in modest circumstances was enough to keep him from seeking his future elsewhere.

Hull spent most of the 1790s serving in the Sedgwick mansion, where he became a valued member of the family. Sedgwick's wife, who was mentally unstable throughout her life according to family stories, fell into a deep depression after multiple pregnancies and her husband's long absences. Her demons prevented her from functioning as mother and wife, and Grippy and Mumbet thus became almost surrogate parents to the Sedgwick children. Catharine Sedgwick, the fifth daughter and ninth child of Theodore and Pamela Sedgwick, later recalled that Mumbet had become "queen of the domain" and "the main pillar of our household," while Grippy was beloved and depended upon for all manner of household services. Only Mumbet "could tranquillize my mother when her mind was disordered [and] the only one of her friends whom she liked to have about her," for "she treated her with the same respect she did when she was sane."[82]

Looking back on her upbringing, Catharine mused that such people as Agrippa Hull and Mumbet, "who surround us in our childhood, whose atmosphere infolds us, as it were, have more to do with the formation of our characters than all our didactic and preceptive education." From Mumbet, Catharine absorbed "a clear and nice perception of justice, and a stern love of it, an uncompromising honesty in word and deed, and conduct of high intelligence, that made her the unconscious moral teacher of the children she tenderly nursed." From Grippy, who had become "a sort of Sancho Panza in the village," she also learned much, especially from his talent in "always trimming other men's follies with a keen perception and the biting wit of wisdom."

The year 1797 was a special one for Agrippa and Jane Hull. Their first child, Charlotte, had been born in 1796, and now came the birth of their first son, James. The year was made all the more sweet when Grippy traveled to New York City to embrace Kościuszko.

Back in Stockbridge after what must have been an emotional reunion, Hull continued to support his growing family, augmented by the birth of a second son, Aseph, in 1802. When the tax assessor made the rounds to levy the state and town taxes in 1799, Hull's assessment put him far below many of the town's well-circumstanced lawyers, farmers, artisans, and shopkeepers but ahead of 64 of the 207 white householders—and first among the 14 black taxable families.

Hull's hard work, and his restraint in spending for any superfluous item—the values upon which the new republic in theory would thrive—are evident in his continued acquisition of property. All around him landlessness afflicted an increasing percentage of white Massachusetts householders. But Hull edged forward to become the wealthiest black villager in Stockbridge. In 1800 and 1801, he added to his homestead, purchasing land from Silas Pepoon, the militia captain under whom he had enlisted during the Shays insurgency, and from another townsman. With Massachusetts moving toward rural capitalism, where more and more men worked for wages on someone else's land, and as the strolling poor filled the countryside drifting from town to town searching for work, Hull carefully saved and enlarged his small farms, becoming as self-sustaining as possible.[83]

Yet on his fifteen acres Hull could not become quite the yeoman farmer that Jefferson idealized—the incorruptible, quintessential American who was self-sufficient in the cultivation of his own land. Grippy could produce some of what was needed for his family and sell, in good years, a small surplus of wheat, bran, and hay in order to make purchases at Stockbridge stores. But bartering his labor for needed items was still sometimes necessary. Piecework—a job here, a job there—became his way of life. Pasturing the Sedgwick family sheep and horses provided a small income. Taking in boarders, such as two indigent women in 1801 and 1802 and stonemasons building a new mill in Stockbridge, brought in a bit more revenue. Moving from town to town in the region to serve as a waiter at weddings, funerals, minister ordinations, and church raisings also added to the cupboard. While Jefferson relied on the labor of others and spent himself deeper into debt, Hull relied on his own labor and practiced self-sacrifice. Living within his means, he cleaved to each of the traditional Puritan values save one: piety. All the others—industry, frugality, modesty, and sobriety—he managed with a geniality and humor that endeared him to white Stockbridgians.[84]

To Grippy's delight, Elizabeth Freeman, his coworker in the Sedgwick household, became his immediate neighbor at his Cherry

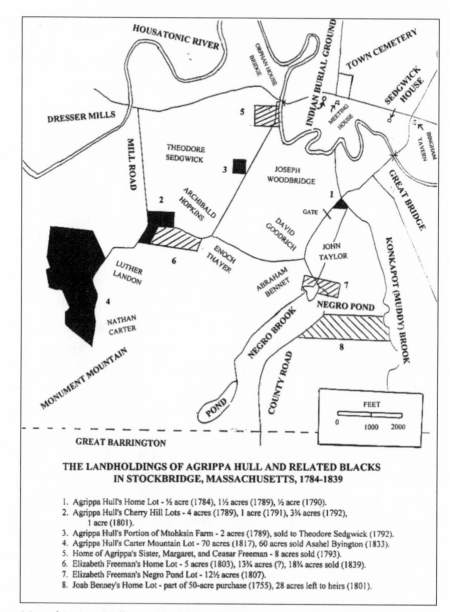

**THE LANDHOLDINGS OF AGRIPPA HULL AND RELATED BLACKS
IN STOCKBRIDGE, MASSACHUSETTS, 1784-1839**

1. Agrippa Hull's Home Lot - ½ acre (1784), 1½ acres (1789), ½ acre (1790).
2. Agrippa Hull's Cherry Hill Lots - 4 acres (1789), 1 acre (1791), 3¾ acres (1792),
   1 acre (1801).
3. Agrippa Hull's Portion of Mtohksin Farm - 2 acres (1789), sold to Theodore Sedgwick (1792).
4. Agrippa Hull's Carter Mountain Lot - 70 acres (1817), 60 acres sold Asahel Byington (1833).
5. Home of Agrippa's Sister, Margaret, and Ceasar Freeman - 8 acres sold (1793).
6. Elizabeth Freeman's Home Lot - 5 acres (1803), 13¾ acres (?), 18¾ acres sold (1839).
7. Elizabeth Freeman's Negro Pond Lot - 12½ acres (1807).
8. Joab Benney's Home Lot - part of 50-acre purchase (1755), 28 acres left to heirs (1801).

Map of Agrippa Hull's Stockbridge landholdings, drawn by Lion Miles of
Stockbridge, Massachusetts. Agrippa Hull's landholdings, which once belonged to
Stockbridge Indians, and the location of his friend Elizabeth Freeman are indicated
on this map.

Hill farm. Her first land purchase was in 1803 for 5 acres, which she bought jointly with Jonah Humphrey, a member of the First Church of Stockbridge who hailed from one of the town's black families that had contributed two members to the American Revolution. In 1807 she added a second property of 12.5 acres just down the county road from Hull's homestead and then purchased Jonah Humphrey's half of their Cherry Hill farm in 1811.[85]

By this time the long association of Hull and Freeman with the Sedgwick family was drawing to a close. Appalled by the radicalism of the French Revolution and disgusted at the rise of the Jeffersonian party, Theodore Sedgwick had turned gloomily conservative by the end of the century. His daughter Catharine remembered how she learned to "look upon a Democrat as an enemy to his country" and at the Jeffersonian party as a malign entity. Her father's friends dreaded the influence on American politics that the French Revolution had wrought. Having never quite recovered from Shays's Rebellion, Sedgwick turned his back on the ideals of the American Revolution, still believing that "the constitutional monarchy of Britain was the safest and happiest government on earth" and hoping that Americans might restore "a strong aristocratic element." Such retrograde thinking sent Sedgwick's political career into eclipse, and it ended when Jeffersonian Democratic-Republicans unseated many Federalist officeholders in the 1800 election. Speaker of the House of Representatives at the end of the Adams presidency, Sedgwick never again held an elective office and remained a sour, bitter defender of the fading Federalist Party.[86]

Perhaps Grippy and Mumbet forgave the politics of the man they had faithfully served so far as his opinions concerned national issues. But reports in Stockbridge newspapers that Sedgwick had been the main drafter of the Fugitive Slave Act of 1793 probably grieved Grippy and Mumbet. Once Sedgwick's politics pervaded the hearth, dining room, and kitchen of his stately Stockbridge home, their allegiance began to subside. Years later, Catharine Sedgwick remembered that "my father's house was one of the few where the domestics were restricted to the kitchen table. 'Oh,' said a woman to me, . . . 'now Catharine, we are all made out of the same clay, we have got one Maker and one Judge, and we've got to lay down in the grave side by side—why can't you sit down to the table together?'"[87]

But that was not to be in the Sedgwick household, where the five black servants ate around the kitchen fire. In a town as small as Stockbridge this must have been common knowledge. How much this bruised Grippy, Mumbet, her daughter "Little Bet," Samson (a runaway slave), and Tip-Top we can only imagine, but Hull could not have been oblivious to Sedgwick's almost morbid fear of Jeffersonian politics. Developing "a thorough distrust of 'the people,'" daughter Catharine recalled, Sedgwick spoke incessantly about ordinary folk as "'Jacobins,' 'sans-culottes,' and 'miscreants.'" Never one to hide his feelings, Sedgwick, his daughter remembered, "dreaded every upward step [that ordinary people] made, regarding their elevation as a depression, in proportion to their ascension, of the intelligence and virtue of the country." His children learned the local saying of the Federalist Congregational minister, "I don't say that every Democrat is a horse-thief, but I do say that every horse-thief is a Democrat!" Many Federalists, called moderate Federalists, were less dismissive in their view of the common man, but her father, Catharine remembered, regarded the "people" as the "'greasy, un-washen multitude' of Rome and of Shakespeare's time."[88] For Hull, who had commanded the respect and affection of high-ranking officers in the Revolution, this must have rubbed hard against his view of himself as a worthy, if ordinary, citizen of Stockbridge.

While Sedgwick was growing ever more conservative, Grippy's politics were shifting in the other direction. Hull had supported the Federalist cause, no doubt in part because of his allegiance to the Sedgwick family but probably also because Northern Federalists supported the abolitionist cause more than Northern Jeffersonians. By 1807 Hull had fully abandoned the Federalist persuasion, presenting the "tea, coffee, plum cake, et cetera, with wine, [and] French cordials" at the wedding reception for the nephew of Barnabas Bidwell, the Jeffersonian lawyer from Stockbridge who replaced Sedgwick in Congress. "One guest whose presence was important," wrote Bidwell's wife, reporting the wedding to her husband in Washington, was "our friend Agrippa Hull [who] rendered himself useful you may be assured." Bidwell and Sedgwick were bitter enemies, and in such a small town as Stockbridge Grippy's new connection with the Bidwell family was, as local legend has told it, enough to put him "out of favor with the Sedgwicks."[89]

Never one to scrape before his employer, Hull left the Sedgwick household a few years after his patron ended his political career with a paroxysm of conservative ranting. There is no indication in the sources if he left of his own accord or if Sedgwick dismissed him. Mumbet left about the same time after Sedgwick's second wife, Pamela, died in 1807. Most of his children were grown by now, and he quickly remarried. Mumbet—"queen of the domain"—was unable to abide Sedgwick's bilious third wife and quietly retreated from half a lifetime of service to the Sedgwicks, finding work as a midwife, nurse, and caretaker. Even before this, she had moved to "her little hut" next to Grippy's Cherry Hill acreage, though she had continued to work in the Sedgwick mansion by day.[90]

Hull was surely delighted by the staunch antislavery position of the Bidwell family, which he served on occasion. Bidwell, replacing Sedgwick in the U.S. Congress, quickly entered the debate over closing the slave trade, offering an amendment that any Africans seized from illegal traders on the high seas would gain immediate emancipation. Although his Washington colleagues rejected the plan, he found support for it at home. His wife, Mary, wrote him that she was "confident you would oppose [the slave trade] with your utmost energy." If Americans did not act quickly to end the commerce in humans, she assured her husband, the nation would "draw down the vengeance of an offended God."[91]

By the time he had shifted his political allegiance, now in his forties, Agrippa Hull had endeared himself to almost everyone in Stockbridge, a town of only about two hundred families in 1800 and only
a bit larger ten years later. "His presence at weddings seemed almost
a necessity," wrote the town's historian. At these events he "wedged
himself and his 'good cheer' into every crowded corner, his im-
promptu rhymes and his courteous jokes . . . always welcome." When
asked why he carved a sign on his pigpen with "a man with a pail of
swill driving the pigs," Grippy replied in verse, "Cuffee on the barn,
whale under his feet, house full of peas and nothing to eat." Grippy's
plainspoken, wry observations allowed him to escape the crueler
markers of race that had become prevalent throughout New England.
Beginning in the 1790s, white New Englanders circulated dialect
jokes and outlandish cartoons to ridicule free blacks and demonstrate
their social inferiority. Reports of Grippy's salt-and-pepper repartee
indicates that he did not have to suffer such satirical attacks.[92]

What was it about this black man who tugged at the emotions of
white villagers at a time when racism was growing? His equanimity,
perhaps, as well as his lack of pretense, and perhaps his insouciance,
zest for life, and good cheer, all of which reminded white villagers of
their better selves. Part of his success, it seems, was that he did not
elbow forward to advocate a reformist agenda. For most black
Americans in the North, reform was a dual issue: dissolving the
racial discrimination that limited their striving for better lives and
helping to end the nightmare of slavery that had trapped their people for generations. Stockbridge's historian, intimate with most families in the village, claimed "he was perfectly free from all airs and
show of consequence. . . . His language was so simple, and his petitions often so peculiarly adapted to the every day needs of his hear-
ers, or of those perishing around him, that a smile was sometimes
provoked from the thoughtless."

Grippy's circumspect manner—pushing his agenda forward with
quiet determination but remaining sensitive to the advantage of not

rubbing too hard against the stiff-necked New England Federalists who still held considerable power in the Berkshire hill towns—served him well. Evidence on his "petitions" is regrettably thin—this is the case for almost all black New Englanders of this era, for they left no letters or essays as part of their legacy—but we have it from Stockbridge's early annalist, Electa Jones, that Hull "felt deeply the wrongs of his nation." Such feelings must surely have sprung from the continuation of slavery, indeed, its rampant growth, in the expanding nation. But as Jones put it, "his feelings rose on the wings of prayer, rather than burst from the muzzle of the musket."[93]

Expressing his feelings "on the wings of prayer" did not happen for a long time after Grippy returned home from the American Revolution. Indeed, he took to religion haltingly. While several black families had joined Stockbridge's First Church, Hull attended only occasionally for some time after the war. But this began to change as he entered his forties. Religion would soon come to occupy an important place in his life as well as in his status in the community.

What may have piqued his interest were two Congregational ministers, one Indian and the other a mixed-race man, who preached in his vicinity in the 1780s and 1790s. The first was Samson Occum, a full-blooded Mohegan, who from 1789 until his death in 1792 taught and preached at Brotherton and New Stockbridge, the villages across the border in New York populated by the Stockbridge Indians who had left Stockbridge, where Hull had known them before the American Revolution. Every winter the Stockbridge Indians returned to their ancient village to build wigwams, make baskets and brooms to sell, honor the gravesites of their ancestors, and light fires on their old hearthstones.[94] This put them almost on Hull's doorstep, for he had purchased his half-acre lot and then systematically extended it through purchase until he was farming on a part of the old Stockbridge Indian village. For several years, then, Hull could not help but see Samson Occum, the Indians' preacher, near his own house.

The other minister of color who seemingly engaged Hull's interest was Lemuel Haynes. Born in 1753 to an enslaved African and a Scottish immigrant servant, Haynes was indentured at five months to a deeply religious farm family in Granville, twenty-eight miles east of Stockbridge. Like Hull, Haynes had served in the Massachusetts army, though he served for a much shorter time. Wielding a pen just as well as a sword, he wrote a stirring essay at age twenty-three on "Liberty Further Extended," in which he called on masters to free their slaves. After the war, Haynes studied for the ministry. Like Phillis Wheatley of Boston, he displayed extraordinary literary abilities that amazed white New Englanders. After arduous study of Latin and Greek, at age twenty-seven he took up the pulpit in Granville, Massachusetts. He was remembered by a latter occupant of the same pulpit as "one of the wonders of the age" because he had risen from "servant-boy" to "spiritual teacher in a respectable and enlightened congregation in New-England."[95]

Unlike Hull, Haynes married a white woman. Though Hull was cut of different cloth than Haynes, Grippy could appreciate the black minister's appeal to people of all kinds. In fact, Haynes and Grippy—one deeply religious, the other an indifferent churchgoer as a young man—touched people in uncannily similar ways. "All classes and ages were carried away with the sweet, animated eloquence of the preacher," Haynes's biographer wrote while Hull was still alive. "You might see children by the wayside, or near the village school-house, arranging themselves in due order to welcome him as he passed, and vying with each other in their tokens of reverence. It was remarkable how singularly he attached to himself the rising generation." Hull certainly heard Haynes preach, probably in about 1785, when the black preacher was completing five years in the Granville pulpit and preparing to move to West Rutland, Vermont, to supply the pulpit there. Or it could have been later, in the 1790s, when Haynes maintained his contacts with his successor at the Granville church and visited there periodically. Stockbridge's early historian, Electa Jones, recalled how Agrippa and the man he was serving—probably Sedgwick—were attending the same church when "a distinguished mulatto preacher" gave the sermon. "On coming out of the house, the gentleman said to Agrippa, 'Well, how do you like nigger preaching?' 'Sir,' he promptly retorted, 'he was half black and half white; I liked my half, how did you like yours?'"[96]

In 1815, England and the United States signed the Treaty of Ghent, ending the War of 1812. Jefferson was seventy-one, Kościuszko was sixty-nine, and Hull was fifty-eight. The European powers at the Congress of Vienna had dashed Kościuszko's dream of a resuscitated and reformed Poland. In the twilight of his life, Kościuszko's wish to see some of Jefferson's slaves freed was close at hand, but he had no way of knowing how his dream would be shattered by the Master of Monticello. In remote Stockbridge, Hull would hear of the death of the man he had served so ably, and later, if he read the newspapers, he would learn of Kościuszko's great betrayal at the hands of his dear friend Jefferson.

5

⚜

Long Endings

TADEUSZ KOŚCIUSZKO spent the last three years of his life in the home of Francis Xavier Zeltner in Soleure, a Swiss provincial capital situated at the foot of the pine-covered Jura Mountains within sight of the rugged peaks of the majestic Alps. Amid the political neutrality of the Swiss republic, it seemed to Kościuszko an ideal place for his retirement. True to form, after the townspeople welcomed him with a procession in his honor, he rejected any additional tributes and insisted upon living as an ordinary citizen.

Time and battle had taken their toll on Kościuszko's body. Although his wounds had largely healed, his health was never better than tolerable. His formerly handsome face was now wrinkled, he was missing many teeth, and his gray hair fell over his forehead and down his shoulders. Yet his eyes were still clear, his voice strong and full, and his irresistible charm intact.[1]

Kościuszko did the best he could in Soleure to maintain his old vigor and stay abreast of events. His old battle wounds kept him from rigorous activity, but he rode a pony around the countryside for exercise, read voraciously in geography and history, and spent hours teaching history, mathematics, and drawing to Emilie Zeltner, the family's twelve-year-old daughter. To the end, charity was never far

Time and his war wounds wrought hard changes on Kościuszko's once-handsome face, but his heart stayed pure. At the time of this drawing, Kościuszko still made his saintly pilgrimages to assist the poor. Xavier Zeltner, drawing of Kościuszko near the end of his life, Kraķow Historical Museum, Poland.

from his mind. "Contrary to custom in Switzerland," the Zeltners' son remembered, "our door had to be kept open the whole day . . . ; it was besieged by the poor, who never went away empty." Walking and riding around the town and the countryside on his black pony, Kościuszko bestowed candies and words of wisdom on residents of all ages and walks of life. On his daily sojourns he brought saddlebags of wine and food for the poor. Kościuszko would ride up to the homes of the impoverished and sick and distribute his gifts. Before the recipients could even recover from their surprise at this kindness, Kościuszko was already back in the saddle, moving on to his next destination. It is recounted that Kościuszko's pony was so accustomed to his master's ways that it would stop every time they met a beggar, traveling craftsman apprentice, or invalid soldier and would not move until the recipient had received his alms.[2]

In his declining years one of Kościuszko's few comforts was to commiserate with Jefferson about Poland's ongoing political plight. For example, in April 1815 he lamented that Czar Alexander's ministers refused to carry out the czar's promise to enlarge the Duchy of Warsaw to Poland's former boundaries. Nor had the czar made good on his pledge to create a constitutional government and to liberate "our poor unfortunate serfs and give them their land." Living in exile, Kościuszko could only deplore the Allied powers' actions at the end of the Napoleonic Wars, "which break their good faith, commit injustices against small states, and treat their people like wolves treat sheep." At this point, Kościuszko abandoned his trust in Europe's leaders.[3]

His life ebbing, Kościuszko settled his worldly affairs in a way he hoped might brighten the future of Eastern Europe's serfs. On April 2, 1817, he wrote a will leaving his Polish estate at Siechnowice to his niece, Katarzyna Estkowa, and her children but stipulating that after his death, the serfs on the estate would become "free citizens and full proprietors of the lands they occupy" and relieved "from all impost, duties, and personal services which they have hitherto owed to the lords of the castle." Consistent with the will he wrote in Philadelphia, he exhorted the freed serfs to school their children in order to prepare them for life as full-fledged citizens. Not knowing just when he would die, he had the terms published in a Paris newspaper on April 21, 1817. This created a public record and spread the word of his decision. His instructions clearly indicate that liberating the serfs was at the forefront of his thoughts in the last months of his life. Freeing the serfs at Siechnowice was the Polish equivalent of his desire to use his American estate to buy the freedom of black Americans held in bondage.[4]

Jefferson must have heard that his Polish compeer had freed his serfs because this was reported in a New York newspaper as early as June 5 and then in newspapers close to Monticello. Two weeks later, aware that his Polish friend was declining and that the twilight years were also upon him, Jefferson urged Kościuszko to "come to Monticello and be one of our family." Unwilling to encroach on his friend's hospitality, Kościuszko declined. Jefferson, in a touching display of friendship, replied that the Pole could build a house or rent one near enough to dine with the former president every day and to "close a life of liberty in a land of liberty, [and] come lay your bones with mine in the Cemetery at Monticello." This would be a perfect way for Kościuszko to manage his American assets while allowing Jefferson "to give you in person . . . assurances of affectionate friendship and support." Kościuszko demurred. Confessing that "my country lies heavy on my heart," he explained that he must remain in Europe to advise and exhort others who still dreamed of a Poland raised from the dead.[5]

Kościuszko's travails ended in the autumn of 1817. Already weakened by a spill from his horse, he took to his bed in early October after an epidemic of typhoid fever struck Soleure. Sensing that death was near, he made an additional will, bequeathing his Swiss funds to the Zeltner family with special allocations to Emilie and the local orphanage. In settling his American estate, he remained confident of his compact with Jefferson. In a final letter to the former president, penned on September 15, 1817, Kościuszko reminded Jefferson of the solemn oath they had made in Philadelphia in the spring of 1798. Of his American assets, he wrote, "after my death you know the fixed destination."[6]

On October 15, 1817, surrounded by Zeltner and a few others, Kościuszko offered blessings to each of his close friends. He then raised himself up, held out his hands to the Zeltners, greeted Emilie with a smile, and, with a gentle sigh, fell back lifeless. He was seventy-one years old.

On his own instructions Kościuszko's funeral was simple. With a group of orphans leading the cortege, six poor men carried the coffin to the Jesuit sanctuary of St. Ursus and Victor Church. The corpse lay in a lead coffin for several months until Czar Alexander I permitted it to be transported to Poland. But Soleure townsmen removed the intestines from his body and buried them in the town cemetery, wanting some part of Kościuszko to remain with them.

His body was placed in a sarcophagus in the Wawel Cathedral in Kraḳow on June 23, 1818. There it continues to rest among the kings, queens, and heroes of the Polish people.[7]

As word of Kościuszko's death reached the outside world, Americans in Paris held a requiem mass on October 31 at St. Roche Church. It was thronged by American and French admirers, many of whom had fought with the Pole in the American Revolution, and by Poles, now living in Paris, who had followed Kościuszko into battle in their Polish homeland. The Marquis de Lafayette spoke eloquently of the respect that even Kościuszko's enemies felt for him and how Americans, Poles, French, and Swiss honored his remains as the "relic of a superior man, a Christian, and a friend of mankind."[8]

Kościuszko's death was mourned in the United States as well. The first brief notice appeared in the *City of Washington Gazette* on December 24, 1817. Major papers quickly picked up the story—the *Baltimore Patriot* on December 26, Philadelphia's *Poulson's American Daily Advertiser* and New York's *Commercial Advertiser* on December 30, the *Alexandria* (Virginia) *Gazette* a day later, and the *Richmond Enquirer* on January 1, 1818. Within two weeks, newspapers up and down the Atlantic seaboard had broadcast the word of Kościuszko's passing.[9]

In the American newspaper accounts, almost all recycled from a translated version of a short obituary in the Paris *Journal de Commerce*, readers were reminded of Kościuszko's stalwart principles, matchless courage, and dedication to the American struggle for freedom and equality. On the floor of the House of Representatives in Washington, Indiana's William Henry Harrison proposed a resolution to honor the memory of the intrepid Pole and urged the erection of a temple where Kościuszko's statue would be placed next to Washington's. "His fame will last as long as liberty remains upon the earth," Harrison told the Senators. The temple never came to be, but in 1825, at the half-century commemoration of the Battle of Bunker Hill, city officials placed in the cavity of the Bunker Hill

Polish citizens made the simple but powerful gesture of carrying dirt from the battlefields where Kościuszko fought to free Poland to create this huge mound on the outskirts of Kraķow. Teodor Baltazar Stachowtcz, *Polish Citizens Creating the Memorial Mound for Thaddeus Kościuszko*, 1859, Kraķow Historical Museum, Poland.

Monument's cornerstone a commemorative medal for Kościuszko along with those celebrating George Washington, John Paul Jones, Benjamin Franklin, and a few others.[10]

The Polish outpouring of emotion was intense and long-lasting. After the fallen hero's body was interred in Kraķow, city officials planned a gigantic commemorative hill to be built just outside the city. Beginning in 1820, men, women, and children brought clumps of earth from Kościuszko battlefields in wheelbarrows, buckets, baskets, and their bare hands to construct the hill, which eventually rose more than one hundred feet. The land sloping down to the Vistula River was to be given as freehold property to veterans who had served under Kościuszko, to form what would be called the Kościuszko Colony.[11] Even today Kościuszko retains an enormously important place in the pantheon of Polish heroes. Postage stamps, currency, and innumerable monuments keep memory of him alive.

As Poles have immigrated to the United States, they have brought that reverence with them and have reified it with scores of statues and community centers around the country.

At the end of 1817 Jefferson learned of Kościuszko's death when translations of the French newspaper account of the Pole's memorial in Paris began to reach the American press. Surprisingly, given the warmth of their relationship, Jefferson remained silent about Kościuszko's death in his correspondence. But this silence did not obviate the fact that the Sage of Monticello was now forced to make a crucial decision. Once the will was probated, Jefferson would have to decide between using the Pole's American assets to purchase the freedom of scores of his own slaves at his Virginia plantations and finding other planters who would accept market value reimbursement for freeing their slaves. On the most intimate level, Jefferson had the opportunity to free and educate his mistress, her children, and other favored plantation slaves of his choice, all the while accepting full compensation for the loss of their labor. To do so would have honored his many pronouncements over the years that slavery was immoral, degrading, and ruinous to the future of the new nation. "What an all-conquering influence must have attended his illustrious example," wrote William Lloyd Garrison many years later, if Jefferson had seized the moment.[12]

The former president had another compelling reason to regard the probating of Kościuszko's will as a godsend. At the time he received news of his Polish friend's demise, Jefferson was mired in debt, his estate headed toward a disastrous collapse. Only two years before, in 1815, he had to sell his precious library—"I cannot live without books," he had said—of almost 6,500 volumes to the Library of Congress, earning more than $23,000 to pay off debts, including nearly $5,000 he had borrowed from Kościuszko's assets.

When his old friend and immigrant neighbor Phillip Mazzei died in Paris the next year, Jefferson was forced to beseech Mazzei's family not to demand money he owed the Italian's estate and temporarily allow him to pay only the back interest on his account. In April 1818, when he caught up on interest in arrears, Jefferson still owed the Mazzei estate $7,400. He also owed the Van Staphorst house, a private bank in Amsterdam, about $6,000, the noxious fruit of a $2,000 loan taken in the early 1790s. In the fall of 1817, as his drought-stricken wheat crop failed, Jefferson was unable to make interest payments to the Van Staphorst bankers' agents in America. These and other large debts, hanging like a millstone around his neck, kept him running from bank to bank seeking extensions on overdue accounts as well as new loans. "To owe what I cannot pay is a constant torment," Jefferson lamented to a friend.[13]

Kościuszko's will offered Jefferson an opportunity to substantially reduce his financial obligations—his estate was now valued at $17,000—but if he freed slaves and took market value compensation from Kościuszko's legacy, he would have to drastically reduce the workforce at his several plantations or hire local free wage laborers to replace emancipated slaves. Would this make it harder in the long term to wrest profits from his decreasingly productive land? (Soil exhaustion had already sent many of his friends reeling into bankruptcy.) With two daughters, their husbands, and his twelve grandchildren on his mind, Jefferson faced the possibility that he could not escape with both his honor and his obligation to family intact.

He was torn: if he decided that he could not carry out the provisions of Kościuszko's will, how could he find an honorable way of abdicating his role as executor? Impossible as it is to weigh the factors preying on his mind, we can identify them. One was his allegiance to the Old Dominion aristocracy and his devotion to sustaining the economic and cultural leverage of the white South in national politics. He also feared offending friends, especially slaveowners already shaken by the actions of others who had released slaves from bondage. Jefferson would not have disagreed with John Adams's characterization of Virginia planters, written a few years before: "Not a bairn in Scotland" nor "a lad upon the highland is more clannish than every Virginian I have ever known."[14]

Interwoven with this loyal attachment to his planter neighbors was Jefferson's hatred of conflict and personal confrontation. The personal attacks he had undergone while serving as Virginia's governor during the Revolution and later as the nation's president had cut him to the core. Borne of this abhorrence of conflict, he had become almost obsessed by the search for personal and political tranquility by the time word of Kościuszko's death arrived. "I wish to avoid all collisions of opinion with all mankind," he had written a friend just a year before.[15]

Yet we can imagine that rumbling through his ever reflective mind was William Short's plea, just a year before, for Jefferson to draw upon his influence to speak out forcefully against the illegal slave trade that was increasing ten years after Congress had outlawed it. Would he only step forward publicly to decry "the infamous traffic in human flesh," Congress might bring it to a halt.[16]

It was not to be. Jefferson could hardly have been more adamant in refusing. "I must turn a deaf ear," he wrote, for "my repugnance to that is insuperable." Unwilling to draw on his prestige, he washed his hands entirely of battling the illegal slave trade and the institution of slavery itself. Sixteen years earlier, he had counseled that "the ground of liberty is to be gained by inches, that we must be contented to rescue what we can get from time to time, and eternally press forward for what is yet to get." But Jefferson had given up on taking part in the business of inching forward. "The present generation," he wrote Short, "will be as able as that which preceded them to do for themselves what is necessary for their own happiness; and that which shall succeed them will do what they shall leave undone."[17]

Jefferson's response to Kościuszko's death came quickly. Within a day or two of receiving word of his friend's passing, he dispatched two letters about the will. One went to William Wirt, his legal advisor, a slaveholder himself and a Washington insider who was now attorney general of the United States; the other went to William Crawford, Secretary of the Treasury. The letters putatively concerned legal proprieties—how Kościuszko's will could be probated properly, whether Jefferson could even function as its executor, and how the very considerable funds now available could be used in a manner consistent with the provisions of the will. But hidden in the language of the letters was the decision Jefferson had already made: that he would not free any of his slaves with Kościuszko's assets.[18]

In writing Wirt and Crawford, Jefferson concealed the precise language of Kościuszko's will, which only he and two close friends had ever seen—John Barnes and John Dawson, who had witnessed the will. The document's language specified that Jefferson was to "employ the whole [of Kościuszko's American assets] in purchasing Negroes from among his own or any others." But in his letter to Wirt, Jefferson was willfully vague; he alluded to his role as executor in "disposing of his [Kościuszko's] funds in a particular course of charity." In a letter the same day to Crawford, Jefferson was similarly opaque, referring only to Kościuszko "making an eleemosynary disposition of his property, of which will he named me executor." Twelve days later, he used the same circumlocution in further correspondence pertaining to the will.

Forecasting his decision that his slaves would never see freedom as Kościuszko had hoped, Jefferson dwelt on the questions of which court would be the proper venue for probating the will and whether he was qualified to serve as executor. He confided to Wirt and Crawford that he had decided to delay proving the will until he heard from Kościuszko's friends, who Jefferson supposed were at the Pole's side when he died and would relay "any particulars which ought to be known." Jefferson then proposed to transfer the execution of the will to the Virginia Court of Chancery, arguing that proving the will would take "a course of time beyond what I can expect to live." However, he supposed that Virginia's district or high court was competent to probate the will and expressed his willingness to appear before the court.

A few days later, Jefferson received a letter that may have increased his foreboding about the complexity of the will. On January 4, John Armstrong, Jefferson's appointee as ambassador to France, had written that Kościuszko had placed a document in his hands in 1806 with instructions not to open it until the Pole's death. It proved to be a second will, which left $3,704 plus interest to Tadeusz Kościuszko Armstrong, John Armstrong's son. The bequest promised to complicate the original plan but hardly overturn it, since the second will plainly stated that the money should come from the funds held by Jefferson in trust for Kościuszko.[19]

Jefferson took no issue with the terms of this bequest but used the opportunity to hint at his unwillingness to serve as Kościuszko's executor. He replied to Armstrong, telling him of Kościuszko's earlier will and reporting that he had written to Wirt and Crawford to ask their advice on the complex process of probating the will of a deceased person with a "residence under one government, his property in another, and his executor in a third." Jefferson stressed that because of these complications, he was not yet ready to serve as executor, again pleading old age. But he assured Armstrong that his son's claim would "meet with no difficulty or delay . . . wherever an authority shall be completed for receiving and paying it."[20]

While he had probably made up his own mind far earlier, it was not until the early spring of 1818 that Jefferson openly declared his decision not to serve as executor of Kościuszko's will. His announcement was provoked by an unexpected letter he received on March 24 from the man with whom Kościuszko spent the last years of his life—Francis Xavier Zeltner. Dated October 29, 1817, Zeltner's letter told the sad news of Kościuszko's death, a fact that Jefferson of course already knew. But jumping off the page was Zeltner's claim to Kościuszko's entire estate. Zeltner asserted that

Kościuszko had left his entire estate to him, including a small bequest to his daughter Emilie, based upon a purported will of 1817. Jefferson had his doubts about Zeltner's claim, since he had received Kościuszko's letter to the contrary only weeks before the Pole's death. But at the very least it promised to complicate the disposal of Kościuszko's American assets.[21]

Jefferson took almost three months to answer Zeltner, not responding until July 23, 1818. Jefferson began his letter by praising Kościuszko effusively, writing that "to no country could that event [the death] be more afflicting nor to any individual than myself. I enjoyed his intimate friendship and confidence of the last twenty years, and during the portion of that time which he spent in this country, I had daily opportunities of observing personally the purity of his virtue, the benevolence of his heart, and his sincere devotion to the cause of liberty."

After these strong words of praise, Jefferson described the 1798 will, which gave all of his assets left in the United States "to the charitable purpose of educating and emancipating as many of the children of bondage in this country, as it should be adequate to." This was the first time that Jefferson had put in writing the precise nature of Kościuszko's largesse—the emancipation and education of slaves—though he did not specify that the will gave Jefferson the opportunity of purchasing the freedom of his own slaves.[22]

Jefferson then revealed to Zeltner that he had decided to forswear his role as the executor of Kościuszko's will. The expert opinions of Crawford and Wirt about his legal capacity to serve and in what court to prove the will had not yet reached him. Nonetheless, he had made his decision. "I had strength and vigor of mind sufficient to undertake the execution of his philanthropic views" twenty years before, he told Zeltner. But the intervening years "now weigh on me so heavily, and have brought me so near the term of all human concerns that it would be imprudent for me to undertake a business of so long execution." These were words strikingly akin to those he had used in turning back William Short's and Edward Coles's pleas over the last few years for the former president to re-take the public stage on behalf of the fast-growing population of en-slaved Americans. But now Jefferson told Zeltner that rather than taking up the executorship of Kościuszko's will, he was searching to find someone else to "ensure a faithful discharge" of Kościuszko's wish to strike a blow against slavery.

Finding a replacement executor of Kościuszko's will was far from a priority for Jefferson. The summer of 1818 passed without his having found one, and then the fall as well. All the while, he must have carefully hidden from his slaves, even from his mistress Sally Hemings, that he had within his grasp the means to free many of them. In the meantime he must have pondered the words of John Taylor, his planter-philosopher friend from Petersburg, Virginia, who had just republished *Arator* in nearby Richmond. Taylor called for the abolition of "this lamentable evil" of slavery and laid down an uncompromising stricture: "To whine over it is cowardly; to ag-gravate it, criminal; and to forbear to alleviate it, because it cannot be wholly cured, foolish."[23]

In November 1818 Jefferson finally took action. Still mindful of the "sacred trust" with Kościuszko, he engaged a friend and close associate, John Hartwell Cocke, to serve as executor. For Jefferson, Cocke was a kindred spirit, almost a son. Through frequent inter-actions in the planning of a state university, Jefferson had learned of Cocke's commitment to the recently founded American Coloniza-tion Society (ACS), an organization that seemed especially relevant to the thorny problem of implementing Kościuszko's will. Initiated by Robert Finley, a New Jersey Presbyterian minister, the ACS had the purported goal of ending slavery gradually and replacing en-slaved people with free white laborers. For their benefit, black Americans already free and those released from slavery in the future should be convinced to immigrate to Africa, where they could set up an independent nation and promote Christianity in a supposedly pagan world. This vision so closely aligned with what Jefferson had argued in *Notes on Virginia* three decades before that word of the ACS's founding must have been welcomed at Monticello as rain upon parched earth.[24]

A man with antislavery instincts and hopes for improving the benighted lives of slaves, Cocke also shared Jefferson's conviction that free people of color probably could not succeed in the United States or mix amicably with whites. The problem of slavery could only be solved through repatriation. The establishment of the ACS possibly tempted Jefferson with the notion of freeing a select number of slaves, taking compensation from Kościuszko's estate, and then, through the offices of the ACS, packing them off to what would soon become the new nation of Liberia. The advantages were multiple. By freeing slaves and assisting in their immigration to Africa, Jefferson would give the ACS an enormous boost of prestige. At the same time, it might gratify Jefferson to see his own doubts about free black capabilities dissolved, and it would reduce his debt substantially thanks to compensation from Kościuszko's bequest. However, there is no surviving evidence that Jefferson actually considered this option. Most likely, as he had expressed it seven years before, when he had been asked about the feasibility of colonization, he "doubted whether many of these people would voluntarily consent to such an exchange of situation."[25]

Such doubts, expressed in 1811, proved to be well-founded by 1819. Early support of the ACS by a few Northern black ministers and secular leaders quickly evaporated as black Americans watched white leaders, in both the North and the South, flock to the idea of repatriating free black Americans. Particularly suspicious, some of the staunchest Southern defenders of slavery were among the white luminaries who had joined the ACS. For ordinary blacks, the ACS smacked of a massive deportation scheme meant to drive them from the land where they had been born. They also believed that the ACS's popularity among white slaveowners and important Southern political leaders was transparent: these men saw the removal of free black Americans as a way to undercut efforts to abolish slavery.

While engaging Cocke as an executor, Jefferson, still waiting for advice about what court was most appropriate for proving the will, pursued legal niceties. Writing Wirt on November 10, 1818, Jefferson repeated his earlier query about the proper court in which he should prove the will and receive authorization for obtaining Kościuszko's funds, held at the time in U.S. bank certificates. But now Jefferson wanted Wirt to know what he had disclosed to Zeltner: that he would not accept the executorship because distributing the assets "will take a longer course of time than I have left of life." But he had engaged Cocke to serve in administering "this sacred and delicate trust disposed of according to the intentions of my dear friend." Above all, Jefferson wanted Wirt to advise him how to transfer the funds to the administrator so as not to make any false step.[26]

Wirt took nearly a year to reply to Jefferson's initial request for advice. When the reply finally came, on January 5, 1819, Jefferson learned that Wirt and Crawford had agreed that the will could be proved in Albemarle County's Superior Court for Jefferson's convenience and that the executor could then withdraw the deceased Pole's funds from the Bank of the United States and use them as the testator provided.[27] In sum, Jefferson was free to prove the will locally.

Jefferson tarried. It took him more than four months to travel the short distance to Charlottesville, where he could prove the will and renounce his executorship. How do we explain such lethargic behavior, especially if the lives of many of Jefferson's slaves, including his mistress and mother of his mulatto children, were at stake? Jefferson himself claimed that he was too frail to pursue the matter. In his letters to Wirt, Crawford, Armstrong, and Zeltner, he explained that the years since he had spent evenings in Philadelphia helping Kościuszko write his will had sapped him of his vigor and brought him to realize that his days were numbered.

To be sure, when he heard of Kościuszko's death, Jefferson was seventy-four and suffering from intestinal disorders and joint stiffness. But Jefferson appeared and acted much younger. He still rode his horse Eagle for two to three hours daily on countryside jaunts, and almost two years later a visiting friend wrote that Jefferson was "strong, active, and in full possession of a sound mind. He rides a trotting horse and sits on him as straight as a young man." As late as 1822, after breaking his arm, he insisted upon his daily horseback rides, leaving visitors amazed at the energy and fast pace with which he toured his property. His hearing and eyesight also remained keen, and his mind was as sharp as ever. Visitors admired the briskness and brilliance of his conversations.[28]

Above all, he wrote constantly, maintaining a correspondence with fellow political figures, including a famed exchange with John Adams that repaired old wounds, and dutifully responding to more than a thousand letters every year. His mind was fully engaged; his commitment to duty was unwavering, at least regarding issues that mattered to him. In fact Jefferson was committing himself to another cause at this very time, and his vigor in pursuing it would have attracted the envy of a man half his age. This was his dream of dreams—the founding of a citadel of higher learning a few scant miles below his mountaintop plantation.

During the days after learning of Kościuszko's death and while lamenting the twilight of his life, Jefferson devoted himself feverishly to the complex politics of creating his "Academical Village," the germ of what was soon to become the University of Virginia. Over the years Jefferson's dream of creating a national university in Virginia had become a personal crusade. In the last months of 1817 he had joyfully joined President James Monroe, former president Madison, and other dignitaries in placing the cornerstone for the first pavilion at what Jefferson called Central College.

Jefferson was supporting the cause of education in other ways as well. With the help of Joseph C. Cabell, his close friend and Virginia legislator, Jefferson drafted bills for establishing elementary public schools, academies, and a university in his beloved Old Dominion. All the while, he worried that Virginia's lawmakers would scoff at the costs of such undertakings as a national depression set in. For a while it appeared that only the elementary schools would survive budget cuts, leaving his pet project, the college, without funds.

By February 1818 it was clear that the battle for the college would be tough, time-consuming, and politically complex. Nonetheless, Jefferson energetically pushed ahead. Although knowing that he had become a lightning rod for criticism of his dream, he worked furiously in assembling data and arguments to neutralize the opposition. Now seventy-five, he rode thirty miles on horseback over two days, accompanied by Madison, to reach Rockfish Gap, where a showdown conference would decide the fate of the university. Full of energy, he presided over the gathering, dominated the proceedings, and achieved his desired result. The man too old to cope with Kościuszko's will had summoned the energy to deal with a far more complex matter—and won the day. The legislature shortly voted to support a state university in Charlottesville, and Jefferson was properly hailed as its father. Aware that the annual grant to the new institution was but $15,000, he pledged his remaining energy and time to making it a living reality.[29]

Though his preoccupation with chartering and building the university contributed to the delay in proving Kościuszko's will, Jefferson was also slowed down because Cocke, the executor he had chosen in late 1818, resigned his position on May 3, 1819. Cocke must have done this with great remorse, for no man commanded his respect and allegiance more than Jefferson. But it is clear from his explanation for quitting that Cocke no longer felt that he could fulfill Jefferson's expectations. Cocke explained that he did so "in the first place from the scarcity of schools about me & 2-ly from the prejudices to me encountered in obtaining admission for negroes— not to mention the effect which might be produced on the minds of

my own people." A day later, Cocke explained how "he declined
administering [the will] on account of some difficulty opposed by
the laws of Virginia, to the charges of the testator."[30]

Cocke's explanation leads to the heart of the matter. His letter indicates that for months he had been trying to find schools in which to
educate slaves in his area, not in Jefferson's county. But soon enough
he encountered hostility from fellow planters in Fluvanna County, to
the southeast of Jefferson's Albemarle County, who learned of
Cocke's plan to educate slaves in preparation for manumission. Also
troubling to Cocke was the thought of how his own slaves would
react at seeing other slaves schooled in preparation for freedom.

There is no way of knowing whose slaves he and Jefferson were
considering as candidates for receiving Kościuszko's largesse, but it
is clear that they were *not* to be their own. Jefferson and Cocke
would certainly have had no trouble finding other plantation owners happy to accept market value for freeing their slaves. All over
Virginia, planters who owned exhausted land were searching for alternatives to what was clearly a losing situation. In Jefferson's Albemarle County, more than a decade before, a visitor portrayed a
"scene of desolation that baffles description," with farms "worn
out, washed and gullied so that scarcely an acre could be found in a
place fit for cultivation." As agriculture in Virginia failed and
planters' debts mounted, slaveowners were ridding themselves of
their slaves at an extraordinary rate. By 1810 the number of free
blacks had grown to about twenty-eight thousand, and in 1819 to
more than thirty-five thousand, about one out of every eight black
Virginians. That number would have been much greater had it not
been for the law passed in 1806 requiring that a person freed from
bondage leave the state within one year or face reenslavement.
However, in 1816, Virginia legislators had bowed to economic, social, and political realities by adjusting that law to allow manumit-
ted people "to petition local courts to exempt them from exile on
the grounds of their 'extraordinary merit' and 'good character.'"[31]

That said, Jefferson certainly knew slaves on his own plantations who could qualify for such exemptions. Indeed, Jefferson's management of his Poplar Forest and Monticello plantations depended on such slaves of "extraordinary merit" and "good character." Why then did Jefferson decide to seek out slaves belonging to other people?

Regardless of whether the slaves belonged to him or to someone else, there was no need to seek out schools for the slaves to be freed in Virginia. Jefferson could easily have freed as many slaves as Kościuszko's bequest allowed for and, in keeping with the terms of the mandate that they be both freed and educated, sent them north to receive an education in Philadelphia. There schools for free blacks had been operating for half a century under the auspices of black churches and the Pennsylvania Abolition Society. Though small, these schools had produced civic-minded black leaders, exactly the kind Kościuszko had envisioned when creating his will.

It seems clear that Jefferson rejected this way of honoring Kościuszko's will for a very specific reason: he did not want to free uneducated slaves (though many of the slaves at Monticello were capable people of steady habits). Both Jefferson and Cocke believed that slaves must be prepared for freedom before emancipation. As early as 1789 Jefferson compared the manumission of uneducated slaves to "abandoning children" because he believed the slovenly habits acquired under slavery could never be erased. Nothing he wrote thereafter suggests that he had changed his mind. But in pursuing his plan to free slaves only after their education, Jefferson was directly violating Kościuszko's mandate to free the slaves first. He was also, however unintentionally, making it impossible to free any slaves at all.[32]

When Cocke wrote in his resignation letter of his "difficulty opposed by the laws of Virginia," he was almost certainly referring to the *Revised Code of the Laws of Virginia* (1819). This code, which consolidated earlier laws passed in 1804, 1805, and 1808, prohibited "all meetings or assemblages of slaves, or free negroes or mulattoes mixing and associating with such slaves at any meeting-house or houses, or any other place or places, in the night or at any school or schools for teaching them reading or writing." Such laws did not prohibit the creation of a school dedicated to teaching free black Virginians, so long as slaves were not involved. But the laws would indeed have prevented Cocke and Jefferson from educating slaves before freeing them in a school setting, though tutoring them individually on one's plantation seemed possible without violating the law. In insisting that slaves not be freed before they had received an education, Jefferson made it impossible to fulfill either component of Kościuszko's mandate.[33]

Having ruled out their own slaves as pioneers for blazing the trail that Kościuszko hoped to lay down, Jefferson and Cocke might have approached slave masters sickened at the ruination of Virginia agriculture who were willing to take compensation for slaves who would be released and then educated—either in Virginia or in the North or West. Cocke does seem to have tried this in his own area, only to be rebuffed by neighboring planters. However, he and Jefferson had specific examples before them demonstrating that Virginia laws, though restrictive, did not block determined planters from freeing and educating their slaves. For example, the Pleasants family of Henrico County, with whom Jefferson had frequent contacts, had been freeing slaves since 1782. Although legal complications delayed the contested manumissions, the Court of Chancery, with the abolition-minded George Wythe presiding, had cleared the way for the manumissions of several hundred Pleasants slaves in 1799. One of Jefferson's cousins, Richard Randolph, as much a part of the Virginia elite as Jefferson, provided another example of how the third president might gratify Kościuszko's fervent desire. Another of George Wythe's protégés, Randolph had penned a will in 1795 that provided for the freedom of his slaves and granted them four hundred acres so they could remain in Virginia as free black farmers. By the time Jefferson learned of Kościuszko's death, it was well-known that the freed Randolph slaves, surrounded by white landowners, were making a modest success of their enclave.[34]

Soon to be governor of Illinois, Edward Coles fulfilled his lifelong dream of ending the curse of slavery by emancipating his bondpeople, an action he hoped Thomas Jefferson would emulate. Mural by unknown artist, 1885, Illinois State House, Springfield, Illinois; photo by Heather Hayes.

Just a month before Cocke had stated insuperable obstacles to fulfilling the role as Kościuszko's executor, Edward Coles, Madison's former secretary and avid abolitionist, had provided still another example of how Jefferson might have grasped the nettle to honor Kościuszko and put into action what he had said so many times was desirable. Returning home from Russia, where he had served as Madison's emissary, Coles acted resolutely to do what he had promised Jefferson in 1814—to free his slaves in such a way

that they might have a decent chance in life. In 1819, after selling
his property in Virginia, packing his possessions, and arranging passage with his twenty-two slaves down the Ohio River, Coles announced to his amazed slaves that they were free. "The effect on
them," wrote Coles, "was electrical. In breathless silence they stood
before me, unable to answer a word, but with countenances beaming with an expression . . . which no language can describe." Reaching Illinois with them, Coles fulfilled his dream of moving from the
slavery-dominated South to what he hoped would be free soil in the
West. There he promised each former slave over age twenty-three
160 acres of land. Later, when he served as governor, Coles would
fight off an attempt to revive slavery in Illinois. But for now he had
blazed a trail for Jefferson and others to follow.[35]

If educating Virginia slaves in preparation for their emancipation
was not possible, if he would not free them and then send them
north, and if he rejected the examples set by Pleasants, Randolph,
Coles, and others, there remained one further possibility. While re-
signing from the executorship, Cocke floated an alternative strategy
for honoring, at least in part, the terms of Kościuszko's will: funnel-
ing the Pole's assets into the American Colonization Society, which
was energetically seeking funds. "I presume the terms of the will give
you no destination that won't admit of your directing the fund to the
accomplishment of the object in the way set forth in the enclosed
paper," Cocke wrote Jefferson. The "paper," it turns out, was the report of Samuel Mills and Ebenezer Burgess, whose reconnoitering
trip to West Africa the year before was meant to pave the way for
sending freed black Americans to their ancestral homeland.[36]

Tempering his resignation, Cocke offered to stay on as executor
if Jefferson would agree to redirect Kościuszko's assets to the ACS
with the proviso that the money was to be used to compensate
slaveowners willing to release slaves who agreed to immigrate to
Africa. Seeking Jefferson's opinion "as to the feasibility of the
scheme of the Colonization Society," Cocke wrote "that could the

Court of Chancery of the state give a new direction to . . . the objects of the colonization society, his objection to administering [Kościuszko's will] would be done away." However, there is no surviving evidence that Jefferson actually considered this option.[37]

With or without a substitute executor of Kościuszko's estate, Jefferson had made up his mind to back out of the trust his Polish friend had placed in him. Just as Cocke's letter of resignation was on its way to him, he wrote his friend that "I [will] prove Kościuszko's will in the district court on Monday and hope that you will relieve me from that task."[38] After Cocke demurred, Jefferson, on May 12, went to the county courthouse himself, where his old friend Archibald Stuart presided over Virginia's eighth circuit court. There he officially unburdened himself of his role as Kościuszko's executor. William Wertenbaker, the court's deputy clerk (whom Jefferson would later appoint as librarian of the University of Virginia in 1824), penned a description of the scene so dramatic that it merits quotation in full:

An illustrious man then and at all times, the observed of all observers, walked into the Court-room. The judge, perceiving that Thomas Jefferson, stately and erect, was standing before him, bowed, and invited him to take a seat upon the bench. To this, Mr. Jefferson replied: "As soon as your Honor shall have leisure to attend to me, I have a matter of business to present to the Court." Immediately, by consent of all parties concerned, the matter then before the Court was then suspended until Mr. Jefferson could be heard. He pulled out of his pocket a paper which he said was the will of his friend, General Tadeusz Kosciuszko; that the will was written in the hand writing of the testator, with which he was well acquainted, and to which fact he was ready to testify on oath. He (Mr. Jefferson) was made executor of the will; but at his time of life it was not in his power to undertake the duties of the office, and that necessity compelled him to decline qualifying. The usual

oath was administered to Mr. Jefferson by the clerk, and the will
was ordered by the Court to be admitted to record.[39]

Such a momentous moment had rarely transpired in the Albemarle County courthouse. The author of the Declaration of Independence, revered Enlightenment figure on both sides of the
Atlantic, former secretary of state under the new nation's first president, and third U.S. president had unceremoniously walked into the
county courthouse on a May morning to relinquish the executorship
of a will drafted by one of the most famous warriors for freedom of
the Western world and to renege on the pledge he made in Philadelphia twenty-one years before. In stepping down from administering
the will of his treasured friend, Jefferson also surrendered the opportunity to free his own children and his mistress, who brought
them into the world, along with dozens of other slaves who toiled
alongside her. All could have gone free at no expense to Jefferson.[40]

The man who had overwhelmed the Rockfish committee assigned to consider the University of Virginia just three years earlier
now relinquished the power to address a central problem of the new
nation. His plans for the university displayed Jefferson's persuasive
powers and illuminated the vast prestige he held among Virginians.
At the courthouse he stood like a diffident yeoman and abandoned
his promise to Kościuszko. "The object of [Kościuszko's] will was
lost," writes Merrill Peterson, the historian who spent his scholarly
life at Jefferson's beloved University of Virginia. "Had Jefferson felt
stronger about the object, he would have ventured the experiment,
despite statutory obstacles and the shortness of years, for the experiment was one he often commended to others and, indeed, one he
may have himself suggested to Kościuszko."[41]

Less than a month after his dramatic appearance in court, Jefferson received a letter that no doubt reassured him that he had made
the right decision in refusing to serve as executor of Kościuszko's
will. Piotr Poletica, the Russian minister to the United States and

previously a visitor at Monticello, wrote him to inquire about yet another claim to Kościuszko's estate. The children of Kościuszko's two sisters, he reported, who now lived in Russian-controlled Poland, were insisting on their rights to their uncle's entire estate. Jefferson replied in a lengthy letter on June 12, 1819, affirming his belief about the validity of the 1798 will and quoting Kościuszko's last letter to him, in which the Pole reminded him of the fixed destination of his American assets.[42]

After receiving Jefferson's account of June 12, Poletica hurried to Monticello to pursue the matter. Jefferson reported his visit to William Short and then his departure on June 21. Six days later, seizing the opportunity to dispense with the burden of executing the will, Jefferson wrote to Wirt. Reviewing the claimants to the will and emphasizing the demands of "foreigners," he sought the attorney general's approval to transfer the will to the federal court in Washington, D.C. He doubted that either Zeltner's family claims or those of the Polish relatives applied to Kościuszko's American property, but it would be up to Armstrong, Zeltner, and the Russian minister to plead their cases in federal court. Jefferson's hands were now washed of the emotion-laden business. It was as if two Polish phantoms, nieces of Kościuszko unknown to Jefferson, had swept onto the stage to rescue the main actor in a morality play where Monticello's master had cast himself in the role of faithless friend. But was he worried that word had reached the ears of his slaves that he had abandoned an opportunity to give many of them their freedom? Masters had been murdered for less than that in the past. We do not know because his slaves' voices are silent in the historical record.[43]

What is known is that Jefferson asked Wirt to become "general Counsel for the trust" and to draw his "compensation . . . from the funds of the testator and that you would advise me in that form." Wirt was a good candidate to do this because he shared many of Jefferson's opinions on slavery and African Americans. He had enjoyed Jefferson's confidence, dating back to 1810, when a private citizen sued the ex-president and Wirt ably defended him. On July 6, the ever faithful Wirt responded, this time promptly, directing Jefferson to send the will and his "relinquishment" to him so that it could be assigned to the Orphans' Court, located in the District of Columbia but governed by the laws of Maryland. He asked if there was "any particular person you would prefer to have appointed [as executor]."[44]

Jefferson did not have anyone immediately in mind to administer Kościuszko's estate. Preoccupied with debt and deeply involved in constructing the first buildings of the University of Virginia, he yet again neglected the matter. In February 1820—seven months after Wirt sent his letter—Jefferson mailed the authenticated will to Wirt. Asking the attorney general to consult with John Barnes, who had managed Kościuszko's estate for more than two decades, Jefferson reaffirmed that Kościuszko had repeated his wish to honor his 1798 will in his letter of September 15, 1817.[45]

Within two weeks of Wirt's receipt of Kościuszko's authenticated will, all of America knew of the tortured disposition of the Pole's bequest. Articles began appearing on March 3, 1820, first in Philadelphia's *Poulson's American Daily Advertiser* and then, over the next few weeks, in several dozen newspapers, even reaching western Massachusetts, where Agrippa Hull would have learned about Kościuszko's bequest from an account in the Pittsfield *Sun*. Some $20,000 from Kościuszko's estate, reported New York's *Daily Advertiser*, was to be used for the purchase of "young female slaves who were to be educated and emancipated," but "the laws of Virginia have prevented the will of Kościuszko being carried into effect." Richmond's *Enquirer*, the only newspaper Jefferson read regularly, reported that the nation's third president was blocked by Virginia's laws that created "difficulties opposed to the wishes of the testator" and that he then had planned to "incorporate the bequest with the funds" of the American Colonization Society.[46]

In all these accounts, the intentions of Kościuszko's will were misreported in three crucial respects while revealing a purported weighty decision of Jefferson's. The newspapers erroneously reported that Jefferson wanted Kościuszko's assets to be given to the ACS, which should use the considerable legacy to purchase the freedom of "young female slaves." This supposed preference of Kościuszko for buying the freedom of young enslaved females was wholly fabricated. At the same time, the newspaper accounts omitted the crucial point that Kościuszko's will gave preference to freeing Jefferson's slaves while also saying nothing about Jefferson's refusal to serve as executor.

These errors and silences appear to have been part of a deliberate campaign waged on Jefferson's behalf. Their source was almost certainly John Hartwell Cocke, who had read his letter to the ACS aloud at a meeting in Washington on January 8, 1820, where he introduced the misrepresentations of the Pole's will. Although the letter itself is now lost, it is quoted extensively in the annual report of the ACS published shortly after the meeting. It is hard to imagine that Cocke rephrased Kościuszko's will for public consumption without Jefferson's consent. Jefferson had himself altered the language of his friend's will only six months before, when he told the Russian minister that Kościuszko wanted his American assets used to purchase "young negroes." In this second retelling by Cocke, the operative clause became "young female slaves." Whether Jefferson was directly involved in the public misrepresentation of Kościuszko's intentions remains unknown.[47]

How Jefferson and Cocke fixed on "young female slaves" as the best candidates for emancipation under the auspices of the ACS is unknown, but it seems likely that this was a strategic decision. In this way, Kościuszko's will would protect the women's yet unborn children, ensuring that their offspring would come into the world liberated. This jibed with the proposal in 1820 of Thomas Mann Randolph, Jefferson's son-in-law and governor of Virginia, to reduce the state's slave population by degrees. Partially spurred by a rumored slave rebellion in Petersburg, Randolph proposed that the state use the tax on slaves to purchase "a fair proportion" of young slaves each year, releasing from bondage "a double proportion of females" over males, in this way arresting the growth of the slave population.[48]

Apart from the significant alteration of Kościuszko's dying wishes, Cocke's letter to the ACS, widely publicized after the annual report reached the newspapers, was phrased so that Jefferson's reputation remained intact, picturing him as a man of good faith who had been thwarted by the laws of his state to honor his old friend. Jefferson's inner turmoil over the entire matter went with him to the grave, for he revealed almost nothing about his personal feelings about reneging on his pledge to his Polish friend, even with his most intimate correspondents.

As Jefferson waited for Wirt to arrange the administration of Kościuszko's estate so the ACS would reap the Pole's largesse, the fiery national controversy over admitting Missouri to the union as a slave state fortified Jefferson's growing attachment to states' rights doctrine that protected slavery. This, in turn, impinged on his thinking about the disposal of the Kościuszko legacy.

By 1819 the nation was once again roiled on the issue of the growth and spread of slavery, with free states and slave states maintaining a shaky political equality in the U.S. Senate. In that year Missouri applied for statehood with an intended constitution that would make slavery lawful. If Missouri came in as a slave state, then the remainder of the Louisiana Purchase might come in as slave states in the future. Jefferson could have spoken out on an amendment introduced by James Tallmadge Jr., a Jeffersonian Republican from New York, which would prohibit carrying any more slaves to Missouri and provide for the release of slaves born after the state was admitted to the union once they reached age twenty-five. Though ten thousand slaves already in Missouri would gain no relief, Tallmadge's amendment nonetheless would set a precedent for a congressionally mandated gradual abolition plan.[49]

Rather than endorse the Tallmadge plan as useful for ending the immediate crisis and potentially solving the national issue of slavery,

Jefferson took a highly defensive stand. Troubled by the fissures in Congress, leery of Supreme Court Chief Justice John Marshall's assertions of federal power, and irritated at how European visitors condemned the American republic for its hypocrisy in maintaining chattel slavery, Jefferson choked at the compromise. For him, it was a terrifying example of how fanatical Northern politicians, in order to dominate the small yeoman farmers (who Jefferson felt resided mostly in the South), were free to bully the Southern states and trample states' rights.

Thoroughly aroused, Jefferson reached out to many about the need to protect the republic as he imagined it. His most famous remark went to John Holmes, a Massachusetts Congressman. The controversy, he wrote, was "like a firebell in the night" that filled him with terror about the American future. "There is no man on earth who would sacrifice more than I would to relieve us from this heavy reproach [slavery] in any practicable way ... if ... a general emancipation and expatriation could be effected; and gradually, and with due sacrifices, I think it might be." But more important than the emancipation of slaves, he contended, were constitutional protections of each state to determine its own future. Thus, for Jefferson, forcing Missouri to plan for gradual emancipation was unconstitutional, while the debate over slavery sapped the bonds between the states. Leaving behind his former opposition to the expansion of slavery, he backed the diffusionist notion that slaves would be better off dispersed throughout the vast trans-Mississippi territories, which would "facilitate their eventual emancipation." Once the cosmopolitan, internationally heralded apostle of universal rights, Jefferson had now become a militant Virginian, elevating property rights and states' rights above the right of African Americans to freedom.[50]

Jefferson's fervent endorsement of states' rights cost him heavily, as men of his own party pelted him in print, sending him into "the deepest political malaise of his entire life." This may partly explain why he did nothing to prod his loyal friend William Wirt to arrange expeditiously the administration of Kościuszko's estate so that the ACS would receive its distribution. Not until July 20, 1821, seventeen months after receiving the Pole's authenticated will from Jefferson, did Wirt find a capable administrator for Kościuszko's American estate—Benjamin Lincoln Lear, a Washington lawyer and son of the well-known diplomat Tobias Lear, who had served as Washington's presidential secretary in Philadelphia.[51]

The record is silent on conversations between Lear and Jefferson in the summer of 1821 about the Kościuszko legacy, but it is clear from a series of letters in September and October of that year that Lear had persuaded Jefferson to endorse the use of the Pole's American assets to create a school for African Americans that would prepare them for a return to Africa. Under this plan the funds, Lear reported to Jefferson, "cannot be appropriated legally to any other purpose . . . [than] for the support of schools." This statement makes it clear that Lear, Wirt, and Jefferson had agreed that emancipating slaves with Kościuszko's money was out of the question, and that using the money for educating black Americans and preparing them for lives in Africa was now the primary goal. Endorsing the plan, Jefferson dispatched the Bank of Columbia certificates and treasury bonds totaling $17,099 to Lear and assured him that he expected the foreign claims on Kościuszko's American estate to be rejected. Nor, he thought, would there be any difficulty in "carrying the trust into execution in this state, nor consequently any danger of public claim on the money."[52]

With this plan agreed upon, Jefferson put the matter aside. Another two years passed before the plan to channel Kościuszko's assets to the American Colonization Society for establishing a Kościuszko School began to move forward. After visiting Jefferson at Monticello in July 1823 to reconfirm the sage's approval, Lear obtained the assistance of Robert Goodloe Harper, a dynamic but mercurial aging revolutionary. Harper had served in the Revolution, imbibed antislavery principles at Princeton after the war, and shifted political orientation from avid Jeffersonian to steadfast Federalist as he established a legal career in the South. Though he vacillated wildly in politics, Harper never wavered in his belief that slavery was a great evil. At the same time he maintained that black Americans, both enslaved and free, were a "useless population . . . which is generally vicious and corrupt," who had to be removed from American society. By 1824 he vowed to devote his remaining years to the education and deportation of slaves. If all went well, the federal government would "provide for the purchase and education of any number, or all, of the children of colour who now are or hereafter shall be born, provided their owners will agree to sell them, and for their transportation at a suitable age to Liberia and other similar settlements."[53]

With Kościuszko's estate dangling like low-hanging fruit, Harper moved to purchase land in Montgomery County, Maryland, halfway between Baltimore and Washington, D.C., for the Kościuszko Seminary Farm. Looking for additional support in June 1824, he addressed Philadelphia merchants, landlords, and lawyers, obfuscating the exact terms of Kościuszko's will, putting a bright face on using the available funds, and shielding Jefferson's decision to resign as executor of the will from coming to light. As reported in the *Philadelphia Recorder*, Harper claimed that the executors of Kościuszko's estate, "owing to debts on the estate, neglected carrying the [Pole's] provision into effect."[54]

Jefferson never suggested that he would offer any of his young slaves for the seminary plan. But his support for it indicates his faith in the American Colonization Society. Satisfied that he had done his best in supporting the aims of the ACS, Jefferson turned his attention to the University of Virginia and the appointment of its faculty.

But later that year he was forced to return to the subject of Kościuszko's bequest when the Kościuszko seminary plan imploded. William Wirt advised Lear not to transfer the Kościuszko funds to

Harper and the ACS. This "compels us to suspend all further proceedings until new resources can be found," Harper wrote New
Haven's Congregational minister, Leonard Bacon. One of the ACS's
key leaders, Eli Ayres, a New Jersey doctor, explained Wirt's decision: "I strongly suppose the Society [ACS] in Washington to be in
the affair of withholding that fund from Harper" because of the
presence in the South of "an intolerable jealousy against elevating
the character of the blacks." Ayres welcomed recent manumissions
by slaveowners in Virginia and Carolina and relished a letter to Lear
from a Georgia widow who offered her slaves to the ACS for emancipation and deportation. But such encouraging signs that might
have helped the Kościuszko Seminary Farm get off to a good start
were for nothing at that point.[55]

The determination to block a plan for black education in the
South, the same situation that John Hartwell Cocke had encountered five years before, reflected the common slaveholders' view that
ignorance was the safeguard of slave docility and the slave system itself. Illiteracy not only distanced slaves from incendiary abolitionist
literature but also allowed slave masters to sidestep "the powerful
equation of literacy with freedom"—the notion that "to read was to
be free." It was a belief that abolitionists and proslavery spokesmen
shared—"that to be a slave was to be kept in ignorance."[56]

Facing this wall of opposition, Lear looked northward to establish a Kościuszko School far from the South. By now Jefferson had
divorced himself from any further involvement in disposing of the
Kościuszko bequest. But washing his hands of the slavery issue
proved more difficult when the beloved Marquis de Lafayette arrived in New York in August 1824, his first visit in forty years, tap-
ping into a deep pool of American affection that bordered on
idolatry. Three months later, on November 4, after an extraordinary series of dinners, effusive celebrations, and parades, where he
was feted in countryside, town, and city by Americans grateful to a
living monument of the American Revolution, Lafayette's en-

tourage, including his son George Washington Lafayette, arrived on Jefferson's doorstep. Escorted by General John Hartwell Cocke, Lafayette approached from Charlottesville, where the "whole place was in gala array in [Lafayette's] honor," as Peter Fossett, then a nine-year-old slave, later recalled. The Jefferson Guards and Virginia militia, made up of schoolboys armed with sharp pointed sticks tipped with pikes, received the French statesman in the town, and they all processed up the hill to Jefferson's retreat. At Monticello, Lafayette and Jefferson fell into each other's arms, sobbing, "My dear Lafayette," "My dear Jefferson." Even the slaves wept at the emotional moment.[57]

The two heroes of the Revolution joined in exuberant festivities at the new University of Virginia, where a huge crowd gathered for a massive dinner. Toasts were raised to Lafayette, to Jefferson, and to the thirteen original states. Recalling the illustrious days in Paris when the French statesman had so ably helped the young republic, Jefferson honored Lafayette by saying that he, as the American emissary in Paris, was the nail and Lafayette had driven it. After such exhausting public celebrations, Jefferson's last in Albemarle County, the men retired to Monticello for rest and conversation.[58]

For eleven days Lafayette stayed at Monticello, sharing meals and earnest conversation with the mansion's master. Lafayette did not hide his bitterness at the growth of slavery and the vast racial gulf that now yawned between whites and blacks. All along his triumphal tour as "the nation's guest," he had made it a point to express solidarity with black Americans. In New York City he had visited the African Free School, and in touring the South he sought out the cabins of slaves and free blacks whom he had known during the Revolution. Just before reaching Monticello, Lafayette had met with James Armistead Lafayette, the Virginia slave who served as a spy and gained his freedom through Lafayette's intercession in 1784. Recalling how black and white men had fought together during the

Revolution, the French celebrity hoped to reconcile the slaveholding republic with the rich hopes of its Revolution.[59]

Speaking openly in the presence of Israel, Jefferson's slave who waited on their tables and stood postilion on his master's carriage, Lafayette lectured Jefferson about the retired president's continued ownership of slaves and his unwillingness to speak out as a revered American leader on the subject. "No man could rightfully hold ownership to his brother man," Lafayette gravely maintained. He had come from France to fight for American independence because he believed "they were fighting for a great and noble principle—the freedom of mankind." Now, decades later, he was grieved "that instead of all being free, a portion were held in bondage." Rebuked, Jefferson contended that slavery should be extinguished but that the proper time had not yet arrived.[60]

It is impossible to know what exactly Jefferson and Lafayette discussed during their two weeks together, but it is almost certain that they spoke of Kościuszko, their deceased mutual friend. Did Jefferson mention the Pole's will, which he had so solemnly pledged to honor a quarter of a century before but had so recently abandoned? We do not know. But Jefferson may well have had a twinge of conscience about Kościuszko's estate when Lafayette pressed his views on human bondage, cudgeling the former president to make a strong stand against slavery.

Lafayette did not soften his displeasure with slavery after Jefferson adopted a defensive posture. The French hero "never missed an opportunity to defend the right *which all men without exception* have to liberty," wrote his secretary, who accompanied him throughout the thirteen-month American pilgrimage. Such forthrightness soon led Virginians to cordon off slaves as the French hero passed through the state from town to town. This became apparent when Lafayette reached Fredericksburg. Slaveowners there were asked to keep their slaves out of sight when the procession made its way through the town, while "all colored people are warned that they are not to appear on any of the streets through which the procession will pass." In Savannah, Georgia, white authorities similarly banned blacks from all celebrations, but that did not stop Lafayette from searching out—after the parade—an old slave he had known nearly half a century before.[61]

After Lafayette's memorable visit, Jefferson stayed abreast of Lear's attempts to use Kościuszko's estate to further the goals of the American Colonization Society. After the decision in 1824 that it was futile to build a school for freed slaves in the South, Lear and the ACS switched their focus to New Jersey, where Presbyterians had earlier planted a small school at Parsippany to train free blacks as African missionaries. Lear found a key ally in the Presbyterian clergyman and politician Theodore Frelinghuysen, a member of and advocate for the ACS. Together they proposed a Kościuszko School in Newark, New Jersey. "One of the principal requisites of the [Kościuszko] will," Lear explained to Jefferson, "is that the slaves shall be purchased and set free," but he considered that his plan accorded with Kościuszko's will "if I can procure them from their masters upon condition of freeing and educating them." Lear would strive to obtain young slaves who would be inexpensive and whose masters were willing to sell. Once educated, it was hoped, many of them would "preach the unsearchable riches of Christ to their heathen brethren [in Africa]—and will yet plant the Cross of Christ in the bosom of that benighted continent."[62]

Lear gave assurances to the ACS that the plans had been vetted and approved by the patriarch of Monticello. No surviving evidence indicates direct communication between Jefferson and Lear since the latter's visit to Monticello in July 1823, but Lear doubtless based his confidence on Jefferson's approval at that time. Jefferson would not, then, have been surprised to read in his favorite newspaper, the *Richmond Enquirer*, on September 5, 1825, that the "Kosciuszko School has lately been formed in Newark, New Jersey," with the comment that the paper's editor had been "authorized to state that this appropriation of the [Kościuszko] fund received the decided approbation of Mr. Jefferson." Unlike Kościuszko, who intended to make a major stroke against slavery with his bequest, Lear had to settle for a small school far away from the areas in which American slaves continued to grow rapidly in number.[63]

His life ebbing in 1825, Jefferson had no further contact with Lear and concerned himself no more with the disposition of the Kościuszko fund. While the University of Virginia remained his abiding passion, he spent much of his remaining energy engaged in last-ditch efforts to stave off creditors. Very few succeeded. An ill-fated lottery scheme failed to raise much money to help pay his debts. By early summer in 1826, Jefferson made his last visits to the university and summoned up enough strength to write John Adams and a few other valued correspondents.

On July 4, 1826, the fiftieth anniversary of the signing of the Declaration of Independence, John Adams and Thomas Jefferson died within hours of each other. While many Americans marveled at the miraculous, simultaneous passing of the two great men, the slaves at Monticello may have held different sentiments. Unlike George Washington, who went to meet his Maker half cleansed of the stain of slavery, Jefferson freed only five enslaved people in his will, all of them members of the Hemings family. Sally Hemings was not one of them. Jefferson pleaded in his will that the newly freed people be allowed to stay in the state. The legislature, respectful of the wishes of the departed president and in no way threatened by such limited emancipation, approved the request so that emancipated members of the Hemings family could support their still-enslaved mother.[64]

Shortly after Jefferson's death, newspapers announced plans for a "school for coloured youth" in New Jersey. Word soon spread of the Kościuszko School, to be named after the "noble champion of Freedom [who] crowned his deeds in the cause of liberty by giving the remuneration due him for service in our revolution to the slaves of our Republic." One such article appeared in the Pittsfield *Sun*, published about twenty miles from Agrippa Hull's Stockbridge residence. The newspaper could easily have reached Grippy, who would thereby have learned of the determination of his old revolutionary officer to help African Americans. If so, he must have thrilled to read: "Yes, our Republic has Slaves, two millions nearly. That some might be rescued from oppression and have their rights, the patriotic Polander whose principles of liberty were too true to be limited by a shade—a color—put the amount owed him by our country in the hands of Mr. Jefferson." Hull could join other Bay Staters who heeded the call of the American Colonization Society to donate money to support the school. In the end it didn't matter because, as we will see, Kościuszko's assets were frozen by new legal complications.

On Monday, January 15, 1827, a bitterly cold morning with snow in the air, planters streamed up the narrow road to Monticello for the beginning of a five-day auction. With the date announced two months before, the crowd was thick. Appetites were whetted by the notice that the hammer would come down on horses and cattle, along with "household furniture, many valuable historical and portrait paintings, busts of marble and plaster of distinguished individuals; one of marble of Thomas Jefferson by Caracci [*sic*]," and Jefferson's polygraph, which for twenty years he used to copy thousands of the letters he wrote. Heightening the tension was the widely circulated announcement that the unfortunate slaves scheduled for the auction block "are believed to be the most valuable for their number ever offered at one time in the state of Virginia."[65]

Thomas Jefferson Randolph, Jefferson's grandson and manager of his grandfather's estates, solemnly witnessed the affair as the brisk bidding began. It was like "a captured village in ancient times when all were sold as slaves," he remembered. Standing on the auction block were 130 "valuable negroes," the living residue of the total of 606 slaves who had toiled during Jefferson's lifetime in five counties where he had owned land.[66] The hammer came down on the "lots" one by one to the highest bidders. Some slaves were sold singly, some as husband and wife, none as complete families so far as the surviving auction receipts indicate.

Could Joe Fossett, Jefferson's invaluable forty-six-year-old blacksmith, take himself from the anvil to witness the auction? Fossett was related to the Hemings clan and was married to Jefferson's favorite cook, noted for her French-Virginian fusion cuisine. By Jefferson's will, Joe would get his freedom on July 4, 1827, six months after the auction. Had Jefferson honored his pledge to Kościuszko, Fossett's wife, Edy, and their eight children—two were infant sons and two others teenage daughters—would have gained their freedom as well. But all of them went under the hammer in at least four separate lots, fetching a total of $1,350. Edy and the two little boys, William and Daniel, became the property of Jesse Scott, which was the best they could hope for, since the light-skinned Scott had been married for more than two decades to Joe Fossett's sister Sally. John R. Jones purchased twelve-year-old Peter. John Winn, a Charlottesville merchant, carried off fifteen-year-old Elizabeth Ann. University of Virginia's Charles Bonnycastle, professor of natural philosophy, who had arrived from England unmarried two years before, bid highest for the comely seventeen-year-old Patsy. No record remains of the purchasers of two other Fossett children. One of them, Peter Fossett, remained a slave for more than twenty years. Sally Hemings, discreetly left unmentioned in Jefferson's will, was apparently withheld from the auction and later quietly freed by Jefferson's daughter, to retire to the rented house in Charlottesville, where her sons, Madison and Eston Hemings, took up life after being freed by their master's will. Four years after Jefferson's death, the federal census taker listed Sally, Eston, and Madison Hemings as whites. Five years later, Sally died at age sixty-two.[67]

Around the nation, newspapers decried the tear-drenched auction. Baltimore's *Niles Register* wished that "Jefferson's slaves had been liberated and removed to the African colony." In the Susquehanna River town of Milton, Pennsylvania, the *State's Advocate* asked how Jefferson, "surely the champion of civil liberty to the American people," left "so many human beings in fetters to be indiscriminately sold to the *highest bidder.*" In biting words, the paper wrote, "Heaven inspired Jefferson with the knowledge 'that all men are created equal.' He was not forgetful—in his last moments he 'commended his soul to God, and his daughter to his country;' but to whom did he commend his wretched slaves?"[68]

Had he witnessed the January auction at Monticello, to be followed by a second sale in 1829, Tadeusz Kościuszko would have shared the dismay of newspaper editors who thought the sordid matter had stained Jefferson's reputation forever. The total proceeds from the 130 slaves, higher than their appraised value, could have been entirely covered by Kościuszko's American estate, which by August 1828 reached $25,516. Mary Jefferson Randolph, Jefferson's granddaughter who several years before had moved to Boston because she and her husband regarded slavery-ridden Virginia as intolerable, declared in a letter to her sister Ellen, "Thank heaven the whole of this dreadful business is over."[69] The auctions at Monticello made moot any possible use of Kościuszko's estate to free the founding father's chattel property, though Jefferson had silently abandoned that promise years before.

Far from the dismal dispersal of Jefferson's human property, Agrippa Hull toiled at his farm in western Massachusetts. Hull was living refutation of Jefferson's doubt that a free black man could survive in the United States. Around the country were innumerable other examples of independent black yeomen, including close neighbors of Jefferson. Having imbibed Kościuszko's revolutionary egalitarianism, Hull had faith in himself, escaping the self-doubt implicit in Jefferson's despair over the potential of blacks.

Every year the Stockbridge tax assessor visited Grippy's Cherry Hill acreage and his small farm along Konkapot Creek to tot up his tax liability. Hull always stood at the top of the small number of black families and ahead of about three of every ten white Stockbridgians. In 1808, the last year of Jefferson's second term as president, Grippy's small orchard of fifteen apple trees still stood; three acres of pasturage and two and a half acres of mowing grass were there to help sustain his horse, a cow, and a few pigs; and the old barn sheltered animals and fodder. Over the next fifteen years Hull increased his property modestly. Sometimes the tax assessor noted an additional horse, or several cows, or a small flock of sheep. Adding to his meager farm income was an annual payment from the town coffers for his work as sexton of the Congregational church. Always brimming with wit and wisdom, he sometimes turned his job of pealing the church bell into a subtle criticism of his fellow citizens. After villagers filed late into the church for evening services one day, Grippy opened the prayer meeting himself: "O Lord, Thou knowest how I comes here and rings de bell and rings de bell, and Thy disciples halt by de way, paying no 'tention to its solemn warning sound."[70]

For Hull, raising and supporting three young children after his wife died sometime between 1803 and 1812 presented challenges far beyond what Jefferson encountered in raising his two motherless daughters. Easing this burden was marriage in 1813 to a woman thirty years his junior. Margaret Timbroke was born in Newport, Rhode Island, in 1789 and had been abandoned in swaddling clothes to a man charged with drowning her. The town hired a Mr.

Ray to support the child, and there she lived until age eighteen, when she came to Stockbridge to live with a Colonel Brown.[71]

Hull married "Peggy" Timbroke in 1813, when she was twenty-four, seven years older than his daughter Charlotte. Peggy soon became as much a fixture as Grippy at weddings and parties of white Stockbridgians. Specializing in root beer, gingerbread, and sugary delectables, she was always "in demand for making the wedding cake for the white families of the town."[72]

In the summer of 1817, just before Kościuszko died, Hull's heart must have leaped upon hearing that Congress was debating a pension to the surviving enlisted men of the Revolution. All of New England buzzed with word of President James Monroe's tour of the Northern states to bind the wounds of a nation divided by the War of 1812 and to promote a pension act to ease the poverty and distress of the aging veterans. Thirty-four years after mustering out of Washington's Continental Army, Grippy was ready, if Congress was willing to pass a pension law, to receive a small stipend for his seventy-four months of service.

Three months before Congress acted on Monroe's proposed pension act, Hull learned that Kościuszko had succumbed to an epidemic of typhoid fever. As American newspapers reported Kościuszko's final days and how all of Europe saluted the incorruptible Pole, Grippy's heavy heart must have found some solace in learning how the officer he had served maintained his humility and generosity to the downtrodden to his last breath.

After it was passed by Congress, Monroe signed the pension bill on March 1, 1818. Aged veterans, clutching discharge papers and other documents, made their way to special courts to apply for a pension. "It is grateful to believe that the few years left to such [men]," wrote Boston's *Weekly Register*, "may be smoothed by the justice of this country. A little while, and no one will remain to tell the story of the revolution." Now fifty-nine, Grippy was among about 3,300 veterans and another 1,700 war widows and orphans who received their pensions. Like all the others, he received a monthly payment of eight dollars. Coming on the eve of the worst depression Americans had ever experienced, it was a welcome, if long overdue, gift from the nation.[73]

Gaining the pension, Grippy shared his satisfaction with a fellow pensioner, the impecunious and blind old black veteran Frank Dunkins, who had enlisted alongside Hull under Captain John Chadwick's company in May 1777 and had boarded with Grippy and his wife since 1814. However, Hull's yearly stipend of ninety-six dollars was short-lived. Beset by fraudulent claims and cost over-runs, the War Department in 1819 stripped from the rolls any pensioner not in dire poverty. Almost exactly twenty-four months after receiving his pension, Hull was dropped from the rolls. Nine months later, he made the 120-mile trip to Boston to appear before a notary public with the help of Stockbridge lawyer Henry Williams Dwight to apply for "a warrant and patent for one hundred acres of land." Unsuccessful in this, Hull would have to wait another eight years to receive his pension.[74]

In the year of Kościuszko's death, Grippy made the largest land purchase of his life—seventy acres of rugged timberland near his Cherry Hill farm. He mortgaged the land to a townsman for seven years to pay the seller. Even after losing his pension, he weathered the severe depression of 1819–22. While Jefferson fell further and further into debt after retiring as president, Hull paid off the mortgage on his seventy-acre timberland while holding fast to his small farms. As late as 1841, Stockbridge's *Weekly Visitor* commended Grippy as a man "free from debt—does not owe a penny" and is "strictly honest in all his dealings with his fellow men."[75]

If Hull's material life was spartan, his village life was not. In 1822, he and his wife, Peggy, celebrated the marriage of their twenty-six-year-old daughter, Charlotte, to Morris Potter from Pittsfield in Stockbridge's Congregational church. Potter's father was part Mohawk and part black, which leads one to imagine that the prospective son-in-law, called a "strong and stalwart husband-man," must have reminded Hull of his upbringing in the village, where Indians were so much a part of community life.[76]

Gaining a son-in-law surely provided some compensation for the loss of Grippy's son James, who died in 1825 at age twenty-seven. It is probably no coincidence that in the same year of his daughter's marriage Grippy joined the Congregational church, during one of the revivals that recurrently struck Stockbridge. Thereafter he was a devout member. "He became hopefully pious, and united with the church," wrote Electa Jones a few years after his death, "evidently enlisting as he had done in the service of his country for better or for worse, as long as life's warfare lasted."[77]

Almost simultaneous with his belated acceptance into the church, he and his wife adopted six-year-old Mary Tilden, whose mother, Betty, toiled as a slave for the Tilden family in New Lebanon, New York, barely five miles from the Massachusetts border. Weary of waiting for New York to give freedom to the dwindling number of slaves, those born to enslaved women who must still remain in bondage until age twenty-one, Mary's mother ran away from her master with her four-year-old daughter. Following a well-trod route of escaped slaves from New York's eastern border to western Massachusetts, Betty Tilden walked across Lebanon Mountain for many days. Probably passing through Pittsfield and Lenox, she finally reached Stockbridge. There she found refuge with the Hulls, who hid her "so that the officers couldn't find her to take her back to Mr. Tilden." Finding work "with some of the good people of the town," Betty paid the Hulls for her daughter's board. The Hulls adopted Mary one year later, just as New York's legislature finally put an end to slavery.[78]

In 1826, the year of Jefferson's death, the War Department began granting pensions to claimants with property not exceeding three hundred dollars in value. Under this administrative ruling Hull reapplied for his annual pension of ninety-six dollars in 1828. But faced with sending in his discharge papers, signed by Washington himself, Grippy balked, fearing they might be lost. "He had rather foregone the pension than lose the discharge," wrote Charles Sedgwick, the son of his former employer. Later that year, Hull and Kościuszko were figuratively reunited. Hull learned that his pension had been granted in recognition of his long service in the Continental Army just as West Pointers erected an impressive monument to the Polish hero of the American Revolution.[79]

EPILOGUE

Long after their deaths, the legacies of Thomas Jefferson and Tadeusz Kościuszko inspired friends of liberty everywhere. Jefferson was rivaled for influence among the founding fathers only by Benjamin Franklin and George Washington; his life and words became touchstones for antebellum Americans who argued on either side of the slavery debate. Defenders of slavery found succor in Jefferson's long-held opinions about black inferiority and his rock-ribbed resistance to any federal attempt to override states' rights in the matter of slavery and its right to exist as the South's principal labor system.

Shortly after the tragedy of the slave auction, Jefferson's descendants began refurbishing his legend. In 1829 Thomas Jefferson Randolph, who since 1815 had managed his grandfather's plantations, published an edition of Jefferson's memoirs, letters, and private diary— or "anas." Designed partly to raise money to pay off the immense debts that had ballooned to more than $100,000 by the time of Jefferson's death, the memoirs quickly became the textbook of republicanism. Ignored by deep-dyed conservatives in New England, the books sold well elsewhere. For adherents to states' rights and, implicitly, the defense of slavery, Jefferson's memoirs became required reading.[1]

Political leaders evoked Jefferson's name and ideas to promote reforms in state and national politics as if he were the fount of wisdom. No better example can be found than in Virginia. Representing the liberal wing of the Virginia legislature, Thomas Jefferson Randolph proposed in 1829 that the state adopt the plan his grandfather had floated in 1824 for the gradual extirpation of slavery. Under this scheme, enslaved children would become property of the state once they reached age twenty-one and then would be colonized outside the United States after their labor had paid for the expenses of their passage. Opponents pointed to Jefferson's own words of doubt in his *Notes on the State of Virginia*, arguing that slavery helped blacks become semicivilized and observing that Jefferson had failed to free his own slaves at his death. Reformers uncovered Jefferson's letter to Edward Coles, in which he had made emancipation the responsibility of the younger generation.

Debate continued but was abruptly halted by Nat Turner's Rebellion in August 1831. The bloody uprising, headed by the charismatic black visionary, shook the Virginia slaveocracy to its roots. Virginia's prolonged debate on what to do about ameliorating slavery ended with the legislature only stiffening the laws to prop up the system of bondage. Never again would Virginia legislators raise the issue of abolition.

For much of the antebellum period, Jefferson's pronouncements on slavery and states' rights became, in the arguments of John C. Calhoun, bulwarks for the doctrine of nullification. The Jefferson that Calhoun prized was the statesman who privileged the protection of Southern mores and slavery over a general emancipation of enslaved Americans. In contrast, African American intellectuals and activists remained steadily critical of Jefferson's views on race and slavery. David Walker's famous *Appeal* was not an isolated condemnation of Jefferson's writing, but was the culmination of years of black disenchantment.[2]

Perhaps more for his valor in Poland than for his service to America, Kościuszko's memory remained alive in the United States as an international freedom fighter. Citizens regularly raised toasts to his memory at July Fourth celebrations, wrote poems in his memory, cited favorite anecdotes, and named schooners, a Hudson River icebreaker, bridges, thoroughbred horses, streets, towns, and counties after him. American newspapers trumpeted a story that Lafayette celebrated Kościuszko's birthday in Paris in 1831, and Americans devoured histories of his revolutionary exploits and worried about the fate of Poland by always linking it to Kościuszko. In 1832 Samuel L. Knapp's historical novel, *The Polish Chiefs: An Historical Romance*, rolled off the press in New York to remind readers about Kościuszko, who "breasted the waves of oppression for the rights of man." In 1838 Knapp published *Tales from the Garden of Kosciuszko*, which made the Polish hero's garden at West Point a major tourist attraction. Along with such popular fare were deeper tributes to Kościuszko's revolutionary zeal, courage, and patriotic selflessness, made all the more relevant by the arrival of Polish exiles in America in 1831. More than a few of these stories appeared in newspapers close to Agrippa Hull's home in Stockbridge, thereby keeping the revolutionary war veteran's memory of Kościuszko alive. For decades after his death, Kościuszko remained in the hearts of Americans.[3]

Kościuszko's financial legacy, however, remained unresolved for decades after his death as competing claimants vied for his estate. Benjamin Lear's plans to use Kościuszko's estate to benefit African Americans were soon thwarted. As Lear prepared to use the Kościuszko fund to support a black school in New Jersey, Kościuszko Armstrong, now an adult and tired of waiting for the bequest he believed was rightfully his, filed suit in 1826 against Lear as executor for the portion of Kościuszko's estate promised him in the Pole's 1806 secondary will.

In court proceedings Lear quoted the letter Kościuszko had written Jefferson just prior to his death in 1817, about the money and how "you know its fixed destination." This statement, Lear contended, was Kościuszko's final word on his estate. Lear argued that Armstrong's will had not been probated by the Orphans' Court or,

as far as he knew, in France. He argued that he therefore had no reason to accept the pleas of the Polish relatives.

With Lear fending off the suit, the case made its way to the U.S.
Supreme Court, which rejected the claims of Armstrong and the Pol-
ish relatives and, on February 27, 1827, remanded the entire affair
back to the Orphans' Court for probate. This action gave the ACS
renewed hope that it would eventually get the money. Kościuszko
Armstrong was undeterred and went on to devise new strategies.
Within the next year he added testimonies from witnesses who saw
Kościuszko swear a will before the American counsel in Paris,
thereby affirming the will and testifying that it had occurred in an
American entity, if not in the actual country.[4]

In August 1829 Armstrong tried a different tack. American
newspapers reported that Armstrong, dissatisfied because Lear refused to give him the bequest of $3,704 plus interest, filed suit to lay
claim to all of the estate. Joining him in this suit were Francis Xavier
Zeltner and Stanislaus Estko, representing Kościuszko's sisters,
Anna and Katarzyna. The claimants contended that the 1798 will
violated contemporary Virginia and Maryland laws that forbade the
education of blacks. This was a clever approach in the wake of Nat
Turner's Rebellion. Frightened by the uprising, the Virginia General
Assembly outlawed meetings of free blacks for the purpose of
preaching or teaching. This measure built upon an 1805 law that
exempted masters of black apprentices from teaching them reading,
writing, and arithmetic. Though the plaintiffs ignored the legality of
the will in 1798, they counted on contemporary animosity among
white Virginians toward black education to win their suit.[5]

It took several years for the case to reach the Supreme Court again.
Lear filed annual statements that demonstrated that the funds were
properly invested and growing. William Wirt remained counsel to the
estate even after Roger Taney succeeded him as U.S. attorney general
in 1829.[6] As the cases traveled through the courts, Lear retained his
hope that the American Colonization Society would receive the funds,

as Jefferson wished. Among Presbyterian luminaries and advocates of the American Colonization Society who listened carefully to Lear's plans were Senator Theodore Frelinghuysen of New Jersey and Francis Scott Key, the composer and brother-in-law of Roger Taney, whose recent appointment as President Andrew Jackson's attorney general owed much to Key's supplications. Sure of the popularity of the proposal, the ACS proudly promoted the Kościuszko School in one of the nation's leading abolitionist magazines.[7]

While news of Kościuszko's will and Lear's plans circulated among Presbyterian proponents of the colonization plan, it is not surprising that African American clerics got wind of it. Among them was the Reverend Samuel Eli Cornish, a New Jersey Presbyterian missionary who in 1827 had founded the nation's first black newspaper, *Freedom's Journal*, in New York City. Devoted to racial uplift, *Freedom's Journal* served as a community billboard, emphasizing the virtues of African Americans to rebut white critics of free blacks and caustically opposing the deportation schemes of the American Colonization Society. Yet Cornish and his allies, who included nearly all the influential blacks of the New York region, had high hopes that Kościuszko's will would fund the proposed black school. "Ten Thousand of the sons of freedom, in this state, soon to be added to our number," wrote Cornish, "will hail the harvest with us." But he argued that the legacy should go not to exporting educated blacks to Liberia but to helping former slaves become their "own masters" within America. Cornish "feared that we shall be defrauded of the money, through a flaw in the instrument." Yet Kościuszko's friendship with African Americans should continue to serve as inspiration: "Let not the WILL, which was in him, be wanting in us for whom he so nobly willed, and with the will we will find the way, and with the way, we shall be sure to find the end, which our father enjoined." While fearing the outcome of the tangled lawsuits, Cornish, like many black antislavery activists throughout the antebellum period, used Kościuszko's legacy as a rallying cry for abolition.[8]

As the case ground through the courts, key participants began to expire. Benjamin Lincoln Lear died in a devastating outbreak of cholera in 1832; William Wirt passed away two years later. At the time of Lear's death, Kościuszko's estate had reached $31,785. Colonel George Bomford, chief of the army ordnance department and a close associate of James Madison and Andrew Jackson, became executor and administrator *de bonis non* (of goods not already administered) of Kościuszko's estate. To protect the interests of the ACS, Theodore Frelinghuysen, a key New Jersey supporter, arranged the appointment of R. S. Coxe to replace Wirt as counsel.[9]

In 1837 the case was rocked yet again—this time by the appearance of an imposter named Henry Lubicz Klimkiewicz, who claimed to be eligible for money from the estate. Because of the distrust emanating from the court cases, Kościuszko's relatives appointed yet another attorney, Major Gaspard Tochman, a veteran of the 1830–31 Polish uprising against Russia. Tochman, ever persistent and faithful to his task, took a number of years to develop his case for the Polish relatives. He used the time to create useful political connections. In July 1847 newspapers in Washington, D.C., announced that Senator Reverdy Johnson and Major Tochman had filed a petition in the Orphans' Court of the District, seeking a show-cause order why Colonel George Bomford, administrator of the estate of Tadeusz Kościuszko, should not immediately distribute what now totaled nearly $50,000 to the Polish heirs of the revolutionary hero (by now, the grandchildren of Kościuszko's sisters).[10]

African Americans continued to follow the case that had promised so much but delivered so little. In 1848 Bostonian abolitionist William C. Nell, who was at work on a book to be titled *The Coloured Patriots of the American Revolution*, contributed an article to Frederick Douglass's newspaper, the *North Star*, in which he reminded the world that Kościuszko had intended the money first entrusted to Jefferson for the education and emancipation of enslaved blacks "to make them better sons and better daughters." His will, said Nell, was a "grateful tribute to the neglected and forgotten colored man," whose plight Kościuszko understood because of the wrongs inflicted upon his country by the Russians. Reiterating Kościuszko's belief that all Americans should be free and equal, Nell admitted that the dreams of the benevolent, plainspoken Pole here had been shattered, leaving black Americans "to stand outside and wait for the crumbs that fall from Liberty's festive board." Regarding Kościuszko as a champion of African American goals, Nell asked bitterly "if any will left to any colored person, had ever been fairly administered by a white person."[11]

Beginning with the news of the petition by Tochman and Johnson in 1847, the *National Era*, an abolitionist newspaper, also reported on the progress of the case, often inserting notices of it alongside coverage of major race-related political disputes. The *National Era* and the *North Star* revived Kościuszko's name during the Hungarian uprising in 1849, reminding readers of Kościuszko's heroism. In articles and poetry, both newspapers invoked Kościuszko's name in glowing tributes to the courage of Kossuth, the Hungarian revolutionary leader. By such use of Kościuszko's legacy, abolitionist newspaper editors linked his dreams of helping black Americans with contemporary battles for the freedom of suppressed nations and serfs in Central and Eastern Europe.[12]

But by 1848 the politics of the abolitionist press had shifted. Coverage of the case included increasingly sympathetic portrayals of Major Tochman and Kościuszko's Polish heirs. Sympathy for the plight of the Poles and Hungarians, despair that African Americans would ever benefit from Kościuszko's estate, and hatred of the methods and goals of the American Colonization Society led the *National Era* to publicize fully the claims of the Polish heirs. Frederick Douglass in particular remarked that the actions of Thomas Jefferson and Benjamin F. Lear had steered use of the money toward the ACS, which Douglass regarded as "an object far enough at variance from the donor's intention."[13]

Meanwhile the case continued in litigation between 1848 and 1851. Tochman and Johnson convinced a circuit court of the District of Columbia that the will benefiting Kościuszko Armstrong was not Kościuszko's last will, clearing the way for consideration of later wills. Two weeks later, on June 26, 1851, a lengthy article in the *National Era* rehearsed the entire case, including the provisions of Kościuszko's 1798 will, and explained how Kościuszko had bequeathed money to Kościuszko Armstrong from his American assets and left to the Zeltners and other European friends over 215,000 French francs. The *National Era*'s coverage indicates the strong interest that abolitionists retained in the fate of Kościuszko's will.[14]

The day of reckoning finally arrived in December 1852, when Chief Justice Roger Taney and the Supreme Court convened to make a final judgment on the case. Taney had been chief justice since Andrew Jackson had appointed him in 1836. Usually a firm advocate of states' rights and a proponent of limited government, Taney veered from his philosophy only in the defense of slavery. In two major cases, *Prigg v. Pennsylvania* (1842) and *Moore v. Illinois* (1852), Taney argued that federal law enabling slave masters to recapture fugitives was superior to any state personal liberty laws. In the case deciding Kościuszko's will, the court focused on whether the 1798 will was still valid, given the later claims. Quickly dismissing the 1798 will, the Supreme Court decreed that the Pole's bequest was void because of "the uncertainty of its dispositions and objects of its bounty." Although the Court based its decision on the existence of multiple and conflicting claims, its reasoning questioned the legitimacy of Kościuszko's emancipation plan. While the decision quoted Kościuszko's 1817 letter to Jefferson stating that "after my death, you know the fixed destination" of the money, Taney and the Court could not fathom how to honor Kościuszko's dying wish to emancipate enslaved blacks or satisfy Jefferson's substitute executors who had tried to implement it, even if circuitously, for many years. Voiding all the wills and declaring Kościuszko's estate intestate, the Court then awarded the entire amount to Kościuszko's Polish descendants. Taney's Court made this deliberation despite the conclusions of a past U.S. secretary of state and attorney general that Jefferson could allot the money as Kościuszko intended. It also ignored Jefferson's conclusion that Zeltner's claim probably had no validity and that Kościuszko Armstrong's bequest was only for a fraction of the estate. Whereas Jefferson had been perhaps unduly cautious, Taney and his Court swept aside previous deliberations. The effect was the same: to disallow Kościuszko's original intentions.[15]

During the cataclysmic events of the 1850s, most of the nation forgot about Kościuszko and his valiant attempt to free Jefferson's slaves. But a few still publicly honored his memory. In a speech on the Kansas-Nebraska Bill of 1854, abolitionist Representative Gerrit Smith, addressing the House of Representatives, excoriated Southern slave power. In his lengthy speech Smith reminded his listeners of the many foreigners who, while opposing slavery, had come to the aid of the United States in its war for independence. Among them was Kościuszko, "at whose fall, freedom shrieked, and who provided in his will, written by himself, that his property in America, should be used by his anti-slavery friend, Thomas Jefferson, in liberating and educating African slaves." Surely, Smith insisted, Kościuszko would not have fought to help give birth to a new nation that would wield its power "on behalf of American slavery." His delicate looks betraying his radical abolitionism, Smith cried out, "How cruel and mean a fraud on those, who fought for American liberty, to use that liberty for establishing and extending American slavery." The Supreme Court's decision about the will did not directly support slavery, but its tone and dismissal of Kościuszko's dreams anticipated Taney's 1857 Dred Scott decision, which exacerbated American tensions and carried the nation one more step down the road to war. For years in Poland, Kościuszko's countrymen held the view that the American Civil War could have been averted if the Polish hero's philanthropic plan had been implemented.[16]

While the Kościuszko will passed through one court after another, Agrippa Hull was steadily building his own legacy within Stock-bridge. By the late 1820s, Hull was advanced in years and slowing in his farmwork. Sorrows as well as joys entered his life. A year after receiving his pension in 1828, Grippy lost his friend of many decades, Elizabeth Freeman (Mumbet). Four doctors visited the venerable lady, finding her alert to the last in her eighty-fifth year and staying up to eleven at night with the doctors. "It beat all, I can tell you," wrote one of them. A month before Freeman died, Catharine Sedgwick visited Mumbet in her "little hut" and wrote of "her faithful friend" finishing a worthy life marked by "a clear mind, strong judgment, a quick and firm decision, an iron resolution, an incorruptible integrity, . . . an unexceptionable fidelity to her engagements, always as she said 'up to the mark,' a strong love of justice stern as Brutus, . . . an astonishing capacity of labor and endurance, . . . and affections stronger than death." Sedgwick's brother Charles wrote the words "Good Mother, farewell" to be inscribed on her tombstone, touching evidence of how she had been at least as much a mother to the brood of Sedgwick children as their deranged natural mother.[17]

The year that Grippy's friend Mumbet died was also the year that David Walker, Boston's fiery free black abolitionist, published his *Appeal to the Colored Citizens of the World*. Born into slavery, Walker had gained his freedom and moved from Charleston, South Carolina, to Boston in the early 1820s, where he was instrumental in forming the Massachusetts General Colored Association in 1828. Grippy was apparently not involved in the growing black abolitionist movement, but unless he was deaf to what people in every part of the country were discussing, he would have heard of Walker's explosive call to arms. In the *Appeal* Walker exhorted African Americans to cast off their passivity and rise up against slavery, lest they add credence to Jefferson's arguments about ineradicable black inferiority—a claim that "in truth injured us more and has been as great a barrier to our emancipation as anything that has ever been advanced against us."

With radical abolitionism surging in the 1830s, fed by Walker's *Appeal* and also by the publication of William Lloyd Garrison's *The Liberator* a year later, Hull studied his conscience and remained a staunch patriot. "He commended efforts for the good of his race, still in bondage," wrote the village historian, but he was "not the man to have taken up arms against the laws of his country which he had fought so long to redeem." Despite his support for keeping the American union intact, Hull favored the harboring of escaped slaves. Referring to the Underground Railroad that was shepherding fugitive Southern slaves toward freedom and safety in the North, Electa Jones remembered that Hull believed, with Moses, that "thou shall not deliver unto his master the servant which is escaped from his master unto thee" and that the runaway slave should be given refuge as "a brother beloved, both in flesh and in the Lord." For the most part, Hull seems to have kept whatever thoughts he may have had about race and slavery limited to bits of folk philosophy he offered up to the people of Stockbridge: "Which is worst—the white black man, or the black white man," Grippy would ask, "to be black outside, or to be black inside?" Or again: "It is not the cover of the book, but what the book contains is the question. Many a good book has dark covers."18

In 1831 Grippy made what was probably his last venture out of Stockbridge. If so, the journey to West Point was a fitting and memorable one. A half century before, he had served with Kościuszko for many months to build the Hudson River fortifications before they went south for the final campaign of the revolutionary war. This time Hull was part of a Stockbridge entourage that visited West Point, now the home of the U.S. Military Academy, which Kościuszko had urged Jefferson to establish. Perhaps Grippy carried with him a few stanzas from the Polish war song that Stockbridge's newspaper had published just before his trip to West Point.

An unknown artist created this oil portrait of Grippy, hanging today in the Stockbridge Public Library. His close-cropped hair thinning and gray, Hull holds a gold-knobbed cane and looks "every whit a man," as his friend Catharine Sedgwick described him. Some local historians in Stockbridge believe the painting was made at West Point when Hull visited there in 1831. Painting of Agrippa Hull, Stockbridge Public Library, Stockbridge, Massachusetts.

> On, hearts of steel; the Russian band are gathering in your
>   native land
> The Cossack's scream has roused the Mother from her dream
> She hears that shout, she knows it well
> Twas raised when Kosciuszko fell
> When Warsaw's streets gave forth a flood of mother's tears
>   and father's blood.[19]

Catharine Sedgwick, who chronicled his visit—as she described it, that of "a pilgrim to a holy shrine"—recounted to the young readers of her *Juvenile Miscellany* that Hull was "slightly bent by the rheumatism, and his locks somewhat grizzled," but beneath his "fleecy locks and black complexion" was "a mind as sagacious as Sancho's [Cervantes's Sancho Panza] and a gift of expression resembling in its point and quaintness that droll sage. He is, however, far superior to Sancho; for with his humor he blends no small portion of the sentiment and delicacy of Sancho's master." He "was one of

The cornerstone of the white marble monument was dedicated on July 4, 1828. Eighty-five years later, Polish Americans contributed money to surmount the monument with a bronze statue of Kościuszko. Among the cadets on a committee to memorialize the West Point hero was Robert E. Lee. Benjamin Latrobe, the architect, suggested an inscription at the monument's base: "Erected by the Corps of Cadets of the USMA. While your river flows and your country exists, no one will be at a loss to understand the Monument, its purpose, and its location." Photograph of Kościuszko monument at West Point Museum, West Point United States Military Academy, West Point, New York.

a large party that included the young, the gay, and the beautiful," wrote Sedgwick, "but he was, as most fitting, the most noticed and honored of them all."[20]

No doubt Hull and the rest of the group visited the Kościuszko monument, erected just a few years before and paid for by West Point cadets who yielded twenty-five cents per month from their slender wages. We can only imagine what raced through Grippy's mind as he gazed at the first sculpted monument to Kościuszko in the world.

And it was Kościuszko the members of the party wanted to hear about. Grippy obliged with pleasure. "If you wish it, young ladies, you shall have a tale; for when it's about the General, love and memory never fail." Then he related the oft-told story of dressing up in Kościuszko's uniform—"his laced coat, his Polish cap, sash, sword and all"—and how he "strutted about, took a book, and stretched myself on the sofa, ordered the servants here and there, and bade one of them bring me a glass of water." Then Kościuszko's return, Grippy's mortification, and the Polish general's open-hearted dismissal of Hull's frolic as a moment to embrace rather than a cause for severe punishment. "He was not a man to enjoy riding on a lame horse," Grippy told the Stockbridgians and, as Catharine Sedgwick recorded the moment, concluded his story of the general, as she had heard it from him many times before in Stockbridge, "by saying, 'he was a lovely man!'"[21]

Following that memorable visit, Agrippa Hull went home. The Stockbridge to which Hull returned in late 1831 was growing slowly but was still a Berkshire village. From 1,540 residents in 1830, it grew to 1,788 in 1840. Stockbridge remained a rural agricultural town, so it is likely that the majority of its black residents were, like Hull, small yeoman farmers who cobbled together an income from crops, animal harvesting, and odd jobs. As he grew older, Agrippa Hull's fortunes were mixed. In 1832 he had to sell most of his mountainous timberland to maintain his family. The tax assessor calculated that his home in the early 1840s was worth about as much as thirty years before. The assessor noted one new change on Grippy's farm. By 1840, at age eighty-one, he had erected a second barn and enlarged his sheepfold. Along with five cows, the most he had ever owned, he had a herd of 128 sheep. For reasons unknown, by 1842 the sheep were gone, and so were several of his cows. Perhaps he was hedging his bets, retreating prudently to what was safe and possible.[22]

By the end of his life, Hull had emerged as a model citizen and something of a village sage. White Stockbridgians held him up as a model for the village's rambunctious youth. In 1831 Catharine Sedgwick described him as "one of the most respectable yeomen of a village in the western part of Massachusetts." In 1841 the local newspaper advised its readers, "if thou art young, imitate this man's example, and you will live many years upon the earth and rejoice in them all." Not only strictly honest and free of debt, "what is more remarkable, he never tasted a drop of ardent spirits. . . . If thou are addicted to the use of strong drink, will you not cease to do evil, and learn, from this man's example, to do well." In the midst of temperance reform, centered in eastern Massachusetts but sweeping west by the 1820s, Hull was a suitable model of a man who harnessed industry to sobriety and lighthearted cheerfulness to community-mindedness.[23]

In the summer of 1844 Francis Parkman, the nation's most famous historian, came across Hull in the yard of the Congregational church after a visit to the Indian burying ground in the village. Finding the "old Negro [who] had been a soldier in W[ashington]'s army" hale and buoyant in his eighty-fifth year, Parkman quickly discovered that Grippy still "remembered all about the Indians" and was trading recollections of them with Oliver Partridge, the octogenarian village doctor and Hull's friend who tended to the burying ground. Noting in his journal that Hull was known as the "African Prince," Parkman settled in to talk with the venerable revolutionary war veteran. Grippy allowed "with a solemn countenance" that "he had four children in the churchyard"—son James had died in 1825, son Aseph in 1836, and two unknown children were apparently buried earlier.

With no grandchildren of his own, Grippy had adopted all the youth of Stockbridge. Parkman scribbled in his journal how the old revolutionary soldier avowed, "But 'these are my children,' stretching his cane over a host of little boys. 'Ah, how much we are consarned to fetch them up well and virtuous.'" Parkman recorded that Grippy was "very philosophical and every remark carried the old patriarch into lengthy orations on virtue and temperance. He looked on himself as father to all Stockbridge." Electa Jones, the village historian, dwelt on the same point: "Never, until the secrets of all hearts are revealed, can the school-boy . . . know how much of his fairness in games, or his safety from the wiles of those older than himself, was in answer to the fervent prayer of this humble servant of God."[24]

Hull's influence spread even beyond Berkshire hill country. The grandson of General John Paterson, writing a half century after Grippy's death, wrote, "As long as he lived, the children and the grandchildren of the officers he had known went frequently to Stockbridge to see him. . . . He would hold the little children on his knees, while the older ones gathered round him. As he grew old, he lived the war over and over again with the children, and would patiently repeat story after story . . . if they wished it." Hull had become one of New England's most venerable links to the revolutionary era. Displaying the Warsaw-manufactured pistol brought from Poland by Kościuszko and a button from the Polish officer's uniform, he spun out his war stories, brightening the day of many and inspiring the youth of the village much as Kościuszko had delighted children four thousand miles away in Soleure, Switzerland.[25]

Self-effacing to his last breath, the man who served as a private in the Continental Army for six years and two months lived out his life on his own terms. In telling the story of impersonating Kościuszko at West Point, he would always say, "From that day to this, I have never tried to play any part but my own." He followed his own moral compass and never reached for more than a modest, honorable place in his society. It was a life less conflicted and compromise-filled than that of the author of the Declaration of Independence, the wartime governor of Virginia, the American minister to France, the vice president, and then president of the United States, the man on a Virginia promontory with thousands of acres and hundreds of enslaved workers answering to his beck and call. It was also a life that the Polish officer he admired and loved would have applauded.[26]

As frost covered the Berkshire mountains in November 1843, Grippy constructed a will. Three white friends witnessed it. He

Margaret Hull, Agrippa Hull's partner of many years, lived in quiet but spare comfort in Stockbridge, where she helped perpetuate his remarkable reputation in local society. Photograph of Margaret ("Peggy") Timbroke Hull, Sedgwick Papers, Massachusetts Historical Society.

named his wife, Peggy, as executor of his will and left her all his worldly possessions—real estate, the weather-beaten cabin, farm animals, "all the wood I may have prepared for the fall," and personal effects. In the event of her remarriage, or after her death, their daughter, Charlotte Potter, was to be the beneficiary.

On May 21, 1848, Agrippa Hull passed away. At the time of his death, he was Stockbridge's last surviving veteran of the American Revolution. His only daughter followed her father to the grave a year later. Why Peggy Hull waited five years after Grippy's death to apply for the monthly pension due to the widows of revolutionary pensioners remains a mystery. Perhaps she was content with home lot and house, an additional twenty-eight acres, and the personal estate of $167.50 that the Stockbridge appraisers of her husband's worldly possessions reported to the probate of wills office.[27]

For twenty-two years the widowed Peggy Hull lived out her life in Stockbridge. Shortly after Grippy's death in 1848, she boarded

Joab Kellis, a Stockbridge-bred black physician, in the small house on Konkapot Brook. Kellis was the grandson of Joab Binney, who had become Grippy's foster father nearly a century before. In 1866, the same year that Kellis died, Mary Hull, the girl she and Grippy had adopted many decades before, came to live with the frail Peggy Hull, now eighty-three, as a caretaker. Peggy had been "made comfortable by a competency left for her few wants" by Agrippa—so went the eulogy published in a nearby newspaper. She was "cared for by devoted kindred of her own color, and respected by everyone, until the flickering lamp of protracted age went out." As respected as her revolutionary war husband, Peggy was remembered by Stockbridgians for her "strong native common sense as well as Christian deportment [that] secured her a warm place in the hearts of all who knew her." On May 15, 1870, she died on the eve of her ninetieth birthday. The Berkshire hills newspaper *Gleaner and Advocate* wrote that the years "had left their infirmities on her wasted frame, but had seemingly ripened her for the better land, where all souls are white in the same garments of imputed righteousness."[28] She was remembered as "a faithful and gentle Christian, in the work of life resolute and cheerful, . . . trusted by parents and loved by children, [and] tenderly remembered by all who knew her."[29]

Thomas Jefferson and Tadeusz Kościuszko remained powerful symbols of freedom in the years after their deaths. In time, Hull too would take his place in local memory, though there was no place for him in the American pantheon, the marbled domain of great white men. His life reminds us that the meaning of freedom and the ways to extend its blessings, in his time and now, take many forms and that many individuals contributed to its creation.

ACKNOWLEDGMENTS

A book that spans the Atlantic and covers so much time could not be written alone. We wish to acknowledge the many contributions of history colleagues and library friends. The staff at innumerable institutions assisted this project. Thanks go to the archivists and librarians at the National Archives in Washington, D.C., and its branch office in Pittsfield, Massachusetts; the Berkshire Athenaeum in Pittsfield, Massachusetts; the Stockbridge (Massachusetts) Public Library; the Stockbridge Town Office; the Massachusetts Historical Society; the American Antiquarian Society; Yale University Library; the New York Public Library; the New-York Historical Society; the Library Company of Philadelphia and the Presbyterian Historical Society in Philadelphia; the Charles Young Research Library at UCLA; and the Thaddeus Kosciuszko National Historic Site in Philadelphia. We also thank the staff of the Thomas Jefferson Papers at Princeton University and Lisa A. Francavilla, managing editor of the *Papers of Thomas Jefferson: Retirement Series*, at the Thomas Jefferson Foundation in Charlottesville, Virginia.

Our heartfelt appreciation goes to several scholars who read full drafts of the manuscript, provided excellent suggestions, and helped us avoid errors. They include Douglas Egerton, Le Moyne College; Peter Onuf, University of Virginia; Barbara Oberg, editor of the Thomas Jefferson Papers at Princeton University; and Brian Porter, University of Michigan. International researchers included Alexandra Ganser, University of Nuremberg; Andrej A. Isserov, Moscow

University; Helene Metz, University of Berne; and Maria Proitsake, University of Stockholm.

Invaluable help on Agrippa Hull and Catharine Sedgwick came from Barbara Allen of the Stockbridge Public Library; James Green of the Library Company in Philadelphia; Emily Piper of Pittsfield; and Laura Lowell and Kimberly Nusco, Massachusetts Historical Society. Lion Miles of Stockbridge was indispensable in unraveling a trail of Agrippa Hull's property transactions and in creating a map of Hull's Stockbridge farm and Elizabeth Freeman's property holdings.

Other scholars who helped with suggestions, translations, and information include Richard Olivas, West Los Angeles College; Alyssa Steppinwall, California State University at San Marcos; Phillip Schwartz, Emeritus of Virginia Commonwealth University; Holly Brewer of North Carolina State University; Robert Nemes, Carol Stevens, and Jill Harsin, Colgate University; Andresz Korbonksi, UCLA; and Robert Gianinni, Independence National Historic Park in Philadelphia. Marian Olivas, National Center for History in the Schools, UCLA, served as website consultant and manuscript format advisor. David Maxey of Philadelphia helped us avoid errors on nineteenth-century law. Nancy Ng Tam and William Hilsman, undergraduate interns at Colgate University, did valuable legwork for this book.

A doff of the hat is owed to Daniel Richter, director of the McNeill Center for Early American History at the University of Pennsylvania, for hosting us at a Friday Afternoon Seminar in March 2007. He, his staff, and the stimulating if critical audience enabled us to sharpen ideas and avoid errors.

Graham Hodges presented excerpts of this book to critical audiences at Peking University, Beijing Foreign Languages University, Ludong University, Dalian University, East China University in Shanghai, Northwest University in Xian, Sichuan University, the University of Macao, the University of Hong Kong, and Jinan University of Guangzhou. He owes thanks for helpful conversations with fellow American Fulbright Scholars in China in 2006–07, including Alan Kulikoff of the University of Georgia, Russell Duncan of the University of Copenhagen, and Mike Urban of the University of Missouri. Chinese scholars who ably critiqued the book include Professors Niu Dayong, Li Jianming, and Wang Lixin of Peking University; Xu Wang of Xiamen University; Gao Chunchang of Ludong University; Zhang Jugou of Nankai University; Zhu Quanhong of East China Normal University in Shanghai; Wen Ren of Sichuan University; Li Cuiyun of Inner Mongolia University, and Wu Jin-ping of Jinan University, along with Hodges's graduate students at Peking University. Hodges is grateful to the Fulbright Foreign Exchange Program for his appointment as Distinguished Fulbright Professor at Peking University in 2006–07.

Much thanks is owed to Lara Heimert, our editor at Basic Books. She believed and invested in this project from the start and worked closely with us throughout. Her scrupulous editing, strong literary critiques, and constant demand for intellectual clarity have shaped and improved this book. We owe much to Brandon Proia and Collin Tracy at Perseus Books Group and Beth Wright of Trio Bookworks as well. Sandy Dijkstra, our agent, proved a true friend during the rough parts of putting this book together. Above all, we owe the most to our wives, Cynthia Shelton and Gao Yunxiang.

NOTES

INTRODUCTION

1. Polish and Polish American biographers of Kościuszko have paid close attention to Kościuszko's friendship with Jefferson, while Jefferson's many biographers have noted it briefly or ignored the relationship altogether. In early biographies of Jefferson, such as William Linn's *Life of Thomas Jefferson* (Ithaca: Mack, Andrus & Woodruff, 1834) and Theodore Dwight's *Character of Thomas Jefferson* (Boston: Weeks, Jordan and Company, 1839), Kościuszko merits no mention, though by 1863 Henry S. Randall noted the Pole's ardent friendship with Jefferson in *The Life of Thomas Jefferson* (New York: Derby & Jackson, 1858). In widely read modern studies such as those by Gilbert Chinard, Nathan Schachner, Saul Padover, Thomas J. Fleming, Willard Sterne Randall, Joseph Ellis, and Garry Wills, Kościuszko never enters the scene. In Dumas Malone's six-volume biography of Jefferson, *Jefferson and His Time* (Boston: Little, Brown, 1948–81), Kościuszko makes cameo appearances.

2. Mikael Dziewanowski's "Tadeuz Kościuszko, Kazimierz Pulaski, and the American War of Independence," in Jaraslaw Pelenki, ed., *The American and European Revolutions, 1776–1848: Sociopolitical and Ideological Aspects; Proceedings of the Second Bicentennial Conference of Polish and American Historians, 29 September–1 October 1976* (Iowa City: University of Iowa Press, 1980), recognizes Kościuszko as a "pioneer of emancipation and a spokesman for racial democracy and justice in eighteenth-century America."

3. Merrill D. Peterson's *The Jefferson Image in the American Mind* (New York: Oxford University Press, 1960) ushered in a new era of Jefferson scholarship. Peterson's *Thomas Jefferson and the New Nation: A Biography* (New York: Oxford University Press, 1970) remains the best single-volume biography of the man. The early biographer quoted is James Parton, *Life of Thomas Jefferson, Third President of the United States* (Boston: J. R. Osgood, 1874).

4. Agrippa Hull appeared in none of the many encyclopedias of American history until a few years ago, when he first surfaced in John A. Garraty and Mark C. Carnes, gen. eds., *American National Biography*, 24 vols. (New York: Oxford University Press, 1999–2002), and in Henry Louis Gates Jr. and Evelyn

Brooks Higginbotham, eds., *African American Lives* (New York: Oxford University Press, 2004). Credit for bringing Hull into public view belongs to Sidney Kaplan and Emma Nogrady Kaplan, whose *The Black Presence in the Era of the American Revolution, 1770–1800* (Greenwich, CT: New York Graphic Society, 1976; rev. ed., Amherst: University of Massachusetts Press, 1989), offered a page and a half of text on Hull along with a full-page reproduction of his portrait in oil.

5. Michel-Rolph Trouillot, *Silencing the Past: Power and the Production of History* (Boston: Beacon Press, 1995), 47.

6. For Jefferson's many biographers, see a "Select Critical Bibliography" in Dumas Malone, *The Sage of Monticello*, vol. 6 of *Jefferson and His Time* (Boston: Little, Brown, 1981; repr., Charlottesville: University of Virginia Press, 2005), 521–35; and Frank Shuffelton, *Thomas Jefferson, 1981–1990: An Annotated Bibliography* (New York: Garland, 1992). To judge by the results of a search using Google, as of August 8, 2006, Jefferson has an unreachable lead over the two other protagonists in this book. About 59,700,000 results are available to inquiring cyber-researchers, and about 50,600 await those interested in Kościuszko, while Hull devotees will receive about 1,070 results.

7. Among the first European biographies of the Polish hero were M. A. Jullien's *Life of Kosciuszko* (Paris, 1823); Constantine Karl Falkenstein's *Tadeusz Kosciuszko* (Paris: F. Didot Freres, 1839); Franciszek Paszkowski, *Dzieje Tadeusza Kosciuszki, Pierwszego Naczelnika Polakow* (Kraŵow: Drukarnia uniwersytetu Jagiellonskiego, 1872); and Tadeusz Korzon, Kościuszko, *Biografia z Dokumentów Wysnuta* (Kraŵow: Nakl. Muzeum Narodowe w Rapperswylu, 1894). Other than brief commemorative treatments, American biographers were led by Miecislaus Haiman, *Kosciuszko in the American Revolution* (New York: Polish Institute of Arts and Sciences in America, 1943), and Miecislaus Haiman, *Kosciuszko: Leader and Exile* (New York: Polish Institute of Arts and Sciences in America, 1946). Recent biographies include James S. Pula, *Thaddeus Kościuszko: The Purest Son of Liberty* (New York: Hippocrene, 1999), and Francis Casimir Kajencki, *Thaddeus Kosciuszko: Military Engineer of the American Revolution* (El Paso, TX: Southwest Polonia, 1998).

CHAPTER 1

1. Thomas Egleston, *The Life of John Paterson, Major-General in the Revolutionary Army, by His Great-Grandson, Thomas Egleston*, rev. ed. (New York: G. P. Putnam's Sons, 1898), 308.

2. Fred Anderson, *The Crucible of War: The Seven Years' War and the Fate of Empire in British North America, 1754–1766* (New York: Vintage Books, 2000), 317–20.

3. Egleston was the great-grandson of Major-General John Paterson, for whom Agrippa Hull served as an orderly for almost two years in the American Revolution. Egleston combed the records of Berkshire County and listened to

stories passed down from revolutionary days in writing his great-grandfather's biography. See Egleston, *Life of Paterson*, v–vii.

4. See William D. Piersen, *Black Yankees: The Development of an Afro-American Subculture in Eighteenth-Century New England* (Amherst: University of Massachusetts Press, 1988), 164, for county population of blacks in 1754 and 1764.

5. George M. Marsden, *Jonathan Edwards: A Life* (New Haven: Yale University Press, 2003), 258; Emilie S. Piper, "The Family of Agrippa Hull," *Berkshire Genealogist* 22 (2001): 3. We are indebted to Richard Olivas, West Los Angeles College, for evaluating the biblical Agrippa and his character.

6. Piper, "Family of Agrippa Hull," 3.

7. Bernard A. Drew, "Joab Benny [Binney] on Evergreen Hill," *Berkshire Eagle*, August 13, 2005, A7; Kenneth P. Minkema, "Jonathan Edwards' Defense of Slavery," *Massachusetts Historical Review* 4 (2002): 43. Edwards presided over the marriage of Rose and Joab in 1751; Electa F. Jones, *Stockbridge, Past and Present; or, Records of an Old Mission Station* (Springfield, MA: S. Bowles, 1854), 238. A blacksmith and tanner, Binney was remembered as "a man of good sense and steady Christian deportment." Rose was admitted to the Stockbridge Congregational Church by Edwards's successor, the Reverend Stephen West, who published an account of her in the *Theological Magazine*, January/February 1797, 191–95, reprinted in Minkema, "Edwards' Defense of Slavery," 45–47; Elias Nason, *A Gazetteer of the State of Massachusetts* (Boston: B. B. Russell, 1874), 278–79; Patrick Frazier, *The Mohicans of Stockbridge* (Lincoln: University of Nebraska Press, 1992). The devastation of the once numerous and proud Mahicans (Frazier uses the alternate spelling "Mohicans") is recounted in chapters 1–9.

8. Kenneth P. Minkema and Harry S. Stout, "The Edwardsean Tradition and the Antislavery Debate," *Journal of American History* 92 (2005): 51; Piper, "Family of Agrippa Hull," 3.

9. Colin G. Calloway, *The American Revolution in Indian Country: Crisis and Diversity in Native American Communities* (Cambridge: Cambridge University Press, 1995), 88–90; Lion G. Miles, "The Red Man Dispossessed: The Williams Family and the Alienation of Indian Land in Stockbridge, Massachusetts, 1737–1818," *New England Quarterly* 47 (1994): 46–76.

10. Piper, "Family of Agrippa Hull," 3.

11. For population, see Ted J. Brasser, *Riding on the Frontier's Crest: Mahican Indian Culture and Culture Change* (Papers in Ethnology Division #13; Ottawa: National Museums of Canada, 1974), 36, cited in Calloway, *American Revolution in Indian Country*, 90–91.

12. Ray Raphael, *The First American Revolution: Before Lexington and Concord* (New York: Norton, 2002), 64; Robert J. Taylor, *Western Massachusetts in the Revolution* (Providence, RI: Brown University Press, 1954), 75, 76.

13. Frazier, *Mohicans of Stockbridge*, 194–98; Calloway, *American Revolution in Indian Country*, 92; Taylor, *Western Massachusetts*, 80–81; Raphael, *First American Revolution*, 205.

14. Benjamin Quarles, *The Negro in the American Revolution* (Chapel Hill: University of North Carolina Press, 1961), 16, 54; Jonathan Smith, "How Massachusetts Raised Her Troops in the Revolution," *Massachusetts Historical Society Proceedings* 55 (1922): 345–70.

15. Jones, *Stockbridge*, 240.

16. One hundred and sixty-two years after Agrippa Hull's enlistment, two great-granddaughters of Stockbridge's famous Theodore Sedgwick described patronizingly how "patriotism even stirred in the breast of Agrippa Hull, the negro servant whom formal Stockbridge [later] employed to serve at banquets." Sarah Cabot Sedgwick and Christina Sedgwick Marquand, *Stockbridge, 1739–1939: A Chronicle* (Great Barrington, MA, 1939), 145; *Massachusetts Soldiers and Sailors of the Revolutionary War*, 17 vols. (Boston, 1896–1908), 8:477. Most Stockbridge men did not sign up until the British unleashed their campaign to capture Fort Ticonderoga in July 1777, and then most men signed up for short periods, often as little as a month or even a week. Charles J. Taylor, *History of Great Barrington, (Berkshire County,) Massachusetts* (Great Barrington, MA: C. W. Bryan, 1882), 248–49; Ray W. Pettengill, trans., *Letters from America, 1776–1779, Being Letters of Brunswick, Hessian, and Waldeck Officers with the British Armies During the Revolution* (Boston: Houghton Mifflin, 1924), 119; Bernard A. Drew, *If They Close the Door on You, Go Through the Window: Origins of the African American Community in Sheffield, Great Barrington, and Stockbridge* (Great Barrington, MA: Attic Press, 2004), 11.

17. Egleston, *Life of Paterson*, 11–14, 50–53; Frazier, *Mohicans of Stockbridge*, 194. A short account of the movements of Paterson's regiment is in Frank A. Gardner, "Colonel John Patterson's [Paterson's] Regiment," *Massachusetts Magazine* 8 (1915): 27–36.

18. Elizabeth A. Fenn, *Pox Americana: The Great Smallpox Epidemic of 1775–82* (New York: Hill and Wang, 2001), 44–55; Egleston, *Life of Paterson*, 57–96. Paterson's regiment of about 600 had been reduced to 220 men by the time they reached Trenton (Egleston, *Life of Paterson*, 66).

19. Gardner, "Patterson's Regiment," 349, 352.

20. Paterson to [Massachusetts] President of Council, May 2, 1777, in Egleston, *Life of Paterson*, 105–6.

21. Thomas W. Baldwin, *The Revolutionary Diary of Colonel Jeduthan Baldwin* (Bangor, ME, 1906), 102, where Baldwin noted his dinner with Colonel Francis Wilkins, Major Hull, General Peterson, and Colonel Kościuszko.

22. James S. Pula, *Thaddeus Kościuszko: The Purest Son of Liberty* (New York: Hippocrene, 1999), 22–23, 36; Miecislaus Haiman, *Kosciuszko in the American Revolution* (New York: Polish Institute of Arts and Sciences in America, 1943), 1–2; Jan Stanislaw Kopczewski, *Kościuszko and Pulaski*, trans. Robert Strybell (Warsaw: Interpress, 1976), 55.

23. This and the next three paragraphs follow Jerzy Lukowski, *Liberty's Folly: The Polish-Lithuanian Commonwealth in the Eighteenth Century, 1697–1795* (London: Routledge, 1991), 12–13, 35–61.

24. Karma Nabulski, *Traditions of War: Occupation, Resistance, and the Law* (New York: Oxford University Press, 1999), 217; Haiman, *Kosciuszko in the American Revolution*, 2.

25. Lukowski, *Liberty's Folly*, 13–18.

26. Nabulski, *Traditions of War*, 221–22; for Linn, see H. C. G. Mathew and Brian Harrison, eds., *Oxford Dictionary of National Biography*, 61 vols. (Oxford: Oxford University Press, 2004), 33:816. The Czartoryski family supplied the core of the school's library of ten thousand volumes, one of Poland's largest; Marian Kukiel, *Czartoryski and European Unity, 1770–1861* (Princeton: Princeton University Press, 1955), 6; Kopczewski, *Kościuszko and Pulaski*, 56–57.

27. Quoted in Pula, *Kościuszko*, 25; for influence of the king and the prosperity of Warsaw see Kopczewski, *Kościuszko and Pulaski*, 55–58. The city grew from about thirty thousand in 1764 to some hundred thousand by the mid-1790s.

28. R. R. Palmer, *The Age of the Democratic Revolution: A Political History of Europe and America, 1760–1800*, 2 vols. (Princeton: Princeton University Press, 1959–64), 1:415.

29. Ibid., 1:411; Pula, *Kościuszko*, 18–20; M. B. Biskupski, *The History of Poland* (Westport, CT: Greenwood Press, 2000), 17.

30. Palmer, *Age of the Democratic Revolution*, 1:416–20.

31. Pula, *Kościuszko*, 26–28; Haiman, *Kosciuszko in the American Revolution*, 2–3.

32. Palmer, *Age of the Democratic Revolution*, 1:30–33, 411–12; Larry Wolff, *Inventing Eastern Europe: The Map of Civilization on the Mind of the Enlightenment* (Stanford: Stanford University Press, 1994), 239.

33. David Brion Davis, *The Problem of Slavery in Western Culture* (Ithaca: Cornell University Press, 1966), 413–17. As a second son, Kościuszko was virtually powerless against his older brother, who held entail over the estate, a right fundamental to gentry rule. Lukowski, *Liberty's Folly*, 174.

34. In *There Are No Slaves in France: The Political Culture of Race and Slavery in the Ancien Régime* (New York: Oxford University Press, 1996), 97–103, Sue Peabody speaks of the "turbulent and ideologically charged atmosphere" in Paris in 1770 and how "arguments for the freedom of slaves . . . took on a new, highly politicized tone"; David Brion Davis, *The Problem of Slavery in the Age of Revolution, 1770–1823* (Ithaca: Cornell University Press, 1975), 48. For Raynal's antislavery campaign, see Davis, *Slavery in Western Culture*, 12–17, 417–21; Lukowski, *Liberty's Folly*, 50–52.

35. Zofia Libiszowska, "Polish Opinion of the American Revolution," *Polish American Studies* 36, no. 1 (1977): 5–16.

36. Kopczewski, *Kościuszko and Pulaski*, 88.

37. Lukowski, *Liberty's Folly*, 197–204; Kopczewski, *Kościuszko and Pulaski*, 95–96; Biskupski, *History of Poland*, 17–18.

38. This and the next three paragraphs follow Pula, *Kościuszko*, 30–38.

39. Ibid., 39–41; Francis Casimir Kajencki, *Thaddeus Kosciuszko: Military Engineer of the American Revolution* (El Paso, TX: Southwest Polonia, 1998), 59–60.

40. Lee, "Address on Slavery," *Virginia Gazette*, March 19, 1767.

41. Paul Finkelman, *Slavery and the Founders: Race and Liberty in the Age of Jefferson*, 2nd ed. (Armonk, NY: M. E. Sharpe, 2001), 113–14.

42. Richard Bland, *The Colonel Dismounted; Or the Rector Vindicated* (1764), quoted in Bernard Bailyn, *The Ideological Origins of the American Revolution* (Cambridge, MA: Belknap Press of Harvard University Press, 1967), 235; Jefferson is quoted in Finkelman, *Slavery and the Founders*, 113.

43. Henry Mayer, *A Son of Thunder: Patrick Henry and the American Revolution* (New York: F. Watts, 1986), 167; for early Virginia slave resistance, see Anthony Parent, *Foul Means: The Formation of a Slave Society in Virginia, 1660–1740* (Chapel Hill: University of North Carolina Press, 2003), chapters 4–5.

44. Stephen B. Weeks, *Southern Quakers and Slavery: A Study in Institutional History* (Baltimore: Johns Hopkins Press, 1896), 214; Paul Finkelman, *The Law of Freedom and Bondage: A Casebook* (New York: Oceana Publications, 1986), 116–23.

45. Gary B. Nash and Jean Soderlund, *Freedom by Degrees: Emancipation in Pennsylvania and Its Aftermath* (New York: Oxford University Press, 1991), 79. Paine's "African Slavery in America" was published in the *Pennsylvania Journal*, March 8, 1775, and was followed by another antislavery essay on October 18.

46. Nash and Soderlund, *Freedom by Degrees*, 80; Samuel Hopkins, *A Dialogue Concerning the Slavery of the Africans* (1776; repr., New York: Arno Press, 1970), 570–71. For a full discussion of Hopkins's Address see Davis, *Slavery in the Age of Revolution*, 290–98.

47. Nash and Soderlund, *Freedom by Degrees*, chapter 3.

48. Pauline Maier, *American Scripture: Making the Declaration of Independence* (New York: Knopf, 1997), 120–22.

49. John Lind, *An Answer to the Declaration of the American Congress* (London: Printed for T. Cadell, J. Walter & T. Sewall, 1776), 107, quoted in Garry Wills, *Inventing America: Jefferson's Declaration of Independence* (New York: Vintage, 1979), 73. For more on Lind's taunting of Americans over slavery, see Christopher Leslie Brown, *Moral Capital: Foundations of British Abolitionism* (Chapel Hill: University of North Carolina Press for the Omohundro Institute of Early American History and Culture, 2006), 130–33, 145.

50. Julian P. Boyd, ed., *Papers of Thomas Jefferson*, 31 vols. (Princeton: Princeton University Press, 1950–2004), 1:130, 353, 363.

51. Robert A. Rutland, ed., *The Papers of George Mason, 1725–1792*, 3 vols. (Chapel Hill: University of North Carolina Press, 1970), 1:277, 289.

52. William James Van Schreeven and Robert L. Scribner, *Revolutionary Virginia: The Road to Independence*, 7 vols. (Charlottesville: University Press of Virginia, 1973–83), 7:454n16.

53. Merrill D. Peterson, *Thomas Jefferson and the New Nation: A Biography* (New York: Oxford University Press, 1970), 110, for first quotation; the second quote is from Jefferson, cited in ibid., 153.

CHAPTER 2

1. Thomas Egleston, *The Life of John Paterson, Major-General in the Revolutionary Army, by His Great-Grandson, Thomas Egleston*, rev. ed. (New York: G. P. Putnam's Sons, 1898), 310.

2. Miecislaus Haiman, *Kosciuszko in the American Revolution* (New York: Polish Institute of Arts and Sciences in America, 1943), 19–21, quoting James Wilkinson, *Memoirs of My Times*, 3 vols. (Philadelphia, 1816), 1:200; Colonel Udney Hay, in letter to George Clinton, August 13, 1777, as quoted in Haiman, *Kosciuszko*, 21.

3. James S. Pula, *Thaddeus Kościuszko: The Purest Son of Liberty* (New York: Hippocrene, 1999), 71–72, borrows the term "labyrinthine hell" from Robert Leckie, *The Wars of America* (New York: Harper & Row, 1968), 170; for a full account of the battle, see Francis Casimir Kajencki, *Thaddeus Kosciuszko: Military Engineer of the American Revolution* (El Paso, TX: Southwest Polonia, 1998), chapter 2.

4. Pula, *Kościuszko*, 77, from Hoffman Nickerson, *The Turning Point of the Revolution, or, Burgoyne in America* (Cranbury, NJ: Scholar's Bookshelf, 2005), 186.

5. George A. Billias, "Horatio Gates: Professional Soldier," in George A. Billias, ed., *George Washington's Generals* (New York: W. Morrow, 1964), 93; testimony of Agrippa Hull in pension file of Stephen Martindale, National Archives, Record Group 15.

6. Quoted in Pula, *Kościuszko*, 100.

7. Egleston, *Life of Paterson*, 140–41, 308. Hull's identification number in Valley Forge National Historic Park database is MA 29655. He is listed in the Fourth Division, John Chadwick commanding, under the Twelfth Massachusetts Regiment of the Second Massachusetts Brigade.

8. James Kirby Martin, ed., *Ordinary Courage: The Revolutionary War Adventures of Joseph Plumb Martin* (St. James, NY: Brandywine, 1993), 62.

9. Louis R. Gottschalk, *Lafayette Joins the American Army* (Chicago: University of Chicago Press, 1937), is the fullest account of this chapter of Lafayette's life.

10. John Laurens to Francis Kinloch, April 12, 1776, quoted in Gregory D. Massey, *John Laurens and the American Revolution* (Columbia: University of South Carolina Press, 2000), 63. Massey details Laurens's early life through the Valley Forge winter in chapters 1–5.

11. For Paterson's involvement in an incipient mutiny, see Wayne Bodle, *The Valley Forge Winter: Civilians and Soldiers in War* (University Park: Pennsylvania State University Press, 2002), 172; Pula, *Kościuszko*, 117–19; Richard K.

Showman, ed., *The Papers of General Nathanael Greene*, 13 vols. (Chapel Hill: University of North Carolina Press, 1976–2005) (hereafter *PNG*). The editors of *PNG* believe that Kościuszko arrived at West Point in March 1778 (5:321).

12. Egleston, *Life of Paterson*, 163–67, for Paterson's role; Laurens's account of the battle is in a letter to his father, June 30, 1778, in Philip M. Hamer et al. eds., *The Papers of Henry Laurens*, 15 vols. (Columbia: University of South Carolina Press, 1968–2003), 13:532–37.

13. Egleston, *Life of Paterson*, chapter 6, relates Paterson's command at West Point; Pula, *Kościuszko*, 109–12, 117–45. The accounts of how Agrippa Hull became Kościuszko's servant have to be combed carefully to extract scattered information about just how, why, and when this happened. The most authoritative source are the military pension records, where great care was taken to verify information given by the veteran applicants before an award was made. However, Hull's application made no mention of his exact assignments in the army, as either Paterson's or Kościuszko's orderly. His pension application states only that at the time of his discharge he was a private in Captain John Chadwick's Company in the Second Massachusetts Regiment of the Massachusetts Line (pension application, June 12, 1828, copy in Stockbridge Public Library, Agrippa Hull file). Yet there is no reason to doubt what many of Stockbridge's most respected citizens told those writing the town's history or biographies of leading townspeople.

14. Electa Jones, Stockbridge's first historian, related that Hull had served Paterson for two years and the remainder of the war "in the service of Kościuszko." Writing while Hull's widow was still alive, Jones was a reliable source. Electa F. Jones, *Stockbridge, Past and Present; or, Records of an Old Mission Station* (Springfield, MA: S. Bowles, 1854), 240. Egleston began his research for a biography of Thomas Paterson, his great-grandfather, three years later. Egleston called Hull a slave who was given to Kościuszko on loan by his great-grandfather, to be returned to Paterson, who freed him after the war. However, Hull's enlistment papers and pension records show that he was free. Egleston, *Life of Paterson*, v–viii, 309–10.

15. William D. Piersen, *Black Yankees: The Development of an Afro-American Subculture in Eighteenth-Century New England* (Amherst: University of Massachusetts Press, 1988), chapter 10.

16. See "Artificers," in Mark M. Boatner III, *Encyclopedia of the American Revolution*, 3rd ed. (Mechanicsburg, PA: Stackpole Books, 1994), 43.

17. Boatner, *Encyclopedia of American Revolution*, 788–93; Lorenzo Greene, "Some Observations on the Black Regiment of Rhode Island in the American Revolution," *Journal of Negro History* 27 (1952): 142–72.

18. Pula, *Kościuszko*, 135–43; Egleston, *Life of Paterson*, chapter 6; Dave Richard Palmer, *The River and the Rock: The History of Fortress West Point, 1775–1783* (New York: Greenwood, 1969), 206–7.

19. Pula, *Kościuszko*, 149–52; Tadeusz Kościuszko to Horatio Gates, March 3, 1779, quoted in Martin I. J. Griffin, "General Tadeusz Kosciuszko," *American*

Catholic Historical Researches, n.s. 6 (1910): 131; Kościuszko to George Washington, August 4 and 7, 1780, quoted in Kajencki, *Kosciuszko*, 117–18.

20. Haiman, *Kosciuszko in the American Revolution*, 99; quote is from Gary B. Nash and Jean Soderlund, *Freedom by Degrees: Emancipation in Pennsylvania and Its Aftermath* (New York: Oxford University Press, 1991), 112.

21. Billias, "Horatio Gates," 100; "A Journal of the Southern Expedition, 1780–1783," *Pennsylvania Magazine of History and Biography* 7 (1893): 287.

22. Boatner, *Encyclopedia of American Revolution*, 169. For Gates's reckless campaign, see Paul David Nelson, *General Horatio Gates: A Biography* (Baton Rouge: Louisiana State University Press, 1976), 218–39.

23. *North Carolina Records*, 14:438, cited in Haiman, *Kosciuszko in the American Revolution*, 102–3; Nathanael Greene to Governor Abner Nash, January 7, 1781; Greene to Washington, January 13, 1781, February 15, 1781, in *PNG* 7:64, 112, 143, 293; "Journal of the Southern Expedition," 287.

24. Sylvia Frey, *Water from the Rock: Black Resistance in a Revolutionary Age* (Princeton: Princeton University Press, 1991), is the best description and analysis of the "triangular war" in the South. André is quoted in Sidney Kaplan and Emma Nogrady Kaplan, *The Black Presence in the Era of the American Revolution, 1770–1800* (Greenwich, CT: New York Graphic Society, 1976; rev. ed., Amherst: University of Massachusetts Press, 1989), 78.

25. Banastre Tarleton, *A History of the Campaigns of 1780 and 1781 in the Southern Provinces of North America* (London, 1787), 89.

26. Frey, *Water from the Rock*, chapter 4; Washington's comment is quoted in Gary B. Nash, *The Unknown American Revolution: The Unruly Birth of Democracy and the Struggle to Create America* (New York: Viking, 2005), 328–29; Massey, *Laurens*, 130–34.

27. Theodore Thayer, *Nathanael Greene: Strategist of the American Revolution* (New York: Twayne, 1960), 290.

28. Boatner, *Encyclopedia of American Revolution*, 1018.

29. See letters from Greene to Kościuszko in *PNG* 6:55, 524, 558–59, 574–75, 580; 7:35–36, 232; for a description of Kościuszko's role in the Battle of Ninety-Six, see *PNG* 9:423–24 and notes.

30. December 28, 1780, and April 15, 1782, in *PNG* 7:9, 9:65; quoted in Robert M. Weir, "'The Violent Spirit,' the Reestablishment of Order, and the Continuity of Leadership in Post-Revolutionary South Carolina," in Ronald Hoffman, Thad W. Tate, and Peter J. Albert, eds., *An Uncivil War: The Southern Backcountry During the American Revolution* (Charlottesville: University Press of Virginia, 1985), 76–77.

31. Kajencki, *Kosciuszko*, 129–30.

32. Thomas Fleming, *Cowpens: "Downright Fighting": The Story of Cowpens* (Washington, D.C.: National Park Service, Department of the Interior, 1988), 58.

33. Boatner, *Encyclopedia of American Revolution*, 297–98.

34. Haiman, *Kosciuszko in the American Revolution*, 111–15; *PNG* 8:324 shows that Kościuszko was near Ninety-Six at Greene's encampment on May 29,

1781. Kościuszko was wounded on June 10 (*PNG* 8:374–75); Greene was still there with Kościuszko on June 20 (*PNG* 8:418–19); a letter from Kościuszko to Gates, July 28, 1781, in Gates Papers, shows that Kościuszko was still in the Ninety-Six district (*PNG* 8:423n3); Boatner, *Encyclopedia of American Revolution*, 805; *PNG* 8:425–26n10, quoting from Roderick Mackenzie, *Strictures on Lt. Col. Tarleton's History of the Campaigns of 1780–1781* (London, 1787), 156; for more on Kościuszko's role in the siege, see *PNG* 8:423–24, 11:101; for black cavalry, see Thomas Parr to Greene, April 27, 1782, in *PNG* 11:127; for black dragoons capturing a Mr. Singleton, see Boatner, *Encyclopedia of American Revolution*, 487n1; for "Coloured Dragoons, all well mounted," in late August 1782, see *PNG* 11:60.

35. Richard Cullen Rath, *How Early America Sounded* (Ithaca: Cornell University Press, 2003), 94–95; Tarleton, *History of Campaigns*, 353–54; Greene to Henry Lee Jr., December 7, 1781, in *PNG* 10:12–13; also pp. 277 and 495 on black spies; and p. 57 for Laurens and his regiment failing to intercept a unit of "British horse" because of the difficulty in obtaining intelligence in the area "peopled for the most part with blacks incapable or unwilling to give information."

36. Greene to Governor Thomas Burke, September 17, 1781, in *PNG* 9:355; Bernard Carmen, "An Uncommon Man's Bicentennial," *Berkshire Courier*, August 15, 1959, puts Hull at Eutaw Springs. Kaplan and Kaplan follow this in *Black Presence*, 43. General Greene wrote to his officers and soldiers the day after the battle that he "conceives himself particularly oblig'd to Col. Koscuzko & Major Forsyth for their voluntary services in the field" (*PNG* 9:306–7); Kajencki, *Kosciuszko*, chapter 9, covers the battle in detail.

37. Colonel Otho H. Williams to Greene, September 16, 1781, in *PNG* 9:353; Dr. James Browne, the officer Agrippa Hull must have served, reported on the wounded to Greene, September 27, 1781; see also Capt. Edward Yarborough to Greene, September 18; Capt. Nathaniel Pendleton to Greene, September 19, in *PNG* 9:401–2, 371, 374–75.

38. Cassandra Pybus, "Jefferson's Faulty Math: The Question of Slave Defections in the American Revolution," *William and Mary Quarterly* 67 (2005): 243–64; for Jefferson and the British invasion of Virginia, see Merrill D. Peterson, *Thomas Jefferson and the New Nation: A Biography* (New York: Oxford University Press, 1970), 203–36.

39. Quoted in Nash, *Unknown American Revolution*, 335; Honyman Diary, June 5, 1781, quoted in Pybus, "Jefferson's Faulty Math," 256. For Jefferson's account of lost slaves, see Edwin Morris Betts, ed., *Thomas Jefferson's Farm Book: With Commentary and Relevant Extracts from Other Writings* (Princeton: Princeton University Press, 1953), 29.

40. Johann von Ewald, *Diary of the American War: A Hessian Journal*, trans. Joseph P. Tustin (New Haven: Yale University Press, 1979), 305, for date.

41. Pybus, "Jefferson's Faulty Math," 252; Lucia Stanton, *Slavery at Monticello* (Charlottesville: Thomas Jefferson Memorial Foundation, 1996), 13.

42. Quoted in Peterson, *Thomas Jefferson and the New Nation*, 242, quoted in Nash, *Unknown American Revolution*, 334–38.

43. Massey, *Laurens*, 202–3, citing Laurens's letter to Washington on December 10, 1781; Greene to Governor John Rutledge, December 9, 1781, in *PNG* 9:22.

44. Massey, *Laurens*, 206–9; *PNG* 10:229–30n4; Greene to Rutledge, January 21, 1782, in *PNG* 10:228–29; Greene pushed the same issue with the Georgia legislature, but, like their South Carolina counterparts, the Georgia lawmakers scorned the proposal (*PNG* 10:506–8, 11:307–9); Pula, *Kościuszko*, 190.

45. Greene to Governor John Mathews, February 11, 1782; Greene to Washington, March 9, 1782, in *PNG* 10:325, 355–56, 471–72; a month later, Greene was still lamenting his men, who were "naked without pay or rum and much discontented" (Greene to Robert R. Livingston, April 12, 1782, in *PNG* 11:35).

46. Haiman, *Kosciuszko in the American Revolution*, 130–35; Pula, *Kościuszko*, 193–97; Massey describes Laurens's nearly suicidal venture and his death at Combahee Ferry on August 27, 1782, in *Laurens*, 225–27; Kościuszko to Greene, September 2, 1782, in *PNG* 11:620; for 1,090 black Carolinians in the Charleston British army, see *PNG* 11:117.

47. Haiman, *Kosciuszko in the American Revolution*, 132–33; Pula, *Kościuszko*, 194; *PNG* 11:680, 12:51; John Markland, "The Revolutionary Service of Capt. John Markland," *Pennsylvania Magazine of History and Biography* 9 (1885): 110–11; Pula, *Kościuszko*, 196–97; *PNG* 12:181, 190–93, for Kościuszko's account of the action and that of two other participants. See also George W. Kyte, "Tadeusz Kosciuszko at the Liberation of Charleston, 1782," *South Carolina Historical Magazine* 84 (1983): 11–21; Alexander Garden, *Anecdotes of the American Revolution*, 3 vols., 2nd ed. (Brooklyn, NY, 1865), 1:79, quoted in Haiman, *Kosciuszko in the American Revolution*, 136.

48. For accounts of the procession, see *PNG* 12:290–93; Joseph Lee Boyle, "The Revolutionary War Diaries of Captain Walter Finney," *South Carolina Historical Magazine* 98 (1997): 148.

49. *PNG* 11:532n7.

50. Pula, *Kościuszko*, 200, quoting Jared Sparks, *Correspondence of the American Revolution*, 4 vols. (Boston: Little, Brown, 1853), 1:72.

51. Jones, *Stockbridge*, 241; Egleston, *Life of Paterson*, 310.

CHAPTER 3

1. "Declaration of Agrippa Hull, April 27, 1818," pension record, M804A, Roll 1363, pp. 0020–0060, National Archives (hereafter NA). Other documents in Hull's pension file confirm this date. For departure from Charleston, see Francis Casimir Kajencki, *Thaddeus Kosciuszko: Military Engineer of the American Revolution* (El Paso, TX: Southwest Polonia, 1998), 177, and Kościuszko to Nathanael Greene, in Metchie J. E. Budka, ed., *Autograph Letters of Thaddeus*

Kosciuszko in the American Revolution: As Well as Those by and About Him (Chicago: Polish Museum of America, 1977), 150, 154. For a full account of the mutiny, see Kenneth R. Bowling, "New Light on the Philadelphia Mutiny of 1783," *Pennsylvania Magazine of History and Biography* 101 (1977): 419–50.

2. Steven Rosswurm, *Arms, Country, and Class: The Philadelphia Militia and the "Lower Sort" during the American Revolution* (New Brunswick, NJ: Rutgers University Press, 1987), 247.

3. Alfred F. Young, *Masquerade: The Life and Times of Deborah Sampson, Continental Soldier* (New York: Knopf, 2004), where Sampson's enlistment and discovery as a woman are fully covered in part 2; Thomas Egleston, *The Life of John Paterson, Major-General in the Revolutionary Army, by His Great-Grandson, Thomas Egleston*, rev. ed. (New York: G. P. Putnam's Sons, 1898), 296–99, for Paterson's three months in the Philadelphia area.

4. Egleston, *Life of Paterson*, 310; Wallace M. West, "Is This Kosciuszko's Pistol?" *Polish Heritage* 46 (1995): 1, 4, 12. Much later, Hull apparently gave the pistol to a friend in Great Barrington, who was the town's first historian; it was passed from there to a family member, then to a buyer at auction, and finally to a gun collector in Sun City Center, Florida, where it rests today.

5. See Electa F. Jones, *Stockbridge, Past and Present; or, Records of an Old Mission Station* (Springfield, MA: S. Bowles, 1854), 40, where she recounts that Hull had spent six years and two months in the Continental Line, which places the date of his discharge in July 1783.

6. James Kirby Martin, ed., *Ordinary Courage: The Revolutionary War Adventures of Joseph Plumb Martin* (Malden, MA: Blackwell, 1993), 160–61; John Shy, ed., *Winding Down: The Revolutionary War Letters of Lieutenant Benjamin Gilbert of Massachusetts, 1780–1783* (Ann Arbor: University of Michigan Press, William L. Clements Library, 1989), 107

7. Revolutionary Claims, July 5, 1828, NA; Martin, ed., *Ordinary Courage*, 162. Historians have generally confirmed Martin's account; see, for example, John Resch, *Suffering Soldiers: Revolutionary War Veterans, Moral Sentiment, and Political Culture in the Early Republic* (Amherst: University of Massachusetts Press, 1999).

8. Bounty Land Warrant Record Card, NA, Warrant #4326. We have not been able to discover why Hull waited until July 1, 1789, to receive his land certificate. Pension applicant, June 1828, File #760, National Archives. For a history of the pension plans, see Resch, *Suffering Soldiers*.

9. Eight years later, Hull petitioned the Court of Common Pleas for help in supporting his mother, whom he had "for many years supported and maintained." Quoted by Emilie S. Piper, "The Family of Agrippa Hull," *Berkshire Genealogist* 22 (2001): 4. For the distressed economy, see Robert J. Taylor, *Western Massachusetts in the Revolution* (Providence, RI: Brown University Press, 1954), chapter 6.

10. Richard E. Welch Jr., *Theodore Sedgwick, Federalist: A Political Portrait* (Middletown, CT: Wesleyan University Press, 1965), chapters 1–2.

11. Arthur C. Chase, *The Ashleys: A Pioneer Berkshire Family* (Beverley, MA: Trustees of Reservations, 1982); Bernard A. Drew, *If They Close the Door on You, Go Through the Window: Origins of the African American Community in Sheffield, Great Barrington, and Stockbridge* (Great Barrington, MA: Attic Press, 2004), 36–40.

12. Theodore Sedgwick, *The Practicability of the Abolition of Slavery: A Lecture Delivered at the Lyceum in Stockbridge, Massachusetts, February 1831* (New York: J. Seymour, 1831), 16; Drew, *If They Close the Door*, 32, for revolutionary service of Bett's husband. Widowed and the mother of a small daughter, Bett is called "spinster" in the first suit, initiated by Sedgwick on May 28, 1781; the record of the case is in James M. Rosenthal, "Free Soil in Berkshire County, 1781," *New England Quarterly* 10 (1937): 783–85. See also Sidney Kaplan and Emma Nogrady Kaplan, *The Black Presence in the Era of the American Revolution, 1770–1800* (Greenwich, CT: New York Graphic Society, 1976; rev. ed., Amherst: University of Massachusetts Press, 1989), 245. Sedgwick's son later called Mrs. Ashley the "shrew untameable."

13. On freedom suit, see Richard E. Welch, "Mumbet and Judge Sedgwick: A Footnote to the Early History of Massachusetts Justice," *Boston Bar Journal* 8 (1964): 13–14; Arthur Zilversmit, "The Abolition of Slavery in Massachusetts," *William and Mary Quarterly* 25 (1968): 620–22; and Elaine MacEacheren, "Emancipation of Slavery in Massachusetts: A Reexamination," *Journal of Negro History* 55 (1970): 290.

14. Catharine Sedgwick describes Elizabeth Freeman and Hull as fellow servants in the Sedgwick house, along with several others. Mary E. Dewey, ed., *Life and Letters of Catherine Sedgwick* (New York: Harper & Bros., 1872), 40–42.

15. For free black life, see Joanne Pope Melish, *Disowning Slavery: Gradual Emancipation and "Race" in New England, 1780–1860* (Ithaca: Cornell University Press, 1998), 84–118.

16. Egleston, *Life of Paterson*, 310. The meeting was recounted much later in stories about Hull: Bernard Carmen, "Bygone Berkshire: An Uncommon Man's Bicentennial," *Berkshire Eagle*, August 15, 1959, 13A; Gerard Chapman, "Agrippa Hull: Stockbridge Immortal," *Berkshire Eagle*, July 15, 1980, 19. Lafayette to President of Continental Congress, February 20, 1778, in Stanley J. Idzerda, ed., *Lafayette in the Age of the American Revolution: Selected Letters and Papers, 1776–1790*, 5 vols. (Ithaca: Cornell University Press, 1977–83), 1:309n; Louis Gottschalk, *Lafayette Joins the American Army* (Chicago: University of Chicago Press, 1937), 149. For Lafayette's itinerary, see Louis Gottschalk, *Lafayette Between the American and the French Revolution (1783–1789)* (Chicago: University of Chicago Press, 1950), chapters 7–10.

17. James Madison to Jefferson, October 17, 1784, quoted in Gottschalk, *Lafayette Between*, 106–7.

18. Liliane Willens, "Lafayette's Emancipation Experiment in French Guiana—1786–1792," in *Studies on Voltaire and the Eighteenth Century*, vol. 242 (Oxford: Oxford University Press, 1986), 349.

19. Patrick Frazier, *The Mohicans of Stockbridge* (Lincoln: University of Nebraska Press, 1992), 16–17, 29–35, 175; Berkshire County Deed Books, Pittsfield Registry of Deeds, Grantee, vol. 19, 452–53 (hereafter PRD).

20. Jones, *Stockbridge*, 241. Jones believed Hull married Darby "not long after the case of Mum Bett had been decided." If this is the case, they deferred having a family for more than a decade. Darby's master was probably Jonathan Ingersoll, who later moved to Stockbridge, where he became a deacon of the First Congregational Church. His genealogy and account books are in Ingersoll Family Papers, Stockbridge Public Library.

21. Leonard L. Richards, *Shays's Rebellion: The American Revolution's Final Battle* (Philadelphia: University of Pennsylvania Press, 2002), 12–15; Taylor, *Western Massachusetts*, 144–45.

22. David P. Szatmary, *Shays' Rebellion: The Making of an Agrarian Insurrection* (Amherst: University of Massachusetts Press, 1980), 102–3; Welch, *Sedgwick*, 49–51. The Battle of West Stockbridge is vividly recreated in Edward Bellamy's *The Duke of Stockbridge: A Romance of Shays' Rebellion* (New York: Silver, Burdett, 1900), chapter 24.

23. Jones, *Stockbridge*, 193–94; other versions are in *The Berkshire Hills*, Federal Writers Project of the U.S. Works Progress Administration for Massachusetts (New York, 1939), 111, and Sarah Cabot Sedgwick and Christina Sedgwick Marquand, *Stockbridge, 1739–1939: A Chronicle* (Great Barrington, MA, 1939), 161–62. Detail is added in Richards, *Shays's Rebellion*, 35–36, and Welch, *Sedgwick*, 49–54.

24. "A Payroll of the Company Turned Out in Alarm at Stockbridge on February 27, 1787," Massachusetts Archives. For accounts of the pillaging of Stockbridge and the final battle near Sheffield, see Jones, *Stockbridge*, 191–94; Richards, *Shays's Rebellion*, 35–36; Szatmary, *Shays' Rebellion*, 110–11; and Welch, *Sedgwick*, 51–55.

25. PRD 28:434–35, 436–47, 437–38, 30:44–45.

26. James S. Pula, *Thaddeus Kościuszko: The Purest Son of Liberty* (New York: Hippocrene, 1999), 203–4; the celebration was described in *Philadelphia Journal*, July 5, 1783.

27. Miecislaus Haiman, *Kosciuszko in the American Revolution* (New York: Polish Institute of Arts and Sciences in America, 1943), 161–62; Pula, *Kościuszko*, 206–7.

28. Theodore Thayer, *Nathanael Greene: Strategist of the American Revolution* (New York: Twayne, 1960), 422; Richard K. Showman, ed., *The Papers of General Nathanael Greene*, 12 vols. (Chapel Hill: University of North Carolina Press, 1976–2005), 13:143n, 161–62, 192–93, 196–97, 319–23, 599. For his two slave plantations, see ibid., 13:219–20. Greene and his family moved to Mulberry Grove, the rice plantation in Georgia, in late 1785, where he would die prematurely six months later at age forty-three.

29. Material on Negro John is in the Archives of the Secret Commission of the Senate of Imperial Russia, Moscow. For his "inseparable companion," see

Columbian Centinel, June 1, 1796, quoted in Miecislaus Haiman, *The Fall of Poland in Contemporary American Opinion* (Chicago: Polish Roman Catholic Union of America, 1932), 232, and in *Philadelphia Gazette and Universal Daily Advertiser*, June 7, 1796. The Warsaw report specified that Negro John "came with him from the United States of America."

30. Kajencki, *Kosciuszko*, 190; Haiman, *Fall of Poland*, 167; on Jefferson and Colonel David Humphreys, see William Howard Adams, *The Paris Years of Thomas Jefferson* (New Haven: Yale University Press, 1997), 47. For James Hemings, see Annette Gordon-Reed, *Thomas Jefferson and Sally Hemings: An American Controversy* (Charlottesville: University Press of Virginia, 1997), 1.

31. Haiman, *Kosciuszko in the American Revolution*, 167; Miecislaus Haiman, *Kosciuszko: Leader and Exile* (New York: Polish Institute of Arts and Sciences in America, 1946), 1.

32. In the vast literature on Kościuszko, historians provide little information on his serfs. Haiman, *Leader and Exile*, 15, mentions "his servants and peasants" at his estate and quotes Kościuszko's letter to his sister about his hopes to free them.

33. Haiman, *Leader and Exile*, 3.

34. Jerzy Lukowski, *Liberty's Folly: The Polish-Lithuanian Commonwealth in the Eighteenth Century, 1697–1795* (London: Routledge, 1991), 111–13.

35. R. R. Palmer, *The Age of the Democratic Revolution: A Political History of Europe and America, 1760–1800*, 2 vols. (Princeton: Princeton University Press, 1959–64), 1:422–24; Norman Davies, *God's Playground: A History of Poland*, 2 vols. (New York: Columbia University Press, 1982), 1:528–30; Jack P. Greene, *Understanding the American Revolution: Issues and Actors* (Charlottesville: University Press of Virginia, 1995), 309–29.

36. Palmer, *Age of the Democratic Revolution*, 1:424.

37. Ibid., 1:426; Zofia Libiszowka, "The Impact of the American Constitution on Polish Political Opinion in the Late Eighteenth Century," in Samuel Fiszman, ed., *Constitution and Reform in Eighteenth-Century Poland* (Bloomington: Indiana University Press, 1997), 233–50.

38. Lukowski, *Liberty's Folly*, 248–49; David Brion Davis, *The Problem of Slavery in the Age of Revolution, 1770–1823* (Ithaca: Cornell University Press, 1975), 92.

39. Palmer, *Age of the Democratic Revolution*, 2:425–29; *Columbian Centinel*, January 4, 1792, excerpted in Haiman, *Fall of Poland*, 55.

40. Haiman, *Leader and Exile*, 5–6.

41. Kościuszko to Michal Zaleski, April 1792, quoted in Pula, *Kościuszko*, 217.

42. Haiman, *Leader and Exile*, 10–11; for fraternization, see chapter 2 in this volume and Caroline Cox, *A Proper Sense of Honor: Service and Sacrifice in George Washington's Army* (Chapel Hill: University of North Carolina Press, 2004), 59–66.

43. Palmer, *Age of the Democratic Revolution*, 2:92; Lukowski, *Liberty's Folly*, 252–55.

44. Quoted in Haiman, *Fall of Poland*, 50–52. The *Western Star*'s coverage of events in Poland was extensive, with five notices appearing in late 1791, seventeen in 1792, fifteen in 1793, and eleven in 1794. For coverage of the Targowica government and the war, see Haiman, *Fall of Poland*, 63–112, and Palmer, *Age of the Democratic Revolution*, 2:92.

45. Palmer, *Age of the Democratic Revolution*, 2:92; Lukowski, *Liberty's Folly*, 254–56.

46. Palmer, *Age of the Democratic Revolution*, 1:433–34, 2:92–93; Lukowski, *Liberty's Folly*, 256–57; Jan Stanislaw Kopczewski, *Kościuszko and Pulaski*, trans. Robert Strybell (Warsaw: Interpress, 1976), 172–73; the quote is from Kościuszko to Felix Potock, September 6, 1792, in Haiman, *Leader and Exile*, 11–12.

47. Quoted in Haiman, *Fall of Poland*, 96; Karma Nabulsi, *Traditions of War: Occupation, Resistance, and the Law* (New York: Oxford University Press, 1999), 214.

48. Pula, *Kościuszko*, 222–25; Haiman, *Leader and Exile*, 13–16; Kopczewski, *Kościuszko and Pulaski*, 174.

49. Haiman, *Leader and Exile*, 3, 15, 17. In leaving Poland, Kościuszko provided that if he died, his sister should inherit his estate and reduce the forced labor of peasants on his estate to two days each year. This put him in the vanguard of serf holders.

50. Kopczewski, *Kościuszko and Pulaski*, 175; Haiman, *Leader and Exile*, 18; Lukowski, *Liberty's Folly*, 257–58.

51. Andrzej Walicki, *The Enlightenment and the Birth of Modern Nationhood: Polish Political Thought from Noble Republicanism to Tadeusz Kosciuszko*, trans. Emma Harris (South Bend, IN: University of Notre Dame Press, 1989), 101–3.

52. Haiman, *Leader and Exile*, 20; Palmer, *Age of the Democratic Revolution*, 2:148–52; Lukowski, *Liberty's Folly*, 260–61.

53. The Manifesto is reprinted in Pula, *Kościuszko*, 307–11. For comments on Kościuszko's dilemma, see Palmer, *Age of the Democratic Revolution*, 2:152–53, and Lukowski, *Liberty's Folly*, 260–62.

54. Lukowski, *Liberty's Folly*, 223n89; quote is from Kopczewski, *Kościuszko and Pulaski*, 177.

55. Hull may have heard of Kościuszko's scrape with death from accounts in seaboard newspapers, such as [Boston] *Columbian Centinel*, January 31, February 7, and April 1, 1795, and *Newport Mercury*, February 8, 1795; the quote is from Stockbridge's *Western Star*, August 7, 1797. Hull possibly heard of the report in newspapers in early February 1795 that "the gallant Kościuszko survived his wounds but a short time; that after his death his head was severed from his body, placed on a pike, and carried through the ranks of the Russian army."

56. Kopczewski, *Kościuszko and Pulaski*, 178–80; Pula, *Kościuszko*, 228–30; on the slaughter of civilians see Palmer, *Age of the Democratic Revolution*, 2:155; J. U. Niemcewicz, *Notes of My Captivity in Russia in the Years 1794, 1795, and 1796* (Edinburgh: W. Tait, 1844), 29–30.

57. *Washington Spy* chronicled Kościuszko's leadership in the issues of July 15; August 14, 19; September 2, 30; November 4, 1794; and January 20, June 23, and November 24, 1795; [Barnabas Bidwell], *An Oration Delivered at the Celebration of American Independence in Stockbridge* (Stockbridge: Loring Andrews, printer, 1795), 10.

58. *Washington Spy*, November 24, 1795; Niemcewicz, *Notes of My Captivity*, 32, 40–48; Pula, *Kościuszko*, 231–34; the notice of Kościuszko's black valet is noted in *Washington Spy*, June 15, 1796, which follows an account from Warsaw dated March 9, 1796.

59. Dumas Malone, *Jefferson the Virginian*, vol. 1. of *Jefferson and His Time* (Boston: Little, Brown, 1948), 396–98; Andrew Burstein, *The Inner Jefferson: Portrait of a Grieving Optimist* (Charlottesville: University Press of Virginia, 1995), 60–63; Fawn M. Brodie, *Thomas Jefferson: An Intimate History* (New York: Norton, 1974), 166–70.

60. Jefferson's draft of a new constitution, written in May and June 1783, is in Julian P. Boyd, ed., *Papers of Thomas Jefferson*, 31 vols. (Princeton: Princeton University Press, 1950–2004), 6:294–305 (hereafter *PTJ*); the clause on slavery is on p. 298; Jefferson to Madison, June 17, 1783, in *PTJ* 6:277–78.

61. Merrill D. Peterson, *Thomas Jefferson and the New Nation: A Biography* (New York: Oxford University Press, 1970), 279–84; Jefferson's quote is on p. 283.

62. Thomas Jefferson, *Notes on the State of Virginia*, ed. William Peden (Chapel Hill: University of North Carolina Press, 1954), vii–xii; Malone, *Jefferson the Virginian*, 373–74.

63. Jefferson, *Notes*, 155; Mason is quoted in Richard K. MacMaster, "Arthur Lee's 'Address on Slavery': An Aspect of Virginia's Struggle to End the Slave Trade, 1765–1774," in *Virginia Magazine of History and Biography* 80 (1972): 151–52n52.

64. Jefferson to Paul Bentalu, August 25, 1786, in *PTJ* 10:296. For slave emancipations in France by administrative order, see Sue Peabody, *There Are No Slaves in France: The Political Culture of Race and Slavery in the Ancien Régime* (New York: Oxford University Press, 1996), 133–35.

65. Adams, *Paris Years*, 11–12; the Lafayette-Jefferson relationship, along with letters between them, can be followed in Gilbert Chinard, ed., *The Letters of Lafayette and Jefferson* (Baltimore: Johns Hopkins Press, 1929); quoted in Jason Lane, *General and Madame de Lafayette: Partners in Liberty's Cause in the American and French Revolutions* (Lanham, MD: Taylor Trade, 2003), 92; quoted in Gottschalk, *Lafayette Between*, 229. Lafayette instituted the purchase of land in French Guiana, a colony with a deeply troubled history. Poorly planned and plagued by excessive heat and a hostile disease climate, the colony had cost the lives of over ten thousand colonists in the previous several decades. Lafayette bought land, hired a manager recommended by Condorcet, and wrote Washington eagerly of his plans, but he did not anticipate immediate emancipation of his slaves, believing that exposure to education and better working

conditions would prepare them for freedom. Harder realities intruded, including raging yellow fever that killed his resident manager. Lafayette turned more of his attention to the unfolding events in France and gave charge of the project to his wife.

66. For Jefferson's friendship with Condorcet, see Adams, *Paris Years*, 134–40; on Condorcet's wide influence on the slavery question, see Richard Popkin, "Condorcet, Abolitionist," in Leonora Cohen Rosenfield, ed., *Condorcet Studies*, 2 vols. (Atlantic Highlands, NJ: Humanities Press, 1984–87), 1:35–48. Jefferson's translation of *Condorcet's Réflexions sur l'esclavage des nègres* is in *PTJ* 14:494–98.

67. Liliane Willens, *Lafayette's Emancipation Experiment in French Guiana, 1786–1792, Studies on Voltaire and the Eighteenth Century 242* (Oxford: Voltaire Foundation, 1986), 345–63; Lloyd Kramer, *Lafayette in Two Worlds: Public Cultures and Personal Identities in an Age of Revolutions* (Chapel Hill: University of North Carolina Press, 1996), 164. On Sharp and the saga of the Black Loyalists, see Graham Russell Hodges, ed., *The Black Loyalist Directory: African Americans in Exile After the American Revolution* (New York: Garland, 1996), passim; Cassandra Pybus, *Epic Journeys of Freedom: Runaway Slaves of the American Revolution and Their Global Quest for Liberty* (Boston: Beacon, 2006), chapters 5, 7, and 9; and Simon Schama, *Rough Crossings: Britain, the Slaves, and the American Revolution* (New York: Ecco, 2006).

68. Jefferson to Chastellux, June 7, 1785, in *PTJ* 8:184; Jefferson repeated all of this to James Monroe and Charles Thomson (*PTJ* 8:229, 245).

69. Richard Price to Jefferson, July 2, 1785; Jefferson to Price, August 7, 1785, in *PTJ* 8:258–59, 356–57.

70. Madison to Washington, November 11, 1785, in W. W. Abbot and Dorothy Twohig, eds., *Papers of George Washington*, Confederation Series, 6 vols. (Charlottesville: University Press of Virginia, 1994), 3:355–56.

71. Jefferson's lengthy interchange with Démeunier is in *PTJ* 10:3–65; quotations on p. 63.

72. Davis, *Problem of Slavery*, 175–76.

73. James Oates, "Why Slaves Can't Read: The Political Significance of Jefferson's Racism," in James Gilreath, ed., *Thomas Jefferson and the Education of a Citizen* (Washington, D.C.: Library of Congress, 1999), 178, 192; Peterson, *Jefferson and the New Nation*, 262.

74. Adams, *Paris Years*, 140; Winthrop D. Jordan, *White over Black: American Attitudes toward the Negro, 1550–1812* (Chapel Hill: University of North Carolina Press for the Institute of Early American History and Culture, 1968), 435.

75. Adams, *Paris Years*, 207–9, 225, 242–47; quote is from Brodie, *Jefferson*, 211.

76. Quobna Ottabah Cugoano, *Thoughts and Sentiments on the Evil of Slavery and Other Writings*, ed. Vincent Carretta (New York: Penguin, 1999). For Cugoano's prominent role among London free blacks and abolitionists, see Stephen Braidwood, *Black Poor and White Philanthropists: London's Blacks and*

the Foundations of the Sierra Leone Settlement, 1786–1791 (Liverpool: Liverpool University Press, 1994). Two years after the publication of Cugoano's book, Richard Cosway supported the publication of Equiano's Interesting Narrative of the Life of Olaudah Equiano.

77. Jefferson to Bancroft, January 26, 1789, in PTJ 14:492–93; Bancroft to Jefferson, September 16, 1788, in PTJ 13:606–8. John C. Miller sees 1788 as the year when "Jefferson's moral revulsion against slavery reached its climax" (Wolf by the Ears: Thomas Jefferson and Slavery [New York: Free Press, 1977], 100).

78. The fullest accounts of Sally Hemings's life are by Gordon-Reed, Jefferson and Hemings, chapter 5, and Lucia Stanton, "Elizabeth Hemings and Her Family," in Free Some Day: The African-American Families at Monticello (Charlottesville: Thomas Jefferson Foundation, 2000), 102–40.

79. Jan Ellen Lewis, "The White Jeffersons," in Jane Lewis and Peter S. Onuf, eds., Sally Hemings and Thomas Jefferson: History, Memory and Civic Culture (Charlottesville: University Press of Virginia, 1999), 127–60.

80. For sale of slaves from 1791 to 1793, see PTJ 22:198–99, 23:33, 116, 253, 255, 24:408–9, 416, 473–74, 25:91, 550–51; Paul Finkelman, "Jefferson and Slavery: 'Treason Against the Hopes of the World,'" in Peter S. Onuf, ed., Jeffersonian Legacies (Charlottesville: University Press of Virginia, 1995), 204–5, and Paul Finkelman, Slavery and the Founders: Race and Liberty in the Age of Jefferson (Armonk, NY: M. E. Sharpe, 1996), 129–31, for the freeing of Robert and James Hemings. For James Hemings's tragic later career see Finkelman, Slavery and the Founders, 160.

81. Philadelphia Freeman's Journal, August 11, 1790. The debate is fully covered in Howard A. Ohline, "Slavery, Economics, and Congressional Politics, 1790," Journal of Southern History 46 (1980): 335–60.

82. Gilbert Imlay, Topographical Description of the Western Territory of North America (London: Printed for J. DeBrett, 1792), quoted in Jordan, White over Black. See also other excerpts from Imlay in Jordan, White over Black, 496–97.

83. General Advertiser, December 28, 1790. Fuller's exploits were lauded in "Account of a Wonderful Talent for Arithmetical Calculation in an African Slave, Living in Virginia," American Museum 5 (1790): 62–63.

84. Quoted in Jordan, White over Black, 451.

85. Ibid., 441, 442, 451–54, quoting from Imlay's A Topographical Description.

86. Banneker's letter was published in Philadelphia in 1792 as "Copy of a Letter from Benjamin Banneker to the Secretary of State with His Answer"; the letter is reprinted in Kaplan and Kaplan, Black Presence, 139–44.

87. All accounts of the Haitian Revolution begin with C. L. R. James's Black Jacobins: Toussaint Louverture and the San Domingo Revolution (New York: Dial, 1938), but the most recent history by Laurent Dubois, Revolution and Slave Emancipation in the French Caribbean, 1787–1804 (Chapel Hill: University of North Carolina Press, 2004), is instructive.

88. Quoted in Jordan, *White over Black*, 378; "Response to the Address of Welcome [in Alexandria]," March 11, 1790, in *PTJ* 16:225.

89. Michael Zuckerman, "The Power of Blackness: Thomas Jefferson and the Revolution in St. Domingue," in *Almost Chosen People: Oblique Biographies in the American Grain* (Berkeley: University of California Press, 1993), 175–218; Rayford Logan, *The Diplomatic Relations of the United States with Haiti, 1776–1891* (Chapel Hill: University of North Carolina Press, 1941); Tim Matthewson, *A Proslavery Foreign Policy: Haitian-American Relations During the Early Republic* (Westport, CT: Praeger, 2003). Jefferson's comment to Monroe, dated July 14, 1793, is in *PTJ* 26:503.

90. Finkelman, *Slavery and the Founding Fathers*, 80–104.

91. Quoted in Peterson, *Jefferson and the New Nation*, 516; Gary B. Nash, *Forging Freedom: The Formation of Philadelphia's Black Community, 1720–1840* (Cambridge: Harvard University Press, 1988), 174–75.

CHAPTER 4

1. Quoted in Fawn M. Brodie, *Thomas Jefferson: An Intimate History* (New York: Norton, 1974), 306–7.

2. Gary B. Nash, *Forging Freedom: The Formation of Philadelphia's Black Community, 1720–1840* (Cambridge: Harvard University Press, 1988), 186–87. The petition is reprinted in Herbert Aptheker, ed., *A Documentary History of the Negro People of the United States*, 2 vols. (New York: Citadel, 1951), 1:40–44.

3. Miecislaus Haiman, *The Fall of Poland in Contemporary American Opinion* (Chicago: Polish Roman Catholic Union of America, 1935), 237.

4. Quoted in Israel Losey White, "Truth About a European Liberalist in America—General Kosciuszko," *Journal of American History* 2 (1908): 370; a slightly different version is in James S. Pula, *Thaddeus Kościuszko: The Purest Son of Liberty* (New York: Hippocrene, 1999), 237.

5. Miecislaus Haiman, *Kosciuszko: Leader and Exile* (New York: Polish Institute of Arts and Sciences in America, 1946), 31–32, for Kościuszko's release. For this quote among many such testimonials, see Haiman, *Fall of Poland*, 230–38. Kościuszko tried to return the czar's flood of rubles in 1798; when the czar refused to accept them, Kościuszko deposited the money in a London bank (Haiman, *Fall of Poland*, 238n7).

6. Niemcewicz mentions the servant three times, as either "Negro John" or "Negro and cook Jean," in the departure from St. Petersburg and later from Stockholm in Julian Niemcewicz, "With Kościuszko Through Sweden," *Acta Sueco-Polonica*, nr 5 (1996): 193–202. We have found no further traces of "Negro John." Kościuszko's passage through Sweden was reported in the United States in the *Tablet of the Times*, May 18, 1797; *Weekly Museum*, July 15, 1797; and *Western Star*, August 7, 1797.

7. For a firsthand account of visiting Kościuszko in Bristol, see Richard Warner, *Literary Recollections*, 2 vols. (London, 1830), 2:132–36. A clergyman

and scientist, Warner found Kościuszko unable to sit upright but still sending "forth a stream of light," indicating "the steady flame of patriotism . . . unquenched by disaster and wounds, weakness, poverty, and exile."

8. Haiman, *Fall of Poland*, 252–55; Pula, *Kościuszko*, 240–41. On Libiszewski see Julian Ursyn Niemcewicz, *Under Their Vine and Fig Tree: Travels Through America in 1797–1799, 1805*, trans. and ed. Metchie J. E. Budka (Elizabeth, NJ: New Jersey Historical Society, 1965), 299n54. *Claypoole's Advertiser*, *Philadelphia Gazette*, and other city newspapers reported Kościuszko's arrival by August 19, 1797.

9. Adam Hochschild, *Bury the Chains: Prophets and Rebels in the Fight to Free an Empire's Slaves* (Boston: Houghton Mifflin, 2005), 185–90, 230–31.

10. Niemcewicz, *Under Their Vine*, 5–11, 295n9; Lyman H. Butterfield, ed., *Letters of Benjamin Rush*, 2 vols. (Princeton: Princeton University Press, 1951), 2:788–89; Haiman, *Leader and Exile*, 47–51; Pula, *Kościuszko*, 241–42.

11. Graham Russell Hodges, *Slavery and Freedom in the Rural North: African Americans in Monmouth County, New Jersey, 1665–1865* (Madison, WI: Madison House, 1997), 114–21; Graham Russell Hodges, *Root and Branch: African Americans in New York and East Jersey, 1613–1863* (Chapel Hill: University of North Carolina Press, 1999), 164, 279.

12. Niemcewicz, *Under Their Vine*, 13; Paul David Nelson, *General Horatio Gates: A Biography* (Baton Rouge: Louisiana State University Press, 1976), 287–88.

13. Winnifred K. Rugg, "Man of Dignity: Agrippa Hull of Stockbridge," *Berkshire Eagle*, May 5, 1950, retold in the *Berkshire Eagle* in 1959 and 1980.

14. Hodges, *Root and Branch*, 166–67, and Shane White, *Somewhat More Independent: The End of Slavery in New York, 1770–1810* (Athens: University of Georgia Press, 1991), 141–47. New York passed a gradual abolition act two years after Kościuszko's visit. Kościuszko must have been puzzled that many members of the Society owned slaves and used them as domestics. The best explanation for this seemingly hypocritical behavior was that younger gentry members of the Manumission Society regarded slave ownership as a perquisite of their rank.

15. Hodges, *Root and Branch*, 174–85.

16. Niemcewicz, *Under Their Vine*, 31; Benjamin Rush to Horatio Gates, August 25, 1797, in Butterfield, ed., *Letters of Rush*, 2:788; Kościuszko to Rush, November 11 and November 13, 1797, in Benjamin Rush Papers, Library Company of Philadelphia.

17. Niemcewicz, *Under Their Vine*, 33, 45; Haiman, *Leader and Exile*, 62–64. The dwelling in which Kościuszko lived is now the Kościuszko National Memorial. Visitors today can step into the second-floor rooms to appreciate the closeness of the Pole's quarters.

18. Philip Hamilton, *The Making and Unmaking of a Revolutionary Family: The Tuckers of Virginia, 1752–1830* (Charlottesville: University Press of Virginia, 2003), 63, 78–80.

19. St. George Tucker to Jeremy Belknap, June 29, 1795, in Massachusetts Historical Society *Collections*, 5th ser., vol. 3 (Boston, 1877), 406.

20. St. George Tucker, "Dissertation on Slavery with a Proposal for the Gradual Abolition of It."

21. Jefferson to Tucker, August 28, 1797, in Julian P. Boyd, ed., *Papers of Thomas Jefferson*, 31 vols. (Princeton, NJ: Princeton University Press, 1950–2004) (hereafter *PTJ*), 29:519.

22. The will is reprinted in Melvin Patrick Levy, *Israel on the Appomattox: A Southern Experiment in Black Freedom from the 1790s Through the Civil War* (New York: Knopf, 2004), 447–49.

23. Jefferson to Martha Jefferson Randolph, December 27, 1797, and February 8, 1798, in *PTJ* 29:596, 30:91.

24. Among scores of Jefferson biographies, most ignore the close relationship. In their magisterial study of the Federalist age, Stanley Elkins and Eric McKitrick make no mention of Kościuszko and the friendship he forged in Philadelphia with Jefferson (*The Age of Federalism* [New York: Oxford University Press, 1993]).

25. "Jefferson by Tadeusz Kosciuszko," in *PTJ* 30:xlii—the drawing follows p. 364; Gaye Wilson, "Thaddeus Kosciuszko, 'Son of Liberty,'" *Monticello Newsletter* 12 (2001): 1–3. When Jefferson was the nation's third president, the bearskin coat was wrapped around the shoulders of Margaret Bayard Smith, a chilled White House guest. Smith noted, "Strange that I, an obscure individual in America, should be wrapped in the same mantle that once enveloped the Czar of Russia—that afterwards long worn by the Hero of Poland and now belongs to one of the greatest men alive."

26. Mathew Carey to Tucker, October 19, 1796, in Lea and Ferbiger Papers, Library Company of Philadelphia. James Green brought this letter to our attention.

27. The *Moniteur* essay was reprinted in *Providence Gazette and Country Journal*, May 20, 1797.

28. Jefferson to Gates, February 21, 1798, in *PTJ* 30:123.

29. Haiman, *Leader and Exile*, 46, 64, 67; for Dombroski and the Poles in Paris, see R. R. Palmer, *The Age of the Democratic Revolution: A Political History of Europe and America, 1760–1800* (2 vols.; Princeton: Princeton University Press, 1964), 1:174; Haiman, *Fall of Poland*, 253; Pula, *Kościuszko*, 249–52. Some Federalists claimed that the money was sent to European banks in Kościuszko's name years before, but it turned out that the sums had long been returned to the United States. Kościuszko regarded what was probably bookkeeping incompetence as a Federalist trick and later urged Jefferson to publish letters detailing the error.

30. Elkins and McKitrick, *Age of Federalism*, 561–75, 590–93, 694–96; Jefferson to Niemcewicz, November 30, 1798, in *PTJ* 30:591; Haiman, *Leader and Exile*, 45, 73–75.

31. For Jefferson-Kościuszko discussions, see Julian Niemcewicz, *Pamietniki Czasow Moich*, ed. Juliana Ursina Niemcewicz (Paris, 1848), 331. For translat-

ing this material we are indebted to Andrej Isserov. For the letter about a passport, see Kościuszko to Jefferson, undated, Massachusetts Historical Society, Jefferson Collection, quoted in Haiman, *Leader and Exile*, 75; *PTJ* 30:194–95.

32. Kościuszko to Jefferson, undated, in Haiman, *Leader and Exile*, 75–76; Pula, *Kościuszko*, 250. The power of attorney, in Jefferson's hand, is in *PTJ* 30:313–14.

33. The original will is in the Jefferson Papers, Massachusetts Historical Society, and is copied from *PTJ* 30:332. A copy of the will is in the Polish National Archives in Warsaw.

34. The second will, dated May 5, 1798, is in *PTJ* 30:332–33.

35. One historian stresses that Jefferson never wavered over the last forty years of his life in believing that slaves were a "captive nation" and that offensive racial mingling, producing children like some of his own, demanded that freed slaves be sent out of the country. The best discussion of this argument is Peter S. Onuf, "Every Generation Is an 'Independant Nation': Colonization, Miscegenation, and the Fate of Jefferson's Children," *William and Mary Quarterly* 57 (2000): 153–70; Tucker, "Dissertation on Slavery," 105.

36. Joanne B. Freeman, *Affairs of Honor: National Politics in the New Republic* (New Haven: Yale University Press, 2001), 247. For the belief of one of Sally Hemings's sons, Madison Hemings, that Jefferson was a man of his word, see Lucia Stanton, "Jefferson Through the Eyes of His Slaves," *William and Mary Quarterly* 57 (2000): 142.

37. For the fur wrap, see *PTJ* 30:331n; for the West watercolor, see Susan R. Stein, *The Worlds of Jefferson at Monticello* (New York: Abrams, 1993), 150.

38. Niemcewicz, *Under Their Vine*, 65–66; James A. Bear Jr. and Lucia C. Stanton, eds., *Jefferson's Memorandum Books: Accounts, with Legal Records and Miscellany, 1767–1826*, 2 vols. (Princeton: Princeton University Press, 1997), 2:981–83; Haiman, *Leader and Exile*, 73–83; Pula, *Kościuszko*, 252; [Portsmouth, New Hampshire] *Oracle of the Day*, November 24, 1798.

39. Niemcewicz, *Under Their Vine*, 84–85, 100–101.

40. Jefferson to Kościuszko, May 7, 1800, in *PTJ* 31:560.

41. Jefferson to Kościuszko, May 30, 1798, in *PTJ* 30:376–77. On a visit to Monticello in 1796, Volney was shocked at the condition of Jefferson's slaves: "demi-nudité misérable et hideuse." Quoted in Michael Knox Beran, *Jefferson's Demons: Portrait of a Restless Mind* (New York: Free Press, 2003), 127.

42. William Short to Jefferson, February 27, 1798, in *PTJ* 30:146–53; George Green Shackelford, *Jefferson's Adoptive Son: The Life of William Short, 1759–1848* (Lexington: University Press of Kentucky, 1993), chapter 1; Andrew Burstein, *The Inner Jefferson: Portrait of a Grieving Optimist* (Charlottesville: University Press of Virginia, 1995), 156–57.

43. Short's appeal to Jefferson and his plan to use free labor in Virginia is rarely mentioned by Jefferson biographers. Even Short's biographer ignores it.

44. Short to Jefferson, August 6 and August 24, 1798, in *PTJ* 30:473–82, 487–96, especially p. 493, where Short spells out how he wished to have tenanted

land distant from areas where slave labor was used or located so that he was not surrounded by slaves.

45. Martyn Lyons, *France Under the Directory* (Cambridge: Cambridge University Press, 1975), 204–10; Palmer, *Age of Democratic Revolution*, 2:334, 336.

46. For the Polish Legions sent to Haiti, see Jan Pachonski and Reuel K. Wilson, *Poland's Caribbean Tragedy: A Study of Polish Legions in the Haitian War of Independence, 1802–1803* (New York: Columbia University Press, 1986).

47. Haiman, *Leader and Exile*, 102.

48. Ibid., 100–103.

49. [John Linn], *Serious Considerations on the Election of a President* (New York, 1800), 12–13, quoted in Anthony Alfred Iaccarino, "Virginia and the National Contest over Slavery in the Early Republic, 1780–1833" (PhD diss., University of California, Los Angeles, 1999), 99.

50. The fullest treatment of Gabriel's conspiracy is Douglas R. Egerton, *Gabriel's Rebellion: The Virginia Slave Conspiracies, 1800–1802* (Chapel Hill: University of North Carolina, 1993)—the quoted passages are from p. 65; see also Gerald Mullins, *Flight and Rebellion: Slave Resistance in Eighteenth-Century Virginia* (New York: Oxford University Press, 1972), 145, 149.

51. Unsigned letter in *Virginia Herald*, September 23, 1800, quoted in Egerton, *Gabriel's Rebellion*, 163.

52. Jefferson to James Monroe, September 20, 1800, in *PTJ* 32:160.

53. Tim Matthewson, *A Proslavery Foreign Policy: Haitian-American Relations During the Early Republic* (Westport, CT: Praeger, 2003), 105, 111. Gordon S. Brown's *Toussaint's Clause: The Founding Fathers and the Haitian Revolution* (Jackson: University Press of Mississippi, 2005) is the fullest treatment of the vacillating American stance.

54. Marie-Jeanne Rossignol, *The Nationalist Ferment: The Origins of U.S. Foreign Policy, 1789–1812*, trans. Lillian A. Parrott (Columbus: Ohio State University Press, 2004), chapter 6; Roger G. Kennedy, *Mr. Jefferson's Lost Cause: Land, Farmers, Slavery, and the Louisiana Purchase* (New York: Oxford University Press, 2003), 177.

55. Jefferson to William Burwell, January 28, 1805, in *PTJ* 8:340–41. In his *The Slaveholding Republic: An Account of the United States Government's Relations to Slavery*, ed. Ward M. McAfee (New York: Oxford University Press, 2001), Don E. Fehrenbacher writes, "One might have expected the author of the Ordinance of 1784 to view the acquisition as a tabula rasa and make some effort to inhibit the spread of the institution [of slavery] into a vast domain still largely free of white settlement. [But] Jefferson as president never lifted his hand against slavery, except in the matter of terminating the importation of slaves. . . . The father of exclusion in the Old Northwest [had become] the father of slavery in Louisiana" (pp. 259–60).

56. Fehrenbacher, *Slaveholding Republic*, 259–61.

57. Annette Gordon-Reed, *Thomas Jefferson and Sally Hemings: An American Controversy* (Charlottesville: University Press of Virginia, 1997), 59–63, along with many other studies.

58. Jefferson to Kościuszko, March 14, 1801, and Kościuszko to Jefferson, undated but in 1801, in Bogdan Grzelonski, ed., *Jefferson-Kościuszko Correspondence* (Warsaw: Interpress, 1978), 60–62.

59. Pula, *Kościuszko*, 266–67.

60. Jefferson to Kościuszko, February 25, 1809, in Grzelonski, *Jefferson-Kościuszko*, 73; Jefferson to Abbé Henri Grégoire, February 25, 1809, in *Thomas Jefferson, Writings*, ed. Merrill D. Peterson (New York: Viking Literary Classics, 1984), 1202.

61. Henri Grégoire, *An Enquiry Concerning the Intellectual and Moral Faculties, and Literature of Negroes*, ed. Graham Russell Hodges (1810; repr., Armonk, NY: M. E. Sharpe, 1997), xv; Jefferson to Grégoire, February 25, 1809, and Jefferson to Joel Barlow, October 8, 1809, in Andrew A. Lipscomb and Albert E. Bergh, eds., *Writings of Thomas Jefferson*, 20 vols. (Washington, D.C.: Thomas Jefferson Memorial Association, 1903–04), 12:254–55, 323–24.

62. For Jefferson's restitution of the borrowed funds, see Bear and Stanton, eds., *Jefferson's Memorandum Books*, 2:1264–65, 1276, 1289, 1307.

63. Jefferson to John Barnes, June 15, 1809, in J. Jefferson Looney et al., eds., *Papers of Thomas Jefferson: Retirement Series* (Princeton: Princeton University Press, 2004–), 1:281; Merrill D. Peterson, *Thomas Jefferson and the New Nation: A Biography* (New York: Oxford University Press, 1970), 924, for estimate of Jefferson's indebtedness upon leaving Washington at about $25,000—equivalent to several millions today. Jefferson to Kościuszko, February 26, 1810, and Kościuszko to Jefferson, March 11, 1811, in Grzelonski, *Jefferson-Kościuszko*, 78–79, 80–81.

64. For the insurrection, see Iaccarino, "Virginia and the National Contest," 136–37; Frank A. Cassell, "Slaves of the Chesapeake Bay Area and the War of 1812," *Journal of Negro History* 57 (1972): 144–155.

65. Donald R. Hickey, *The War of 1812: A Forgotten Conflict* (Urbana: University of Illinois Press, 1989), 244–45.

66. The proclamation is in Christopher T. George, "Mirage of Freedom: African Americans in the War of 1812," *Maryland Historical Magazine* 91 (1996): 434; Susan Cooper Guasco, "Confronting Democracy: Edward Coles and the Cultivation of Authority in the Young Nation" (PhD diss., College of William and Mary, 2004), 94–99; Iaccarino, "Virginia and the National Contest," 138–51; George, "Mirage of Freedom," 428–50; John N. Grant, "Black Immigrants into Nova Scotia, 1776–1815," *Journal of Negro History* 48 (1973): 253–70; Robin W. Winks, *The Blacks in Canada: A History* (Montreal: McGill-Queen's University Press, 1971), 114–41.

67. Quoted in Peterson, *Jefferson and the New Nation*, 934.

68. Dumas Malone, *The Sage of Monticello*, vol. 6 of *Jefferson and His Time* (Boston: Little, Brown, 1981; repr., Charlottesville: University of Virginia Press, 2005), 113–23. No comments on the slave flight to the British survive in Jefferson's extant correspondence.

69. The account of Coles in the current paragraph and the next follows Kurt E. Leichtle, "Edward Coles: An Agrarian on the Frontier" (PhD diss., University of Illinois–Chicago, 1982), 9–21; facsimiles of the letters between Coles and Jefferson are in E. B. Washburn, *Sketch of Edward Coles, Second Governor of Illinois, and of the Slavery Struggle of 1823–24* (1882; repr., New York: Negro Universities Press, 1969), 21–30.

70. Leichtle, "Edward Coles," 40–41; Guasco, "Confronting Democracy," 70–71.

71. Drew R. McCoy, *The Last of the Fathers: James Madison and the Republican Legacy* (New York: Cambridge University Press, 1989), 310–12, quotes on pp. 310–11.

72. Edward Coles to Jefferson, July 31, 1814, in Coles Papers, Princeton University Library, printed in "Letters of Governor Coles," *Journal of Negro History* 3 (1918): 158–60; see also Leichtlen "Edward Coles," 61, and Guasco, "Confronting Democracy," 99–100.

73. Jefferson to Coles, August 25, 1814, in Jefferson, *Writings*, 1343–46; Guasco, "Confronting Democracy," 99–101. On Pitt and Fox, see David Brion Davis, *The Problem of Slavery in the Age of Revolution* (Ithaca: Cornell University Press, 1975), 180–84.

74. A current explanation of Jefferson's unwillingness to play the role of statesman that he had advocated in *Notes on the State of Virginia*—"With what execration should the statesman be loaded, who, permitting one half the citizens thus to trample on the rights of the other?"—holds that "he could not risk jeopardizing civic community, and therefore the very possibility of moral action, by alienating fellow-citizens who were equally endowed with inalienable rights." This depiction of Jefferson's stance focuses on Jefferson's insistence in 1802 that "the habits of the governed determine in a great degree what is practicable." Ari Helo and Peter Onuf, "Jefferson, Morality, and the Problem of Slavery," *William and Mary Quarterly* 60 (2003): 601–8; Jefferson's letter to P. S. Dupont de Nemours, January 18, 1802, is quoted on p. 608; Jefferson to Short, January 3, 1793, in *PTJ* 15:15.

75. Jefferson to Coles, August 25, 1814; Coles to Jefferson, September 26, 1814; Guasco, "Confronting Democracy," 105–8.

76. Malone, *Sage of Monticello*, 323; Brodie, *Jefferson*, 424, for Danton's maxim.

77. Haiman, *Leader and Exile*, 105–6; Marian Kukiel, *Czartoryski and European Unity, 1770–1861* (Princeton: Princeton University Press, 1955), chapters 9–10.

78. Haiman, *Leader and Exile*, 103–4; Pula, *Kościuszko*, 267; *Berkshire Star*, March 3, 1816.

79. Quotes are in Pula, *Kościuszko*, 268–69, and Haiman, *Leader and Exile*, 106; Kościuszko's letters to Jefferson on the Polish plight, dated March 14 and October 16, 1815, brought a sympathetic response from Jefferson.

80. Pula, *Kościuszko*, 268–69.

81. The town meeting of neighboring Sheffield in 1774 voted "to take into consideration the present inhuman practice of enslaving our fellow creatures, the natives of Africa." Lillian E. Preiss, *Sheffield: Frontier Town* (Sheffield, MA: Sheffield Bicentennial Committee, 1976), 129, quoted in Glendyne R. Wergland, "Women, Men, Property, and Inheritance: Gendered Testamentary Customs in Western Massachusetts, 1800–1860" (PhD diss., University of Massachusetts, Amherst, 2001), 172–74; Graham Russell Hodges and Alan Edward Brown, eds., *Pretends to Be Free: Runaway Slave Advertisements from Colonial and Revolutionary New York and New Jersey* (New York: Garland, 1994), 64, discuss New York slaves fleeing to New England.

82. Mary E. Dewey, ed., *Life and Letters of Catharine M. Sedgwick* (New York: Harper & Brothers, 1871), 29, 40–42, 73; Mary Kelley, ed., *The Power of Her Sympathy: The Autobiography and Journal of Catharine Maria Sedgwick* (Boston: Northeastern University Press, 1993), 89.

83. The birth of Charlotte Hull is derived from the record of her death on January 7, 1849, where her age is given as fifty-two years, six months. The transition to "rural capitalism" in western Massachusetts in this period is explored by Christopher Clark in *The Roots of Rural Capitalism: Western Massachusetts, 1780–1860* (Ithaca: Cornell University Press, 1990), chapter 2; for Bay State's strolling poor, see Douglas L. Jones, "Poverty and Vagabondage: The Process of Survival in Eighteenth-Century Massachusetts," *New England Historical and Genealogical Register* 133 (1979): 243–53; and Ruth Herndon, *Unwelcome Americans: Living on the Margin in Early New England* (Philadelphia: University of Pennsylvania Press, 2001).

84. Catharine Sedgwick Daybook, Sedgwick Papers, vol. 9, pp. 38, 50, 52, Massachusetts Historical Society, for services to Sedgwick family in 1790 and 1794; for ordination dinner and church raising, *Congregational Church Memorials, Lee, Massachusetts* (Lee, MA, 1858), 58. The *Stockbridge Selectmen's Book, 1792–1827* records many accounts paid to Hull for sheltering homeless men and women. Stories of Grippy passed down in Stockbridge lore are laced with his humor. One recounts that, when serving dinner at an August Sedgwick gathering, Mrs. Sedgwick ordered him "to be sure to serve the peas with the chicken." When Grippy carried in the chicken, Mrs. Sedgwick, seeing no peas, reproved him. Grippy replied, "It's 'yes ma'am, no ma'am, if you please; it's inside the chicken you'll find the green peas'" ("A Sedgwick Story, as Told by a Former Librarian [Miss Goodwin]," Agrippa Hull file, Ms. 5.535, Massachusetts Historical Society.

85. Electa F. Jones, *Stockbridge, Past and Present; or, Records of an Old Mission Station* (Springfield, MA: S. Bowles, 1854), 242–43, has a brief notice of

Humphrey; for Freeman's land purchases, Berkshire County Deed Books, Pittsfield Registry of Deeds, 46:98, 392–93.

86. Dewey, ed., *Life and Letters*, 34–35; for her father's politics in the Jeffersonian era, see Richard E. Welch Jr., *Theodore Sedgwick, Federalist: A Political Portrait* (Middletown, CT: Wesleyan University Press, 1965), chapters 14–16. In his "Political Will and Testament," written upon leaving office, Sedgwick characterized the Jeffersonians as "our own degenerate citizens and Jacobin renegadoes from other countries" (Sedgwick Papers, Box 10, folder 2, Massachusetts Historical Society).

87. Dewey, ed., *Life and Letters*, 21.

88. Catharine Sedgwick described the Sedgwick black servants and her father's view of Jeffersonians in "Recollections of Childhood," in ibid., 35, 65, 73n.

89. Welch, *Sedgwick*, 213; list of Stockbridge voters, 1800, Sedgwick Papers, Box 8, folder 13, Massachusetts Historical Society; Mary Gray Bidwell to Barnabas Bidwell, October 24, 1807, private collection, Palo Alto, California, copy in Berkshire Athenaeum, Pittsfield, Massachusetts; story told in 1949 by Edith Tracy that Mrs. Alexander Sedgwick, a descendant of Theodore Sedgwick, had told her this many years before. Written testimony in Stockbridge Public Library, Agrippa Hull file. Bidwell's biting pamphlet "The Honorable Mr. Sedgwick's Political Last Will and Testament" (n.p., 1800) added to the mutual hatred of Stockbridge's two most important lawyers, who lived across the street from each other.

90. Dewey, ed., *Life and Letters*, 42, 73n.

91. Mary Bidwell to Barnabas Bidwell, December 23, 1805, and Barnabas Bidwell to Mary Bidwell, February 5, 1806, in Bidwell Family Papers, Sterling Library, Yale University.

92. Jones, *Stockbridge*, 241; papers lent to Miss Parsons in August 1929 by Mrs. Henrietta Crockett, great-great-niece of Peggy Hull, Agrippa Hull File, Stockbridge Public Library; Joanne Pope Melish, *Disowning Slavery: Gradual Emancipation and "Race" in New England, 1780–1860* (Ithaca: Cornell University Press, 1998), 170–73.

93. Jones, *Stockbridge*, 241–42.

94. Patrick Frazier, *The Mohicans of Stockbridge* (Lincoln: University of Nebraska Press, 1992), 244, citing Timothy Woodbridge, *Autobiography of a Blind Minister* (New York, 1856), 37.

95. For Haynes's parentage and upbringing, see Richard D. Brown, "'Not Only Extreme Poverty, but the Worst Kind of Orphanage': Lemuel Haynes and the Boundaries of Racial Tolerance on the Yankee Frontier, 1770–1820," *New England Quarterly* 61 (1988): 505–9; Ruth Bogin, "'Liberty Further Extended': An Antislavery Manuscript by Lemuel Haynes," *William and Mary Quarterly* 40 (1983): 85–105; Timothy Mather Cooley, *Sketches of the Life and Character of the Rev. Lemuel Haynes* (New York, 1837), 66.

96. It is almost certain that the "distinguished mulatto preacher" was Lemuel Haynes, since he was the only widely known and admired minister of color in

this region of New England. Jones, *Stockbridge*, 242, for Grippy's quip. Some of Haynes's letters back to Elihu Atkins, his successor in the pulpit at Granville, are in Cooley, *Sketches of Haynes*, 82–93.

CHAPTER 5

1. James S. Pula, *Thaddeus Kościuszko: The Purest Son of Liberty* (New York: Hippocrene, 1999), 268–69, 271.

2. Ibid., 271–73; "The Last Years of Kościuszko," *Harper's New Monthly Magazine* 37 (1867): 481; Xavier Zeltner, "Personal Reminiscences of Kosciuszko," *U.S. Military Magazine* 4 (1865): 136–46.

3. Kościuszko to Jefferson, Soleure, April 1816, Jefferson Collection, Massachusetts Historical Society; Miecislaus Haiman, *Kosciuszko: Leader and Exile* (New York: Polish Institute of Arts and Sciences in America, 1946), 105; Pula, *Kościuszko*, 272–73.

4. Kościuszko's will releasing his serfs was reprinted first in the Paris *Moniteur* on April 21, 1817. Kościuszko's early biographers, as well as literary journals such as the *Museum of Foreign Literature, Science, and Art*, August 1835, recirculated the provisions of the will.

5. Kościuszko's will freeing his serfs was translated for publication in American newspapers, such as the *New-York Daily Advertiser* on June 5, 1817; *New York Columbian* and Washington's *Daily National Intelligencer* on June 6; and Norfolk, Virginia's *American Beacon and Commercial Diary* on June 17. For the exchange of letters that followed: Jefferson to Kościuszko, June 15, 1817, Herbert R. Strauss Collection, Newberry Library, Chicago; Kościuszko to Jefferson, September 15, 1817, Jefferson Collection, Massachusetts Historical Society.

6. Kościuszko to Jefferson, September 15, 1817.

7. Pula, *Kościuszko*, 274–75; Haiman, *Leader and Exile*, 115, 117.

8. The conclusion of Lafayette's eulogy is in Pula, *Kościuszko*, 275.

9. Dumas Malone notes that Jefferson regularly read the *Richmond Enquirer* (*Sage of Monticello*, vol. 6 of *Jefferson and His Time* [Boston: Little, Brown, 1981; repr., Charlottesville: University of Virginia Press, 2005], 528). For other newspaper accounts beyond those mentioned in the text, see *Alexandria Herald*, January 2, 1818; *Albany Argus*, January 9, 1818; *American Mercury*, January 13, 1818; *New Bedford Mercury*, January 16, 1818; *Massachusetts Spy, or Worcester Gazette*, January 21, 1818; and *Niles' Weekly Register* and *Weekly Visitor and Ladies Museum*, January 24, 1818. The *Essex Patriot*, February 21, 1818, published a letter from Kościuszko to Pennsylvania's John Dickinson, written in 1783, in which the Pole wrote of how he had come to America to "change his slavery for liberty" in a war in which "three millions of people, without money, . . . have shaken off the yoke of a people like England." This letter has eluded all Kościuszko biographers, so far as we can determine.

10. Harrison is quoted in Pula, *Kościuszko*, 276; for Bunker Hill medal, [Boston] *Centinel*, June 20, 1825.

11. Haiman, *Leader and Exile*, 117; Pula, *Kościuszko*, 276–77; *Baltimore Patriot*, April 7, 1821.

12. John Barnes to Jefferson, December 30, 1817; Francis Xavier Zeltner to Jefferson, October 29, 1817, and Jefferson to Zeltner, July 23, 1818. Kościuszko's will is never mentioned in the Jefferson studies of Dumas Malone, Joseph Ellis, Garry Wills, Connor Cruise O'Brien, Fawn Brodie, Andrew Burstein, and many others. The main treatments are by Polish American historians, notably Haiman, Francis Casimir Kajencki, and Pula. Among American historians, John C. Miller, *Wolf by the Ears: Thomas Jefferson and Slavery* (New York: Free Press, 1977), and Merrill Peterson, *Jefferson and the New Nation: A Biography* (New York: Oxford University Press, 1970), have brief notices of Kościuszko's death and the disposition of his will, though both contain errors. Garrison is quoted in David Brion Davis, *Was Thomas Jefferson an Authentic Enemy of Slavery? An Inaugural Lecture Delivered before the University of Oxford on 18 February 1970* (Oxford: Clarendon, 1970), 4.

13. On financial problems in this period, see Malone, *Sage of Monticello*, 175–79, 301–13, 509–10; and Herbert E. Sloan, *Principle and Interest: Thomas Jefferson and the Problem of Debt* (New York: Oxford University Press, 1995), 218–21.

14. John Adams to Benjamin Rush, November 11, 1807, in John A. Shutz and Douglass Adair, eds., *The Spur of Fame: Dialogues of John Adams and Benjamin Rush, 1805–1813* (San Marino, CA: Huntington Library, 1966), 106.

15. Jefferson to Charles Yancey, 1816, quoted in Andrew Burstein, *Jefferson's Secrets: Death and Desire at Monticello* (New York: Basic Books, 2005), 233.

16. William Short to Jefferson, July 18, 1816, Massachusetts Historical Society *Collections*, ser. 7, vol. 1 (Boston, 1900), 258–61.

17. Jefferson to Charles Clay, January 27, 1790, in Julian P. Boyd, ed., *Papers of Thomas Jefferson*, 31 vols. (Princeton: Princeton University Press, 1950–2004) (hereafter *PTJ*), 16:129; Jefferson to Short, August 10, 1816, in Jefferson Papers, Library of Congress.

18. Jefferson to William Wirt, January 5, 1818; Jefferson to William Crawford, January 5, 1818, in Jefferson Papers, Library of Congress.

19. John Armstrong to Jefferson, January 4, 1818, in Jefferson Papers, Library of Congress.

20. Jefferson to Armstrong, January 17, 1818, in Jefferson Papers, Library of Congress; Pula, *Kościuszko*, 286, for wording of will. Jefferson referred to Kościuszko's "disposing of his property in the U.S. to a charitable purpose of which will he made me executor." On Armstrong see C. Edward Skeen, *John Armstrong, Jr., 1758–1843: A Biography* (Syracuse: Syracuse University Press, 1981).

21. Zeltner to Jefferson, October 29, 1817, in the National Archives; "Notarized Statement of Will of General Tadeusz Kościuszko, Oct. 10, 1817, Soleure, Switzerland," is in the National Archives, RG 21, Entry 115, Case File 913. The will left fifty thousand French francs from funds held in England and the rest of

his money there to General Buszkoyski. These funds were derived from the money Czar Paul I had given Kościuszko in 1797, which had remained untouched in England. The will also referred to other money banked with friends in Zurich and Soleure and specifically willed his "carriage and horse" to the Zeltners. Nowhere are the American assets mentioned in this will.

22. Jefferson to Zeltner, July 23, 1818, in William K. Bixby and Worthington Chauncey Ford, eds., *Thomas Jefferson Correspondence* (Boston, 1916), 239–41. It is not clear why Jefferson took nearly three months to respond to Zeltner's letter.

23. John Taylor, *Arator: Being a Series of Agricultural Essays, Practical and Political, in Sixty-Four Numbers*, 4th ed., rev. and enl. (Petersburg, VA: Whitworth & Yancey, 1818), quoted in Susan Dunn, *Dominion of Memories: Jefferson, Madison, and the Decline of Virginia* (New York: Basic Books, 2007), 55.

24. Cocke's intimate relations with Jefferson as a member of the university's board of visitors is treated in Malone, *Sage of Monticello*, passim. Jefferson expressed his approval of the ACS plans to Thomas Humphreys on February 8, 1817, Paul Leicester Ford, ed., *The Writings of Thomas Jefferson*, 10 vols. (New York: G. P. Putnam's Sons, 1892–99) (hereafter *WTJ*), 10:77. On the creation of ACS see P. J. Staudenraus, *The African Colonization Movement, 1816–1865* (New York: Columbia University Press, 1961); Douglas R. Egerton, "'Its Origin Is Not a Little Curious': A New Look at the American Colonization Society," in *Rebels, Reformers, and Revolutionaries: Collected Essays and Second Thoughts* (New York: Routledge, 2002), 93–107.

25. Jefferson to John Lynch, January 21, 1811, in *WTJ* 9:303–4. Jefferson was fully confirmed in his view of the reluctance of black Virginians to leave the place of their birth. In a census of free blacks living in Albemarle County in 1833, it was found that almost none were willing to go to Liberia.

26. Jefferson to Wirt, November 10, 1818, in Jefferson Papers, Library of Congress.

27. Wirt to Jefferson, December 28, 1818, in Jefferson Papers, Library of Congress.

28. Merrill D. Peterson, ed., *Visitors to Monticello* (Charlottesville: University Press of Virginia, 1989), 90. The comment is from the sober-sided Maryland Quaker Isaac Briggs. Even five years later, Duke Bernhard of Saxe-Weimar-Eisenach found Jefferson "in conversation . . . very lively, and his spirits, as also his hearing and sight, seemed not to have decreased at all with his advancing age. I . . . would have taken him for a man of sixty" (Peterson, ed., *Visitors*, 105).

29. Malone, *Sage of Monticello*, 261–82.

30. In response to John Armstrong's letter of March 1, 1819, concerning Kościuszko's bequest to his son, Jefferson promised he would prove the will on May 5 in Charlottesville, where the administration of it would be committed to Cocke—"the most diligent, correct, and worthy man in the world." Armstrong to Jefferson, March 1, 1819; Jefferson to Armstrong, March 12, 1819, in Jefferson

Papers, Library of Congress. Cocke's letter of withdrawal, May 3, 1819, is in the Papers of Thomas Jefferson, Alderman Library, University of Virginia.

31. There is nothing in the correspondence to indicate that Jefferson was ready to put forward any of his several hundred slaves as candidates for freedom. For soil exhaustion, see Dunn, *Dominion of Memories*, 20–29, quote on p. 23.

32. Jefferson to Edward Bancroft, January 26, 1789, in *PTJ* 14:492–94.

33. The *Revised Code of the Laws of Virginia* is quoted in Philip J. Schwarz, *Slave Laws in Virginia* (Athens: University of Georgia Press, 1996), 54.

34. James Kettner, "Persons or Property: The Pleasants Slaves in the Virginia Courts, 1792–1799," in Ronald Hoffman and Peter J. Albert, eds., *Launching the Extended Republic: The Federalist Era* (Charlottesville: University Press of Virginia for the United States Capitol Historical Society, 1996), 136–55; Melvin Patrick Ely, *Israel on the Appomattox: A Southern Experiment in Black Freedom from the 1790s Through the Civil War* (New York: Knopf, 2004), chapters 1–2.

35. Kurt E. Leichtle, "Edward Coles: An Agrarian on the Frontier" (PhD diss., University of Illinois–Chicago, 1982), 74–76. The quoted passages are from [Edward Coles], *History of the Ordinance of 1787 by Edward Coles* (Philadelphia, 1856).

36. Cocke to Jefferson, May 3, 1819; see Staudenraus, *American Colonization Movement*, chapter 4, for full account of the Mills-Burgess "mission of inquiry."

37. Armstrong to Jefferson, November 6, 1819, in Jefferson Papers, Library of Congress, citing a letter from Cocke to Armstrong, October 11, 1819. We have not found Cocke's letter to Armstrong.

38. Jefferson to Cocke, May 3, 1819, in Henry E. Huntington Library, San Marino, CA.

39. "Statement of William Wertenbaker, Deputy Clerk of the Circuit Court of Albemarle," May 1819, *Scribner's Monthly* 17, no. 4 (February 1879): 614–16.

40. Jefferson estimated the value of slaves in 1824 on "an average of two hundred dollars each, young and old" (Jefferson to Jared Sparks, February 4, 1826, in *WTJ* 16:10). For more on slave prices, see Robert McColley, *Slavery and Jeffersonian Virginia*, 2nd ed. (Urbana: University of Illinois Press, 1973), 24; Robert W. Fogel and Stanley Engerman, eds., *Without Consent or Contract: The Rise and Fall of American Slavery, Markets in Production: Technical Papers*, vol. 1 (New York: Norton, 1992), 37.

41. Haiman, *Leader and Exile*, 125; Pula, *Kościuszko*, 290–91; Burstein, *Jefferson's Secrets*, 38–40; Peterson, *Jefferson and the New Nation*, 1000.

42. Poletica to Jefferson, May 27, 1819; Jefferson to Piotr Poletica, June 12, 1818 [1819], Russian Archives, copy in Jefferson Papers, Library of Congress. Jefferson had probably already received William Short's letter of May 25 telling of Poletica's desire to see Jefferson regarding the disposition of Kościuszko's will. Short's letter is in *MHS Collections*, ser. 7, vol. 1 (Boston: Massachusetts Historical Society, 1900), 277–81.

43. Jefferson to William Short, June 29 [?], 1819, *MHS Collections*, ser. 7, vol. 1, 285–86; Jefferson to Wirt, June 27, 1819; Lucia Stanton, "The Other End of the Telescope: Jefferson Through the Eyes of His Slaves," *William and Mary Quarterly* 57 (2000): 139–52, for what we do know from the written and oral testimony of Jefferson's slaves.

44. Jefferson to Wirt, June 27, 1819; Wirt to Jefferson, July 6, 1819; for the suit of Edward Livingston against Jefferson, see Malone, *Sage of Monticello*, 55–73.

45. Armstrong to Jefferson, November 6, 1819; Jefferson to Armstrong, November 19, 1819; Jefferson to William Wirt, February 5, 1820, all in Jefferson Papers, Library of Congress. See also Jefferson to Archibald Stuart, January 18, 1820, seeking a signature for an endorsed copy of the will (in Bixby and Ford, eds., *Thomas Jefferson Correspondence*, 253); and Jefferson to Wirt, February 20, 1820, with the "official copy of the will with the necessary authentications."

46. Among many newspapers that reported this, most were copying from *Poulson's Daily Advertiser*, such as the *New-York Daily Advertiser*, March 6; *New Bedford Mercury*, March 10; *New-England Palladium*, March 10; *Boston Recorder*, March 11; *Richmond Enquirer*, March 14, 1820.

47. *The Third Annual Report of the American Society for Colonizing the Free People of Colour of the United States* (Washington, 1820), 16. We have not found Cocke's letter to the ACS. The incoming letters of the ACS were not preserved for this year by its secretary, Elias Caldwell, though his successor, R. R. Gurley, faithfully preserved the correspondence after assuming office in 1824. See Staudenraus, *African Colonization Movement*, 305.

48. William H. Gaines, Jr., *Thomas Mann Randolph: Jefferson's Son-in-Law* (Baton Rouge: Louisiana State University Press, 1966), 124–25; Randolph's proposal is in his message to the Virginia legislature on December 4, 1820, in *Journal of the House of Delegates . . . 1820* (Richmond, 1821), 10–11. Randolph's plan got nowhere with the Virginia legislature.

49. Don E. Fehrenbacher, *The Slaveholding Republic: An Account of the United States Government's Relations to Slavery*, ed. Ward M. McAfee (New York: Oxford University Press, 2001), 263–65.

50. Jefferson to John Holmes, April 22, 1820, in *WTJ* 15:248–50; Malone, *Sage of Monticello*, 328–44; Miller, *Wolf by the Ears*, 221–33; Dunn, *Dominion of Memories*, 43–44, 66.

51. Peterson, *Jefferson and the New Nation*, 997; Wirt to Jefferson, July 20, 1821, in Jefferson Papers, Library of Congress.

52. Benjamin Lincoln Lear to Jefferson, September 19, 1821; Jefferson to Lear, September 25, 1821; Lear to Jefferson, October 4, 1821, in Jefferson Papers, Library of Congress.

53. Lear's visit to Monticello in July 1823 is mentioned in William Wirt's letter to Jefferson, July 20, 1823, Jefferson Papers, Massachusetts Historical Society; quote is from Staudenraus, *American Colonization Movement*, 111; on

Harper, see Eric Robert Papenfuse, *The Evils of Necessity: Robert Goodloe Harper and the Moral Dilemma of Slavery*, Transactions of the American Philosophical Society, 87, pt. 1 (Philadelphia: American Philosophical Society, 1997). Harper's statement is on p. 67.

54. *Notes on the State of Virginia*, Queries 18 and 14. Jefferson to James Heaton, May 20, 1826, quoted in Peter S. Onuf, *Jefferson's Empire: The Language of American Nationhood* (Charlottesville: University Press of Virginia, 2000), 174. For Jefferson's assessment of the moral incapacity of slaves and the impossibility of integrating them into white society after giving them their freedom, see Ari Helo and Peter Onuf, "Jefferson, Morality, and the Problem of Slavery," *William and Mary Quarterly* 60 (2003): 583–614.

55. Robert Goodloe Harper to Leonard Bacon, November 8, 1824, reprinted in Papenfuse, *Evils of Necessity*, 144–49.

56. James Oakes, "Why Slaves Can't Read: The Political Significance of Jefferson's Racism," in James Gilreath, ed., *Thomas Jefferson and the Education of a Citizen* (Washington, D.C.: Library of Congress, 1999), 182, 180.

57. Eli Ayres to Leonard Bacon, August 4, 1825, in Bacon Papers, Yale University Library; Malone, *Sage of Monticello*, 402–5; Lucia Stanton, *Free Some Day: The African-American Families of Monticello* (Charlottesville: Thomas Jefferson Foundation, 2000), 97–98. For Cocke escort, see Edgar Ewing Brandon, comp., *Lafayette, Guest of the Nation: A Contemporary Account of the Triumphal Tour of General Lafayette Through the United States in 1824–1825, as Reported in the Local Newspapers*, 3 vols. (Oxford, OH: Oxford Historical Press, 1957), 3:127–38.

58. Malone, *Sage of Monticello*, 408.

59. Lloyd Kramer, *Lafayette in Two Worlds: Public Cultures and Personal Identities in an Age of Revolutions* (Chapel Hill: University of North Carolina Press, 1996), 218.

60. Miller, *Wolf by the Ears*, 273–75; for Israel's recollection of Lafayette's strictures on slavery, see Fawn M. Brodie, *Jefferson: An Intimate History* (New York: Norton, 1974), 461–62; and Stanton, "Jefferson Through the Eyes of His Slaves," 144. After gaining his freedom in the 1830s, Israel adopted Jefferson as his surname. "The Memoirs of Israel Jefferson" are reprinted in Annette Gordon-Reed, *Thomas Jefferson and Sally Hemings: An American Controversy* (Charlottesville: University Press of Virginia, 1997), 247–53.

61. Auguste Levasseur, *Lafayette in America in 1824 and 1825, or Journal of a Voyage to the United States*, 2 vols. (Philadelphia: Carey and Lea, 1829); emphasis in original. *Virginia Herald*, November 27, 1824, quoted in J. Bennett Nolan, *Lafayette in America Day by Day* (Baltimore: Johns Hopkins Press, 1934), 259; Kramer, *Lafayette in Two Worlds*, 218; the incident of Lafayette visiting a slave in Savannah was described in Levasseur's travelogue.

62. For the Parsippany school, see Marion Thompson Wright, *The Education of Negroes in New Jersey* (New York: Teacher's College Bureau of Publications, 1941), 80–88.

63. "Address of Theodore Frelinghuysen, before the New-Jersey Colonization Society," *Western New York–Baptist Magazine*, February 1825, 257–62; "African School," *African Repository*, November 1825, 276–77, for report from the New Jersey African School directors on applying the Kościuszko funds to their enterprise; "Circular in Behalf of the African Education Society" (dated August 26, 1826), *Philadelphia Recorder*, September 23, 1826; *Report of the Proceedings at the Formation of the African Education Society . . . Dec. 28, 1829* (Washington, D.C., 1830). For ACS editorial extolling the virtues of the school, see *The Friend: A Religious and Literary Journal*, August 1, 15, 1829, and *Report of the Proceedings of the African Education Society*, 15.

64. Stanton, *Free Some Day*, 65, 95, 124–25, 141–46.

65. *Niles Register*, November 11, 1826, 167–68; similar announcements of the auction were widely published—for example, in *Baltimore Patriot*, November 6; *Eastern Argus*, November 14; *Republican Star*, November 14; *Rhode Island Republican*, November 16; *New Hampshire Sentinel*, November 17; and *Connecticut Courant*, November 20.

66. Quoted in Lucia Stanton, "Those Who Labor for My Happiness: Thomas Jefferson and His Slaves," in Peter Onuf, ed., *Jeffersonian Legacies* (Charlottesville: University Press of Virginia, 1993), 147; *Monticello Newsletter* 16 (Winter 2005): 1–3.

67. Stanton, "Those Who Labor," 168–70; for Daniel Webster's 1824 description of Edy Fossett's cooking, Stanton, "Those Who Labor," 165; Gordon-Reed, *Jefferson and Hemings*, 206–9; Brodie, *Jefferson*, 466–67.

68. *State's Advocate*, date unknown but reprinted in *New York Telescope*, December 30, 1826.

69. Benjamin Lear's four accounts of the fund were filed with the District of Columbia Court with copies kept by the ACS, where they can be found in the ACS Papers, Kościuszko File, Library of Congress. The fourth report, on February 5, 1831, reported that the fund had reached $27,991. Quote is from Stanton, "Those Who Labor," 147.

70. In the State Tax of 1809, Hull's tax liability exceeded that of sixty-three white householders. *Stockbridge Selectmen's Book, 1792–1827*, and manuscript tax assessors' lists for Stockbridge are the basis of this account of Hull's small farm and its comparison to Mumbet's. Hull also advertised in local newspapers for strayed sheep (*Berkshire Star*, October 24, 31, November 7, 1816) and wandering heifers (*Berkshire Journal*, October 20, November 12, 19, 26, December 3, 1829). Katharine M. Abbott, *Old Paths and Legends of the New England Border: Connecticut, Deerfield, Berkshire* (New York: Putnam's Sons, 1907), 222–23.

71. Electa F. Jones, *Stockbridge, Past and Present; or, Records of an Old Mission Station* (Springfield, MA: S. Bowles, 1854), 241, says Hull married Margaret "some years after [Jane Darby's] death," which suggests a death date shortly after birth of Aseph or perhaps one of the two other children who did not survive infancy. Two accounts of Peggy Timbroke Hull were passed down by her

descendants: "Papers Lent to Miss Parsons in Aug. 1929 by Mrs. Henrietta Crockett, Widow of Wellington" and great-great-niece of Peggy Hull; "Paper Written by Miss Galpin for Miss Goodrich" (as told in 1904 by Mary Gunn, the adopted daughter of Agrippa and Peggy Hull), Bowker-Hoffman Papers, both at Stockbridge Public Library. The marriage of Agrippa and Margaret in February 1813 by the Reverend Ephraim Swift is noted in depositions taken to support Margaret's application for a pension in 1853.

72. "Paper Written by Miss Galpin."

73. John Resch, *Suffering Soldiers: Revolutionary War Veterans, Moral Sentiment, and Political Culture in the Early Republic* (Amherst: University of Massachusetts Press, 1999), chapter 4; quote is on p. 121. Hull's award is in Roll 1363, 21–3199.

74. Glendyne R. Wergland, "Women, Men, Property, and Inheritance: Gendered Testamentary Customs in Western Massachusetts, 1800–1860" (PhD diss., University of Massachusetts, Amherst, 2001), 184; Dunkins Pension File #34773, which includes a testimonial from Agrippa Hull, is in the National Archives. For Dunkins's war service, see *Massachusetts Soldiers and Sailors in the War of the Revolution*, 17 vols. (Boston, 1896), 5:36, 53. Note from Pension Office, August 1853, in Hull file, notes that he was paid up to March 4, 1820, and "then dropped from the Roll"; Resch, *Suffering Soldiers*, chapter 5, for amended law; nearly nineteen thousand veterans received their pensions under the 1818 act, though death and the means test reduced that number to about twelve thousand by 1822 (Resch, *Suffering Soldiers*, 277n45).

75. *Weekly Visitor*, March 25, 1841, quoted in Emilie S. Piper, "The Family of Agrippa Hull," *Berkshire Genealogist* 22 (2001): 5. For Hull's 1817 land purchases and mortgage, see Berkshire County Deed Book 59:142, 242–43. In 1825 he mortgaged all his property to secure $350 from the Massachusetts Life Insurance Company and paid off the loan with interest over the next seven years (Deed Book 68:656–59).

76. Piper, "Family of Agrippa Hull," 5.

77. Jones, *Stockbridge*, 40.

78. One of Mary's descendants was still relating this story in 2004 (conversation with Elaine Gunn). Bernard A. Drew, *If They Close the Door on You, Go Through the Window: Origins of the African American Community in Sheffield, Great Barrington, and Stockbridge* (Great Barrington, MA: Attic Press, 2004), 17 and n99; "Paper Written by Miss Galpin."

79. William Glasson, *Federal Military Pensions in the United States* (New York: Oxford University Press, 1918), 76. John C. Dann, ed., *The Revolution Remembered: Eyewitness Accounts of the War for Independence* (Chicago: University of Chicago Press, 1980), xvi. Not until 1832 did Congress pass a general pension law stripped of means tests. Charles Sedgwick to Acting Secretary of State Richard Rush, June 12, 1828, quoted in Sidney Kaplan and Emma Nogrady Kaplan, *The Black Presence in the Era of the American Revolution, 1770–1800* (Greenwich, CT: New York Graphic Society, 1976; rev. ed., Amherst: University

of Massachusetts Press, 1989), 43. For monument, Pula, *Kościuszko*, 277; a bronze statue of Kościuszko was added to the monument in 1913.

EPILOGUE

1. Merrill D. Peterson, *The Jefferson Image in the American Mind* (New York: Oxford University Press, 1960), 19–20, 30–34, 71; Thomas Jefferson Randolph, ed., *Memoir, Correspondence and Miscellanies from the Papers of Thomas Jefferson*, 4 vols. (Charlottesville: F. Carr, 1829). The correspondence included four letters from Jefferson to Kościuszko, but nothing about the will. See Andrew A. Libscomb and Albert E. Burgh, eds., *The Writings of Thomas Jefferson*, 20 vols. (Washington, D.C.: Thomas Jefferson Memorial Association of the United States, 1903–04), 3:395, 422, 495, and 4:140.

2. Peterson, *Jefferson Image*, 48–63; for African American views, see Manisha Sinha, "Black Radicalism in the Age of Revolution," *William and Mary Quarterly* 64 (2007): 157–58.

3. For poems and children's stories, see *The Young Gentleman and Lady's Museum, Being a Collection of Elegant, Entertaining, and Instructive Pieces Calculated to Improve Young Persons* (Hallowell, ME: N. Cheever, 1811); *Connecticut Courant*, May 19, 1828; *Berkshire Journal*, March 31, 1831. For horses, see *Charleston Courier*, March 7, 1828. For the schooner and icebreaker, see *Baltimore Patriot*, August 18, 1831; *Pittsfield Sun*, December 2, 1840. For Lafayette's celebration of Kościuszko's birthday, see *Vermont Gazette*, April 20, 1830; *Rhode Island American Statesman and Providence Gazette*, April 6, 1830. For July 4 celebrations, see *Salem Gazette*, September 3, 1830; *Chestertown (MD) Inquirer*, July 15, 1831; *Pittsfield Sun*, July 14, 1836. For histories, see *Vermont Gazette*, May 5, 1830 and October 20, 1834. For anecdotes, see the *Watch-Tower*, May 31, 1830, among dozens of other cites. For Poland, see *Essex Gazette*, February 5, 1830; *Connecticut Courant*, March 1, 1831; *Vermont Gazette*, March 22, 1831; *Baltimore Patriot*, April 2, 1831; *Pittsfield Sun*, April 14, 1831; *Norwich Courier*, May 4, 1831; *Watch-Tower*, June 6, 1831. For lady love, *Barre Gazette*, July 23, 1841. For use of Kościuszko's republicanism in this era, see Karma Nabulski, *Traditions of War: Occupation, Resistance, and the Law* (New York: Oxford University Press, 1999), 214–24. *The Polish Chiefs* thoroughly erased Kościuszko's abolitionism and his American bequest while turning Agrippa Hull into "Joseph Cotton," a "broad-shouldered, long-armed, and bow-legged" young man "with a head that seemed large enough for a giant of seven feet"; Samuel L. Knapp, *The Polish Chiefs: An Historical Romance* (New York: G. H. Evans, 1832), and Samuel L. Knapp, *Tales from the Garden of Kosciuszko* (New York: West and Trow, 1838). For the Polish exiles, see Jerzy Lerski, *A Polish Chapter in Jacksonian America* (Madison: University of Wisconsin Press, 1958).

4. Armstrong against Lear, Administrator of Kościuszko, Supreme Court of the United States, 25 U.S. 169; *Reports of Supreme Court Cases Argued and Decided in the Supreme Court of the United States*, 14 vols. (Rochester: Lawyer's

Co-operative Publishing Company, 1918), vols. 6, 7, 8, 8:49–72; James Pula, *Thaddeus Kościuszko: The Purest Son of Liberty* (New York: Hippocrene Books, 1999), 291–93. For the ACS's renewed hope, see *African Repository and Colonial Journal*, October 1835, 10.

5. Tommy Lee Bogger, *Free Blacks in Norfolk, Virginia, 1790–1860: The Darker Side of Freedom* (Charlottesville: University Press of Virginia, 1997), 138.

6. *Baltimore Patriot*, August 14, 1829; "Complaint of Kościuszko Armstrong," April 1, 1829, Chancery Dockets, Rule 53, Box 83:90; Answer of Benjamin L. Lear to Kościuszko Armstrong, December 1830, Chancery Decrees, Rule 3, Box F3, Case File 90, NA; Pula, *Kościuszko*, 292; Walker Lewis, *Without Fear or Favor: A Biography of Chief Justice Roger Brooke Taney* (Boston: Houghton Mifflin, 1965), 43.

7. *Reports of Supreme Court Cases* 4:14. For Key and Taney, see Lewis, *Without Fear or Favor*, 117–20. For early abolitionist mention, see *Genius of Universal Emancipation*, December 2, 1826.

8. *Freedom's Journal* (New York), June 8, 15, 1827.

9. For Wirt's death, see Anya Jabour, *Marriage in the Early Republic: Elizabeth and William Wirt and the Companionate Ideal* (Baltimore: Johns Hopkins University Press, 1998), 161–62; John K. Marian, "George Bomford," in John A. Garraty and Mark C. Carnes, gen. eds., *American National Biography*, 24 vols. (New York: Oxford University Press, 1999–2002), 3:151–53. For hiring of Coxe, see *Religious Intelligencer*, September 26, 1835, 267–68. In attempting to raise money for the Kościuszko School, religious journals such as the *Religious Intelligencer* peddled the idea that Kościuszko provided that his assets "should not be used until an equal amount should be raised in the United States to be added to it" (September 26, 1835, 267).

10. Tochman also kept the flame of Kościuszko's memory burning brightly by delivering public lectures about a third Polish uprising against Russia in 1842–44. Samuel Tyler, *Memoir of Roger Brooke Taney: Chief Justice of the Supreme Court of the United States* (Baltimore: J. Murray, 1872), 72–73, 249; Lewis, *Without Fear or Favor*, 242–43.

11. William C. Nell, "The Kościuszko Tribute to Colored Americans," *The North Star* (Rochester, NY), March 17, 1848.

12. *National Era* (Washington, D.C.), October 14, 1847, June 8, 1848, October 11, 1849, January 24, October 3, 1850, August 31, 1854; *North Star*, December 18, 1851, February 12, 1852.

13. *North Star*, March 17, 1848; *National Era*, May 16, 30, 1850, April 17, 1851. See January 16, 1851, for a human interest story about Kościuszko.

14. *National Era*, June 12, 26, September 4, 1851.

15. Taney's Court believed in the plans the American Colonization Society envisioned for blacks, having two years earlier appended to a decision a lengthy appeal to free African Americans that they leave the country. For this case, see James Birney, ed., *Examination of the Decision to the Supreme Court of the*

United States in the Case of Strader, Gorman, and Armstrong vs. Christopher Graham . . . Concluding with an Address to Free Colored People Advising Them to Remove to Liberia (Cincinnati: Truman & Spofford, 1852).

16. "Speech of Gerrit Smith on the Nebraska Bill," *National Era*, May 11, 1854. For a vivid portrayal of Smith, see John Stauffer, *The Black Hearts of Men: Radical Abolitionists and the Transformation of Race* (Cambridge: Harvard University Press, 2002); Israel Losey White, "Truth About a European Liberalist in America—General Kosciuszko," *Journal of American History* 2 (1908): 371. A Newark journalist, White reprinted Kościuszko's will with Jefferson as its executor.

17. Mark Hopkins, quoted in Bernard A. Drew, *If They Close the Door on You, Go Through the Window: Origins of the African American Community in Sheffield, Great Barrington, and Stockbridge* (Great Barrington, MA: Attic Press, 2004), 33; Mary Kelley, ed., *The Power of Her Sympathy: The Autobiography and Journal of Catharine Maria Sedgwick* (Boston: Massachusetts Historical Society, 1993), 125; Timothy Kenslea, *The Sedgwicks in Love: Courtship, Engagement, and Marriage in the Early Republic* (Boston: Northeastern University Press, 2006), 32. Kenslea discusses Mumbet's role as mother and Pamela Sedgwick's psychotic condition in chapter 1.

18. Peter P. Hinks, *To Awaken My Afflicted Brethren: David Walker and the Problem of Antebellum Slave Resistance* (University Park: Penn State University Press, 1997). For the comment on Jefferson, see James Oakes, "Why Slaves Can't Read: The Political Significance of Jefferson's Racism," in James Gilreath, ed., *Thomas Jefferson and the Education of a Citizen* (Washington, D.C.: Library of Congress, 1999), 177. Electa Jones, *Stockbridge, Past and Present; Or, Records of an Old Mission* (Springfield: S. Bowles, 1854), 242; she quotes the biblical passages Deuteronomy 23:15 and Philemon 16.

19. *Berkshire Journal*, March 31, 1831.

20. "West Point by Miss Sedgwick," *Juvenile Miscellany*, January/February 1833, 237–45; the quoted passage is on p. 242. Sedgwick described the visit to West Point in a letter to her niece in August 1831; Catharine Sedgwick Papers, Box 1, folder 14, Massachusetts Historical Society. We are indebted to Laura Lowell for finding this letter.

21. "West Point by Miss Sedgwick," *Juvenile Miscellany*, 243–45.

22. Berkshire County Deed Books, Pittsfield Registry of Deeds, Grantee, 78:559–60, 81:521–22; the population data are from the federal decadal censuses. The number of black Stockbridgians reported in the *Berkshire Journal*, December 2, 1830, was seventy-six rather than sixty-four.

23. *Weekly Visitor*, March 25, 1841, quoted in Emilie S. Piper, "The Family of Agrippa Hull," *Berkshire Genealogist* 22 (2001): 5; for temperance in Massachusetts, see George F. Clark, *A History of the Temperance Reform in Massachusetts, 1813–1883* (Boston: Clara & Caruth, 1888).

24. The year before, Hull wrote his will leaving his estate to his daughter after his wife died or remarried and called "Charlotte Potter, my daughter and only

remaining child." Mason Wade, ed., *The Journals of Francis Parkman*, 3 vols. (New York: Harper, 1947), 1:260; Jones, *Stockbridge*, 241.

25. Thomas Egleston, *The Life of John Paterson, Major-General in the Revolutionary Army, by His Great-Grandson, Thomas Egleston*, rev. ed. (New York: G. P. Putnam, 1898), 10; the button, given by Mrs. Henrietta Crockett, the great-great-niece of Peggy Timbroke Hull, is in Pleasant Valley Sanctuary, Lenox, Massachusetts.

26. "West Point by Miss Sedgwick," 245.

27. Will of Agrippa Hull, Berkshire County Probate Records #7171, Pittsfield, Massachusetts; Peggy's application and supporting documents are in the Agrippa Hull file, National Archives.

28. Piper, "Family of Agrippa Hull," 5.

29. Tombstone inscription written by Miss Jennie Pomeroy, Stockbridge Public Library, Hull file.

INDEX

313